NAPA & SONOMA
ENCOUNTER

Napa & Sonoma Encounter

Published by Lonely Planet Publications Pty Ltd
ABN 36 005 607 983

Australia	Head Office, Locked Bag 1, Footscray, Vic 3011
	☎ 03 8379 8000 fax 03 8379 8111
	talk2us@lonelyplanet.com.au
USA	150 Linden St, Oakland, CA 94607
	☎ 510 250 6400
	toll free 800 275 8555
	fax 510 893 8572
	info@lonelyplanet.com
UK	2nd fl, 186 City Rd
	London EC1V 2NT
	☎ 020 7106 2100 fax 020 7106 2101
	go@lonelyplanet.co.uk

This title was commissioned in Lonely Planet's Oakland office and produced by: **Commissioning Editor** Suki Gear **Coordinating Editor** Saralinda Turner **Coordinating Cartographer** Andy Rojas **Layout Designer** Aomi Hongo **Assisting Editors** Daniel Corbett, Helen Koehne **Assisting Cartographers** Eve Kelly, Peter Shields **Managing Editor** Bruce Evans **Managing Cartographer** Alison Lyall **Cover Designer** Katy Murenu **Project Manager** Fabrice Rocher **Managing Layout Designer** Sally Darmody **Thanks to** Amanda Sierp, Anna Spruce, Brian Turnbull, Brice Gosnell, Diana Duggan, Glenn Beanland, Indra Kilfoyle, Jessica Boland, Joshua Geoghegan, Martin Heng, Melanie Dankel, Michael Ruff, Paul Sampson, Tom Hall

ISBN 978-1-74179-446-5

Printed through Colorcraft Ltd, Hong Kong.
Printed in China.

HOW TO USE THIS BOOK

Color-Coding & Maps

Color-coding is used for symbols on maps and in the text that they relate to (eg all eating and drinking venues on the maps and in the text are given a green knife and fork symbol). Each Wine Country valley also gets its own color, and this is used down the edge of the page and throughout that regional section.

Review Listings

Winery reviews are listed geographically in each valley chapter from south to north. All other reviews are listed alphabetically.

Send us your feedback We love to hear from readers — your comments help make our books better. We read every word you send us, and we always guarantee that your feedback goes straight to the appropriate authors. The most useful submissions are rewarded with a free book. To send us your updates and find out about Lonely Planet events, newsletters and travel news visit our award-winning website: *lonelyplanet.com/contact*

Note: We may edit, reproduce and incorporate your comments in Lonely Planet products such as guidebooks, websites and digital products, so let us know if you don't want your comments reproduced or your name acknowledged. For a copy of our privacy policy visit *lonelyplanet.com/privacy*.

ALISON BING

When not scribbling notes on menus and grazing her way across NorCal valleys, Alison is writing for Lonely Planet's *San Francisco, California* and *Italy* guides, and gourmet and art magazines including *Cooking Light* and *Flash Art*. She divides her time between San Francisco and a hilltop town in Tuscany, which looks a lot like Napa, only older and less likely to wear flip-flops. Alison holds a bachelor's degree in art history and a masters degree from the Fletcher School of Law and Diplomacy, a joint program of Tufts and Harvard Universities – perfectly respectable credentials she regularly undermines with opinionated culture commentary for magazines, news outlets and radio.

ALISON'S THANKS

Alison offers thanks in Wine Country quantities: magnums to fellow members of Slow Food SF, Cook Here & Now and Sanchez Writers Annex; special reserve Jeroboams to cartographer Alison Lyall, project manager Fabrice Rocher and editor Saralinda Turner, and Encounter champions Heather Dickson and Brice Gosnell; sparkling Methuselahs to honored designated drivers Yosh Han, Sahai Burrowes, Luke Hass, Kristin Sgroi, Alexei Wachman, Natasha Nicholson and Erin Archuleta; and a Balthazar to Suki Gear, every writer's dream editor. Finally, a Nebuchadnezzar should do the trick for the Bing family and Marco Flavio Marinucci, whom I can't toast enough.

THE PHOTOGRAPHER

Jerry Alexander is a highly credited food and travel photographer who was born and raised in the Napa Valley. When he's not traveling the world Jerry and his wife, Thanaphon, divide their time between their Wine Country vineyard and their recently completed home in Chiang Mai.

Cover photograph A Napa Valley vineyard flaunts its cloak of mist and sunlight, Charles O'Rear/Corbis **Internal photographs** p48 courtesy di Rosa Preserve; p53 Deborah Jones; p103 John McJunkin, courtesy of Freestone Vineyards; p17 *Running through the woods* by Robert Hudson (foreground) and *Camp of Landscape Artists* by Roy De Forest (wall); p77 *Blue Tree 2*, Sonoma 2004 by Claude Cormier, Architectes Paysagistes Inc; p105 Ceramic mural tile wall of Lucy and Charlie Brown in the Charles M Schulz Museum's Great Hall; p176 *Rock Pools, Melted Stone*, 2000 (floor) and drawings from the Earth and Snow Series,1993, pigment extracted from seeds, pigmented snow allowed to melt on paper by Andy Goldsworthy (side walls), and untitled oil painting, 1983 by Per Kirkeby (back wall). All photographs by Lonely Planet Images and by Jerry Alexander, except p10, p27 Wes Walker; p43, p51 John Elk III; p157 Lee Foster.

All images are copyright of the photographers unless otherwise indicated. Many of the images in this guide are available for licensing from **Lonely Planet Images**: www.lonelyplanetimages.com

Enchant your taste buds with toasty bubbles from Schramsberg (p46)

CONTENTS

THE AUTHOR 03

THIS IS WINE COUNTRY 07

HIGHLIGHTS 08

**WINE COUNTRY
  CALENDAR** 23

ITINERARIES 27

THE VALLEYS 32

>NAPA VALLEY 36

>SONOMA VALLEY 68

>RUSSIAN RIVER VALLEY 96

>DRY CREEK VALLEY 120

>ALEXANDER VALLEY 136

>ANDERSON VALLEY 146

WINE-TASTING BASICS 157

SNAPSHOTS 164

> ACCOMMODATIONS 166

> SPAS 170

> WINERIES 172

> CUISINE 174

> ART & ARCHITECTURE 176

> OUTDOOR ACTIVITIES 178

> SHOPPING 179

> CHILDREN 180

> PICNICS 181

> AFTER DARK 182

> FOR NONDRINKERS 183

> HANDS-ON 184

BACKGROUND 185

DIRECTORY 192

INDEX 202

Why is our travel information the best in the world? It's simple: our authors are passionate, dedicated travelers. They don't take freebies in exchange for positive coverage so you can be sure the advice you're given is impartial. They travel widely to all the popular spots, and off the beaten track. They don't research using just the internet or phone. They discover new places not included in any other guidebook. They personally visit thousands of hotels, restaurants, palaces, trails, galleries, temples and more. They speak with dozens of locals every day to make sure you get the kind of insider knowledge only a local could tell you. They take pride in getting all the details right, and in telling it how it is. Think you can do it? Find out how at **lonelyplanet.com**.

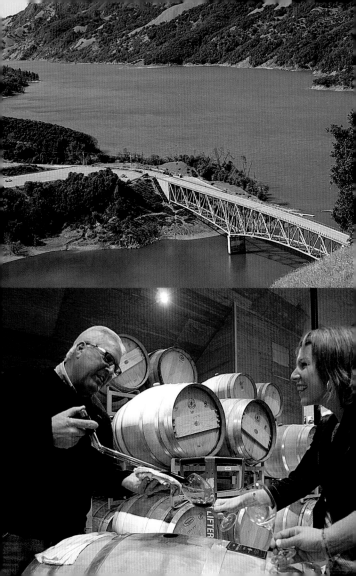

THIS IS WINE COUNTRY

Other wine regions around the world work just as hard, but this one has all the fun. Consider permission granted to roll in the mud, drink inside a Zoroastrian temple, walk through 1000-year-old redwoods and feast on nine-course organic meals, just because you can.

Anything goes and everything grows in these six valleys, and that's the way it's been for 150 years. Prospectors came for gold and stayed for grapes, bringing boot-stomping good times to rural stagecoach outposts. The varied coastal valley microclimates made everyone feel at home, whether they came from Italy or Patagonia, Australia or Alsace – not that it was always easy to put down roots in NorCal, with its turbulent geologic history of volcanic eruptions and earthquakes. Only the most adventurous immigrants and idealistic hippies stood their ground here, creating an experimental green polyglot farming ecosystem that has come to define California on the plate, inside the glass and in the popular imagination.

Pity the folks back home enduring glum happy hours with house reds and brie wedges: you'll be discovering authentic Thai spring rolls made with Sonoma-grown lemongrass and Anderson Valley Dry Gewürztraminer, or taco-truck carne asada off Hwy 101 to pair with your Alexander Valley Cab. These are the Wine Country moments that make foodies and wine aficionados wax rhapsodic and taciturn surfers utter the ultimate NorCal benediction: 'Right on.'

Yet for all its cultivated fields and finely tuned palates, the West still has its wild side. Old-growth sequoias stand tall in Russian River and Anderson Valleys thanks to conservation initiatives pioneered by rebel lumber barons, and wild trout are making comebacks with sustainable farming practices. When the yellow mustard blooms and wildflowers take over the hills, you'll be glad you came for the wine and stayed for the countryside.

Top Detour to Lake Sonoma for hiking, boating and the annual steelhead-trout spawning frenzy (p133) Bottom Discovering the intricacies of oak and age at Robert Young winery (p138)

> 1 Discover the best vintage yet 10
> 2 Find out just how fresh you can get at NorCal's top restaurants 12
> 3 Slip into something more comfortable: volcanic mud 14
> 4 Breathe in pure air and awe amid ancient redwood groves 16
> 5 Get up close and personal with the wildest art in the west 17
> 6 Explore the hidden valley that convinced the ultimate adventurer to settle down 18
> 7 Take creative detours and go with the Boho flow 19
> 8 Find your architectural niche and drink in it, too 20
> 9 Pack gourmet picnics and join the foodie festivities 21
> 10 Follow your bliss along California's laziest river 22

Garlic grows for gastronomic glory in the French Laundry (p56) kitchen garden

>1 WINE, WINE, WINE
DISCOVER THE BEST VINTAGE YET

Now is a good time for a drink in Wine Country. The wines they're pouring are radically different from wines you might've sipped only a decade ago – and it's not merely a matter of vintage. In the 1990s, a blight of phylloxera forced vintners to tear out acres of infested vines, which led to some soul searching. Vintners began questioning their own methods, and thinking ahead to a time when people would ask the same questions about wine they were already asking about food: what exactly is in this, how was it grown and what does that mean for the planet? Some pioneering NorCal vintners took the initiative and began the long process of reinventing their wines, from dirt to cork.

Some changes you can tell at a glance or a sniff. Rows of vines that were once kept artificially tidy with weed-controlling herbicides are now riots of flowering ground cover enjoyed by grazing sheep, keeping weeds in check and ecosystems in balance. Owls, ladybugs and specially trained golden retrievers are now valued members of winery pest-control teams at newly certified organic vineyards (see boxed text, p162). Century-old wineries gleam with solar panels and waste-water–recycling equipment, and if the fertilizer pile smells like herbal tea, maybe that's because it is: nutrient-rich mulches are phasing out

industrial chemicals at biodynamic wineries (see boxed text, p162). And these aren't just small-time ventures helmed by hippies – landmark Napa and Sonoma wineries are installing owl boxes and beehives.

Bucolic splendor is nice, but how does it taste? Wines produced using new vines and pioneering methods have gotten through that awkward transitional phase and matured a few years, and should be ready in time for your arrival. Pour some in your glass, and you might notice traces of silky purple silt at the bottom – more wines are deliberately left unfined and unfiltered, and have an extraplush mouthfeel. Many vintners are manipulating their wines as little as possible these days – after all the trouble they've taken to grow better grapes, they want you to taste them in their natural glory.

So go ahead: swirl, sniff, and swish at any of the 100-plus wineries recommended in this book. Instead of the usual white-to-red progression, try a vertical tasting to compare new releases to 'library wines' produced a year or two earlier: amazing what a difference a year can make, and how a winemaker can capture that in a bottle. Or go horizontal and try Cabs from different vineyards by the same winemaker– you're literally drinking in the scenery. And if you're so inclined, don't be shy about asking 'what exactly is in this, how was it grown and what does that mean for me and the planet?' These days, your pourer will be glad you asked, and should be ready with some tasty answers.

HIGHLIGHTS

>2 FARM-TO-TABLE DINING

FIND OUT JUST HOW FRESH YOU CAN GET AT NORCAL'S TOP RESTAURANTS

Shameless name-dropping is to be expected on Wine Country menus, but it's not all about top chefs and prestigious wineries. Wine Country farmers are now established food celebrities, snagging top menu billing with organic butternut squash from the Patch community garden (p88), certified humane Redwood Hill goat cheese (p87) and biodynamic Philo Apple Farm chutney (p156). In agriculturally endowed California, people can afford to be picky about their food – so restaurants are smart to name local sources on the menu as up-front guarantees of freshness, quality, environmental responsibility and community reinvestment. To find restaurants emphasizing local produce, look up 'locavore' (sourcing ingredients locally) in the 'Eat' subindex of this guide: until you've been personally introduced to local produce, you haven't really eaten in California.

Collaborations between farmer and chef go even further in Wine Country, where restaurants are located not in skyscrapers but amid

fields and ranches. Since chefs and farmers are neighbors here, you'll hear menu consultations happen casually over beer or at farmers markets held five days a week, nine months a year. More than just local sourcing, creative collaboration defines farm-to-table dining. Farmers report to chefs when peaches will be hitting their prime; chefs ask farmers to grow lemon verbena for a dish they have in mind; and come summertime, fresh peaches with lemon-verbena shortbread appear on the dessert menu.

The distance from farm to table is shrinking from a couple of miles to a few feet in Wine Country, at restaurants cultivating kitchen gardens and making their own artisan foods. Chef de cuisine Timothy Hollingsworth of French Laundry (p56, kitchen above) keeps a close eye on peas in the restaurant's 5-acre garden until their shoots reach peak tenderness. Chefs also share menu bylines with head gardeners at Sonoma staples Ubuntu (p52) and Zazu (p105), and budget-conscious eateries like Diavola (p143) and Bovolo (p132) justifiably boast about their in-house charcuterie-makers. Taste the results for yourself: restaurants that grow their own or cultivate close partnerships with producers earn a 'farm-to-table' distinction in this book.

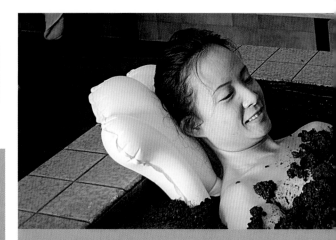

>3 CALISTOGA MUD BATHS

SLIP INTO SOMETHING MORE COMFORTABLE: VOLCANIC MUD

Napa bistros and tasting rooms are all about elegant refinement, but a wallow in warm Calistoga mud is pure primordial glee. Start feet first: the ticklish feeling of volcanic sludge squishing between your toes is cause for a squeal, and seems to take years of sidewalk-pounding off your soles. Slurping sounds are inevitable no matter how gracefully you attempt to slide into the bath, or however briskly the bath attendant applies glorious glop to your arms and legs. By the time you're in up to your neck, you should feel as giddy as a kid in a mud puddle. After 20 minutes unwinding in your mud bath, you may find that you've regressed to a state of primeval ooze, and need help finding your feet.

The sensation is positively prehistoric, and no wonder: this goo goes back about eight million years, when Mt Konocti erupted and left the Calistoga region bubbling with geothermal springs and coated with fine volcanic silt. The aroma of the mud remains

intoxicatingly ancient, like a whiff of something from the back of a cave – musky, fossilized and sulfuric – though often it's mixed with grass-scented peat for heat retention and texture. Most mud baths come with your choice of aromatherapy, usually soothing Sonoma lavender or invigorating eucalyptus.

Native Californian Wappo people have enjoyed restorative muddy wallows in Calistoga for 500 years, but if you can't get a booking for this weekend, blame Sam Brannan. The real-estate speculator and professional loudmouth who jumpstarted the Gold Rush by shouting 'Gold! Gold! Gold!' in the streets of San Francisco kicked off the Calistoga spa craze in 1862, with broad claims that murky, mineral-rich local hot springs could cure rheumatism, arthritis and even drunkenness. Calistoga spas still allude to the 'detoxifying' properties of local mud, though no reliable medical study can confirm or deny the health benefits, and those with medical conditions should check with their doctors before wallowing. Spas typically flush baths with boiling water, stir and reheat mud between uses – but for the squish-squeamish, Lavender Hill Spa (p62) offers silty single-use volcanic baths and Solage (p62) has slather-on mud treatments.

>4 REDWOOD FORESTS

BREATHE IN PURE AIR AND AWE AMID ANCIENT REDWOOD GROVES

Vineyards may be the ultimate NorCal drinking backdrop, but to really let your inner Californian rip, head into the wilds of Anderson Valley (p155) and Russian River (p114). Breathe in that redwood-rarified air, and as you exhale, out might slip the classic Californian exclamation: Duuude! These old-growth trees are the tallest living species on Earth, up to 1400 years old, higher than a football field is long and with such impressive girth that you couldn't bear-hug them if you tried.

Some 130 years ago, similar awestruck moments overcame lumber barons Colonel James Armstrong and Joshua P Hendy, who stopped the axes from felling these magnificent redwood groves. Their conservation efforts preceded state conservation laws by almost 50 years, and were considered tantamount to madness after the Gold Rush went bust in the 1870s, when wood was the next obvious natural resource to be exploited. Redwoods were falling so hard and fast that Guerneville was nicknamed 'Stumptown,' and residents complained that the unholy creak of crashing trees and shouts of 'Timber!' kept them up at night. More than any skyscraper or cathedral, these preserved groves of majestic *sequoia sempervirens* are California's greatest monuments, testaments to pioneering Californian ecologists' best natural instincts.

> 5 DI ROSA PRESERVE

GET UP CLOSE AND PERSONAL WITH THE WILDEST ART IN THE WEST

The most prestigious and outrageous private collection of contemporary Californian art started with bagels and wine. In the 1960s, newspaper reporter Rene di Rosa started buying Beat collages made by fellow regulars at San Francisco's Coexistence Bagel Shop – and when Rene and his wife Veronica bought a Carneros winery with family money, their local art collection exploded all over the house, outbuildings, the cellar and eventually the vineyards. When the vineyards became valuable, they were sold to pay for more art from artists then working in the San Francisco Bay Area, from the creepy Tony Oursler projection pulling faces in the wine cellar to an early Robert Bechtle experiment in pure form on his living-room ceiling. Today the collection of breakthrough contemporary works at the nonprofit di Rosa Preserve (p47) is worth untold millions, but still you're invited into the house to snoop at bathtubs overflowing with installations and visit outlandish art in its natural habitat outdoors, with peacocks strutting amid the sculpture.

>6 JACK LONDON STATE HISTORIC PARK

EXPLORE THE HIDDEN VALLEY THAT CONVINCED THE ULTIMATE ADVENTURER TO SETTLE DOWN

A man of many words – 1000 a day minimum – author Jack London needed only two to sum up his 1400-acre Sonoma farmstead: 'Beauty Ranch.' He began farming the Valley of the Moon in 1905, when *White Fang* would soon make him the best-selling author in American history. Sustainable farming wasn't a novel concept, but London provided the celebrity needed for these ideas to take root in California. He reforested and terraced eroding hillsides, poured manure down slopes to avoid chemicals and built a humane 'Pig Palace' for his livestock. 'I believe the soil is our one indestructible asset,' he explained. 'I am rebuilding worn-out hillside lands that were worked out and destroyed by our wasteful California pioneer farmers… Everything I build is for the years to come.'

Today London's words ring true in this thriving park (p90), including his farmhouse and the House of Happy Walls, where his wife, Charmain, lived after his death. Polynesian war clubs line the stairs to Charmain's fabulous Bohemian boudoir, while downstairs are some of London's 600 rejection letters. Peek into the farmhouse library to see where London hung his trademark hat, wrote using then–high-tech Dictaphone and typewriter, and kept his priorities straight: 'I devote two hours a day to writing and ten to farming…my work on this land, and my message to America, go hand in hand.'

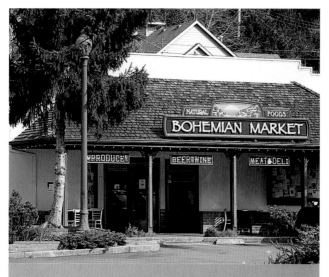

>7 BOHEMIAN HIGHWAY

TAKE CREATIVE DETOURS AND GO WITH THE BOHO FLOW
No better name could be given to this eccentric 12-mile stretch of highway winding from organically grown Freestone to good-time Guerneville, with plenty of quirks along the way in Occidental and Monte Rio. Farmers markets with *taiko* drums (p107), historic 1970s crafts galleries (p111), bountiful organic bakeries (p111) and a retro movie theater with gourmet hot dogs (p113) make the journey along Bohemian Hwy a destination in itself. While the exclusive all-male Bohemian Grove is closed to the public, the beaches at Monte Rio (p113) and downtown Guerneville (p115) welcome anyone up for a splash in the Russian River. Take a bike (p197) or motorcycle or at least your own sweet time, and you'll see why this route through the redwoods has inspired frolicking in otherwise industrious lumberjacks, yule-wreath makers, railroad builders and even US presidents.

>8 WINE COUNTRY ARCHITECTURE

FIND YOUR ARCHITECTURAL NICHE AND DRINK IN IT, TOO

Eclectic would be a polite way to describe the wild style of Wine Country, which includes retired Victorian bordellos in Alexander Valley, original California Mission adobes in Sonoma, genuine-imitation Tuscan fortifications in Napa, French-slate faux chateaux in Sonoma, saloon-style clapboard storefronts in Anderson Valley and innocent gingerbread-trimmed farmsteads in Dry Creek. Sometimes neighboring wineries don't seem to belong in the same valley, or even the same planet: Quixote's quirky Hundertwasser golden onion domes and tree-sprouting rooftops (p41, pictured above) are just down Silverado from Persian-minimalist Darioush (p39), which looks like the world's first Zen–Zoroastrian temple. Hall's Frank Gehry tasting room (p45) is still in the works but, meanwhile, modern architecture fans are content to argue over whether the hilltop tasting room at Arista (p102) looks more like a bunker or a birthday cake.

>9 FARMERS MARKETS & ARTISAN EATS

PACK GOURMET PICNICS AND JOIN THE FOODIE FESTIVITIES

Grapes are a given but the cheese is hard to believe in Wine Country. No self-respecting corner deli here would be seen without local handcrafted goat *crottins* or aged dry jack in stock, and artisan cheese pairings at local wineries would easily upstage any lesser hooch. Fromageries Andante and Pug's Leap draw cult-like followings and crowds at farmers markets, but Sonoma cheese is no foodie fad: Vella Cheese (p90) has been a gourmand magnet for 75 years.

Lactose-intolerant drinkers have a reason to celebrate too: Wine Country food artisans are branching out and providing new pairing possibilities. Larger stores like Oakville Grocery (p58, pictured above) and Glen Ellen Market (p93) are stocking locally cured charcuterie, and honey, herbs and handmade chocolates are the latest specialties alongside Sonoma's classic lavender and cheese. Wildcrafting (harvesting wild food) is a local passion, and you'll spot wild mushrooms, sage and sea vegetables on market shelves and on hikes – but leave the mushrooming to the pros, as some local species are poisonous.

Local farmers are featuring their own produce in gourmet treats, and you'll find Gravenstein apples in Ace-in-the-Hole ciders (p109) and Mom's apple pies (p110). All this bounty turns farmers markets into festive foodie events, so don't be surprised when a picnic pit stop turns into a true country hoedown.

> 10 ADVENTURES ON THE RUSSIAN RIVER

FOLLOW YOUR BLISS ALONG CALIFORNIA'S LAZIEST RIVER

Turtles tan, Great Blue Herons meditate and the otters are always kidding around: there's never any rush on the Russian River. Even after spring rains speed up the rapids, this river is slow and mellow, ideal for tubing at places like Johnson's Beach (p115) or a good upper-body workout in a canoe (p118) or inflatable kayak (p129). Parents can teach their kids to doggie-paddle without fear of currents, and kiddies areas at Johnson's Beach (p115) and the summertime boardwalk at Monte Rio (p113) make for instant playdates.

The Russian River occasionally overflows in spring but is back to a blithe burble by summer, when lazy days are spent angling for bass downstream by Monte Rio or for a date upstream near Guerneville. Russian River is gay-friendly and family-oriented too, so your nearest and dearest will never feel like fish out of water here – go Guerneville for more teen activities and GLBT nightlife, or head to Monte Rio for riverside retreats with tiny tots and family flicks at the Rio (p113).

>WINE COUNTRY CALENDAR

No matter when you arrive in Wine Country, you're just in time for a drink. There's always something to toast: mustard fields and top chefs in winter, apple blossoms and movie stars in spring, revolution-aries and lavender in summer, cowboys and tractors in fall. Local websites can help you plan your trip around a Wine Country festival, especially www.winecountry.com for Napa; www.sonomavalley.com for Sonoma Valley; www.101things.com for Anderson Valley; www.bohemian.com or www.russianriver.com for Russian River and Dry Creek; and www.wineroad.com for Alexander Valley. Or you can count on kismet and locals spilling secrets over drinks – especially if you're buying.

Swing into Calistoga in March for jazz, blooms and a bloomin' good time (p24)

JANUARY

Winter Wineland

www.wineroad.com

Obliterate New Years' resolutions with food and wine pairings, winery tours and corks popping on new releases at 100+ wineries along Russian River and Dry Creek – all for $40.

FEBRUARY

Cloverdale Citrus Fair

www.cloverdalecitrusfair.org

Party like it's 1892 with blacksmith demos, bake-offs, a Citrus Fair Queen pageant and the historically kitsch Citrus Expo, featuring Roman temples, coral reefs and other scenes built with oranges.

MARCH

Mustard, Mud & Music

www.calistogajazz.com

When yellow mustard flowers run riot in the vineyards, Calistogans take to the streets with jazz, wine and mud-slinging – and offer deals on mud facials and new-release wines.

Taste of Yountville

www.yountville.com

The ultimate foodie block party: amuse-bouche from 15 top restaurants, vintages from 20 wineries and a rare opportunity to tour French Laundry's (p56) pristine garden.

APRIL

Sonoma International Film Festival

www.sonomafilmfest.org

Hit the red wine–stained carpet the first week of April for Wine Country's biggest indie film fest, with proceeds benefiting local arts programs.

Apple Blossom Festival

www.sebastopol.org

Community flower power takes over Main St as free-spirited Sebastopol celebrates its apple-orchard roots amid Wine Country vines.

MAY

Annual Legendary Boonville Beer Festival

www.avbc.com

Four hours of live music and *bahl hornin'* (good drinking) kick off at 1pm on the first Saturday in May, when more than 70 breweries come together and turn on the taps for local charities.

Napa Valley Cinco di Mayo

www.napavalleycincodemayo.com

Mariachis warble, ponies prance and petticoats twirl as Calistoga celebrates Mexico's independence with kid-friendly, alcohol-free entertainment the first Saturday in May.

JUNE

Harmony Fest

www.harmonyfestival.com

Think globally, funk locally with acts such as George Clinton, Michael Franti and India.Arie, and frolic in the Eco Village, Goddess Grove and Beer & Wine Garden.

Cinco de Mayo Mexican celebration (p24)

Russian River Blues Festival

www.omegaevents.com

Blues musicians like Earl Thomas, Los Lonely Boys and the Fabulous Thunderbirds get fans in Guerneville wailing about the woman who done them wrong – until she pours them another Pinot.

JULY

California Wine Tasting Championships

www.greenwoodridge.com

It's a fight to the finish in Philo mid-July, as novice and expert wine-tasters attempt to identify wines in just one swish.

AUGUST

Gravenstein Apple Fair

www.gravensteinapplefair.com

Celebrate Sonoma's August harvest in Sebastopol with 125 local artisans plus wine, beer, heritage foods and an apple pie–eating contest (preferably not in that order).

SEPTEMBER

Mendocino County Fair

www.mendocountyfair.com

Yee-haw! Mid-September Boonville becomes a live-action Western, with rodeos, sheep-dog trials, square dances and marathon spinning and knitting sessions.

WINE COUNTRY CALENDAR

Napa Wine and Crafts Faire

www.napadowntown.com/napawine
andcraftsfaire.html

Bottles, corks and wine-stained wood get
creatively repurposed at this juried showcase
for Napa's best crafts and specialty foods –
plus wine.

OCTOBER

Sonoma County Harvest Fair

www.harvestfair.org

Stomp to win at the World Championship
Grape Stomp competition, or just grab some
wine and hit the hay rides at Santa Rosa's
harvest hootenanny.

NOVEMBER

Holiday Open House

www.heartofsonomavalley.com

So much wine, so little time... Discover new
favorites in a late-November weekend of
cave tours, food pairings and new releases
poured by the winemaker at 20 Sonoma
Valley wineries, all for $30.

WINE COUNTRY RUN-DOWN

Napa Valley Marathon (www
.napavalleymarathon.org) You can't
booze en route, but winners receive their
weight in Napa wines. The February race
is limited to 2300 registrants — look for
date announcements online.

Human Race (www.humanracenow
.org) Ten thousand serious runners,
stumbling pirates, and jokers in
champagne-bottle costumes cover 3km or
10km through Santa Rosa in May, raising
$1 million plus for 400 nonprofits.

Vineman 70.3 (www.vineman.com)
July's half-iron man triathlon includes
a 1.3-mile swim in Guerneville plus a
56-mile bike ride and 13-mile run along
Dry Creek. Oof.

DECEMBER

Calistoga Lighted Tractor Parade

www.calistogavisitors.com

Rudolf's nose can't compare to 50 antique
tractors, trucks and construction vehicles all a-
twinkle with holiday lights as they roll down
Main St on the first Saturday in December.

Keep the doctor away with cider, jam and jelly from Philo Apple Farm (p156)

ITINERARIES

Bubbly for breakfast, luxurious spa treatments, tours of world-class art collections, afternoons floating downriver and ultrafresh feasts prepared by top chefs: your daily Wine Country agenda would be the envy of millionaires. And you can do it on a budget, all while supporting sustainable businesses that preserve the region's natural wonders.

ONE DAY IN NAPA

Toast the good life with sparkling wine at Domaine Carneros (p38) around 10am, before your di Rosa Preserve tour (p47) to see Wine Country at its weirdest: haughty peacocks perch on fallen angels and needy paintings plead 'Don't ever leave me' as you walk away. Graze Napa's Oxbow Market (p52) for a locally produced lunch and browse Napa's most original designs at Betty's Girl (p51) and Nest (p50) before hitting the Silverado Trail: Darioush (p39) and Quixote (p41) for far-out architecture, Stag's Leap (p41) and Phelps (p45) for premium wines, and Frog's Leap (p43) and Casa Nuestra (p45) for good times. Wallow in a Calistoga mud bath and dine farm-fresh at Jolé (p67), or unwind at the Silverado Brewing Company (p63) and Cameo Cinema (p64) with the locals.

TWO DAYS IN NAPA & SONOMA

Get in on the action with sparkling-wine tours at Schramsberg (p46), dungeon barrel tastings at Castello di Amorosa (p46) and tasting menus by top chefs-in-training at the Culinary Institute of America (p63). Taste pioneering biodynamic wines at Grgich (p44) and witness the Gehry tasting room under construction at Hall (p45), then head to the Hess Collection (p40) for Napa's best art-and-wine pairings. Swing over to Sonoma for Mission architecture and mineral-spring spas, then Glen Ellen for B&Bs, dinner at the Fig Café (p92) and morning hikes the next day in magnificent Jack London Park (p90). Break for lunch at Vineyards Inn (p95) and port at Kaz (p75), and return to San Francisco via Santa Rosa's Sonoma County Museum (p104) and farm-to-table dining at Zazu (p105).

Top Get frilled to kill at Betty's Girl (p51) **Bottom** Beneath its peaceful exterior, Alexander Valley (p136) boasts an unruly past

FORWARD PLANNING

Three weeks before you go Book your B&B and Calistoga mud-bath treatment (boxed text, p62), reserve bikes or bike tours (p197) for Napa, Sonoma Valley and Dry Creek, and make dinner reservations at acclaimed restaurants in Healdsburg and Yountville – it's probably too late for French Laundry (p56), but maybe not Cyrus (p133) or Ad Hoc (p54)...
One week before you go Call ahead to book tastings and tours at wineries that require appointments, reserve your table at Sonoma Valley restaurants, find last-minute deals at spas and B&Bs, and check the *North Bay Bohemian* online (www.bohemian.com) and www.101things.com for the lowdown on free events, live music and upcoming festivities in Wine Country.
The day before you go Pack your effervescent ibuprofen tablets and eat a hearty dinner so you can hit the ground drinking, check out what's in season in the Bay Area at www.cuesa .org/seasonality to whet your appetite for farm-fresh food, and see what's playing tomorrow night at Wine Country's historic one-screen cinemas in case you just need to vegetate after your first full day of wine tasting.

ONE WEEK IN WINE COUNTRY

Tack four days onto the three days described above, heading west from Santa Rosa to the Russian River Valley. Follow the Hot Summer Day itinerary (below), then kick off the next morning with a bubbly tasting at Iron Horse (p99). Head to Graton to browse antiques, art and funerary urns before lunch at Underwood Bar (p119) or its sister across the street. Save room for dessert at Mom's Apple Pie (p110), then take W Dry Creek Rd to Porter Creek (p101) for biodynamic Pinot, Hop Kiln (p102) for gourmet vinegar and Preston (p126) for organic wines and snacks. Dine at Scopa (p134) and sleep in Healdsburg and, the next day, take Oakville Grocery (p134) picnic fixings to tastings at award-winning Amphora (p124), sustainable Unti (p123) and biodynamic Truett-Hurst (p125). Hike around Lake Sonoma (p133) and return via Geyserville for tastings at Meeker (p141) and Locals (p140) before pizza at Diavola (p143). Overnight at a Cloverdale B&B, then follow the Anderson Valley on a Budget itinerary (opposite) to finish off a week well spent.

HOT SUMMER DAY

Rent a convertible and head for the coastal mists and redwood forests of the Bohemian Hwy, starting with a delicious breakfast at Wild Flour (p111) and cool-weather Chardonnay at Freestone (p98). Stop in Occidental for beach bags made from billboards at Renga Arts (p111) and picnic supplies at Bohemian Market (p112), then flop on Monte Rio Beach (p113) or head to Johnson's Beach (p115) to float downriver on rented inner tubes. Clean up at Sumbody Spa (p108) before dinner and a movie at Saint Rose (p110) or the Rio Theater (p113), and take heated film debates to Rainbow Cattle Co (p117) or Barley & Hops (p112).

ANDERSON VALLEY ON A BUDGET

The finer things in life are free (or cheap) in Anderson Valley, from natural wonders to fantastic wine tastings. Stop at Meyer (p148) for free bocce and port, or head straight to Boonville's Anderson Valley Brewing Company (p152) for a $5 tour with free tastes of eight brews. Break for bargain lunches at Boonville General Store (p154) or hit Boont Berry Farm (p153) for supplies and a picnic amid old-growth redwoods at Hendy Woods (p155). Stop by Philo Apple Farm (p156) for $1.50 organic cider and a free orchard hike before taking on tastings at Toulouse (p149), Navarro (p150) and Lazy Creek (p150), and a hearty dinner at Lauren's (p154). Camp in Hendy Woods or backtrack to Cloverdale's motels and value-priced Victorian B&Bs (p169).

FOR NONDRINKERS

Russian River, Sonoma Valley and Carneros are Wine Country's best bets for teetotalers. Outdoor adventures abound around Russian River – ambitious vacationers can turn a three-day weekend into a mellow version of the Vineman half-triathlon (p26) with tubing on the river, biking along scenic West Dry Creek Rd and hiking through the giant redwood groves at Armstrong Woods (p114). Time-travel is possible at Sonoma's historic sites, hot springs and pristine Jack London Park (p90), and visitors hallucinate without help at the surreal Cornerstone Sonoma (p76) and sculpture-strewn di Rosa Preserve (p47). Farmers markets are an all-natural feast for the senses, while county fairs offer rodeos, sheepdog trials and other Wild West adventures minus the saloons. For more inspiration, check out the Snapshots chapter (p183).

>1 Napa Valley   36
>2 Sonoma Valley   68
>3 Russian River Valley   96
>4 Dry Creek Valley   120
>5 Alexander Valley   136
>6 Anderson Valley   146

Stag's Leap District once shushed French critics with its California Cabs (p189)

THE VALLEYS

Twenty-two distinct groups of Native Californians once lived in NorCal Wine Country, with customs and languages that changed from one valley to the next – even today, you might think people are speaking different languages across the six main valleys of the region.

While Napa tasting-room regulars rave about 'Rutherford dust' in a glass of Cabernet, in Anderson Valley they're busy *bahl hornin'* Pinot (enjoying Pinot Noir, as spoken in the local lingo of Boontling). But anywhere you go in Wine Country, people are proud to see you enjoying the fruits of their labor, and one thing is universally understood: Bottoms up, dude!

Here's what to look for in the six main valleys:

Napa Valley Taste the good life with prize Cabernets and cult Meritages, Tuscan castles and Persian palaces, mud baths and nine-course tasting menus.

Sonoma Valley The breakaway Bear Flag Republic still thinks independently with biodynamic wineries, organic olive oil drizzled on ice cream and a community farm in the heart of downtown Sonoma.

Russian River Valley Pinots taste like violets, otters act like clowns and nature-loving bikers unpack organic picnic supplies from their Harleys along the Bohemian Hwy.

Dry Creek Valley Breakthrough Syrahs and Sangioveses are served in garages and caves along tree-lined West Dry Creek Drive, California's scenic bike route for boozers.

Alexander Valley The Wild West's glory days live on with Victorian inns, Zins that survived Prohibition, winter Citrus Fairs and summertime farmers markets.

Anderson Valley Escape the summer heat and Chardonnay-centric hordes of Napa and Sonoma, and chill out in the redwoods with excellent Dry Gewürztraminer in the more alternative part of Wine Country.

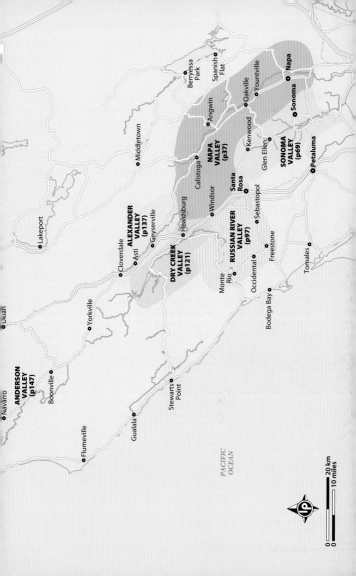

>NAPA VALLEY

The most glamorous stretch of farmland in America, Napa Valley attracts 4.7 million visitors a year expecting to be wined, dined, soaked in hot-springs spas and tucked between crisp linens. Yet 35 years ago, this 5-by-35-mile strip of stagecoach stops seemed forgotten by time.

Grapes have grown here since the Gold Rush, but grape-sucking phyl-loxera bugs, Prohibition and the Great Depression reduced 140 wineries

NAPA VALLEY

🍷 WINERIES

Artesa	1	B6
Casa Nuestra	2	C2
Castello di Amorosa	3	B2
Chateau Montelena Winery	4	B1
Darioush	5	D5
Domaine Carneros	6	B6
Etude	7	C6
Frog's Leap	8	C3
Girard Winery	9	A5
Goosecross Cellars	10	C4
Grgich Hills	11	C3
Groth	12	C4
Hall	13	C3
Hess Collection	14	C5
Honig	15	C3
Joseph Phelps	16	C3
Mondavi	17	C3
Mumm Napa	18	C3
Piña	19	C4
Quixote	20	D4
Robert Sinskey	21	D4
Round Pond	22	C3
Rubicon Estate	23	C3
Schramsberg	24	C2
Stag's Leap Wine Cellars	25	D4
Vincent Arroyo	26	B1
Wine Garage	27	D2

📷 SEE

di Rosa Preserve	28	B6
Ma(i)sonry	29	A5

Napa Valley Museum	30	A6
Nest	31	D5
Old Faithful Geyser	32	B1
Petrified Forest	33	B1
St Helena Farmers Market	34	C3

🏃 DO

Bale Grist Mill Park	35	C2
Calistoga Bikeshop	36	D2
Calistoga Spa Hot Springs	37	D2
Dr Wilkinson's Hot Springs	38	D1
Golden Haven Hot Springs	39	D1
Indian Springs	40	D1
Lavender Hill Spa	41	C2
Safari West	42	A1
Spa at Carneros Inn	43	C6
Spa Solage	44	D1

🛍 SHOP

Calistoga Pottery	45	C2
Lolo's	46	A3
Mudd Hens	47	D1
Napa Premium Outlets	48	C6
Napa Soap Company	49	A3
Napa Valley Olive Oil	50	B3
Woodhouse Chocolate	51	A2

🍴 EAT & DRINK

Ad Hoc	52	A6
Boon Fly Café	(see 43)	
Bouchon	53	A6
Buster's	54	C2
Cook	55	A2
English Garden Tea Rooms	56	D2
French Laundry	57	A5
Go Fish	58	A3
Jolé	59	D1
La Luna Taqueria	60	C3
Long Meadow Ranch	61	C3
Market	62	A2
Model Bakery	63	A2
Moore's Landing	64	C6
Napa Valley Coffee Roasting Company	65	A2
Oakville Grocery	66	C4
Paninoteca Ottimo	67	A6
Redd	68	B6
Silverado Brewing Company	69	C2
Taylor's Automatic Refresher	70	A3
Wine Spectator Greystone Restaurant at the Culinary Institute of America	71	C3
Yo El Rey	72	D2

⭐ PLAY

Cameo Cinema	73	A2
Lincoln Theater	(see 30)	
Pancha's	74	A5

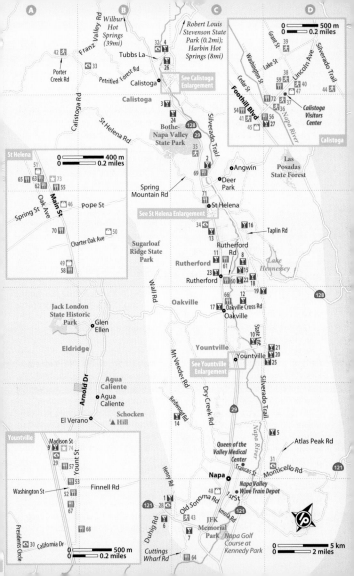

Map labels and locations

A
- 42 🏕
- Porter Creek Rd

B
- Wilbur Hot Springs (39mi)
- Franz Valley Rd
- 32 4
- Tubbs La
- 33
- Petrified Forest Rd
- Calistoga
- **Calistoga**
- St Helena Rd
- Calistoga Rd
- 3
- 24
- Bothe-Napa Valley State Park
- 35
- Spring Mountain Rd
- See Calistoga Enlargement

C
- Robert Louis Stevenson State Park (0.2mi); Harbin Hot Springs (8mi)
- See Calistoga Enlargement
- Silverado Trail
- 128
- 29
- 2
- 69
- Angwin
- Deer Park
- 71
- St Helena
- 34
- 13
- 16
- Taplin Rd
- Rutherford Rd
- 11
- 61
- 8
- 23
- 60 22
- **Rutherford**
- 66
- 12
- 17 Oakville Cross Rd
- Oakville
- 10 State Ln
- **Yountville**
- Yountville
- 128
- Lake Hennessey
- Las Posadas State Forest
- 19
- 18
- 21
- 20
- 25
- Silverado Trail
- 5
- Atlas Peak Rd
- 31
- Monticello Rd
- 121

D
- 500 m
- 0.2 miles
- Grant St
- 39
- Lincoln Ave
- Silverado Trail
- Lake St
- 38
- 59
- 40
- 47
- 44
- Washington St
- Cedar St
- 72
- 37
- **Foothill Blvd**
- 54
- 36
- 41
- 56
- 27
- 45
- Napa River
- Calistoga Visitors Center
- Calistoga

St Helena Enlargement
- 400 m
- 0.2 miles
- 51
- 65 63 73
- 62 55
- Main St
- Oak Ave
- 46
- Pope St
- Spring St
- 70
- Charter Oak Ave
- 50
- 49
- 58
- See St Helena Enlargement

Jack London State Historic Park
- Glen Ellen
- Eldridge
- Agua Caliente
- Agua Caliente
- Arnold Dr
- El Verano
- Schocken Hill
- Sugarloaf Ridge State Park
- Wall Rd
- Mt Veeder Rd
- See Yountville Enlargement
- Redwood Rd
- 14
- Dry Creek Rd
- Napa River
- 29

Yountville Enlargement
- 9
- Madison St
- 74
- 29
- 57
- Yount St
- 53
- 52
- Washington St
- Finnell Rd
- 67
- 68
- 30
- California Dr
- Presidents Circle
- 500 m
- 0.2 miles

Lower section
- Queen of the Valley Medical Center
- Trancas St
- Napa Valley Wine Train Depot
- **Napa**
- 48
- 1
- 1st St
- 26
- Henry Rd
- Old Sonoma Rd
- 43
- JFK Memorial Park
- 6
- 7
- Imola Rd
- Duhig Rd
- 121
- Cuttings Wharf Rd
- 64
- Napa Golf Course at Kennedy Park
- 121
- 5 km
- 2 miles

THE VALLEYS

NAPA VALLEY

in the 1890s to around 25 by the 1960s. However, when Napa wines took top honors at a 1976 blind tasting in Paris, the wine-drinking world took note. Independent, family-owned wineries still cluster around Calistoga and off the Silverado Trail, though most Napa vineyards are now owned by global conglomerates and sell for $275,000 an acre.

Longtime locals recall when Sally Schmitt opened a restaurant in Yountville's laundry in 1979, with all-California wines and 'fancy' $10 mains; today, reservations are essential at the landmark French Laundry, run since 1994 by Thomas Keller (p56). With so many acclaimed restaurants, Valley residents have earned a new nickname: 'Napkins.'

WINERIES

Ⓨ DOMAINE CARNEROS

Map p37; ☎ 800-716-2788, ext 234; www.domainecarneros.com; 1240 Duhig Rd, Carneros; tasting with snacks $15; ☽ 10am-6pm

When French Champagne powerhouse Taittinger Reims bought this Carneros estate in 1987, connoisseurs frothed with indignation: how could a Cuvée come from a California swamp? Winemakers Eileen Crane and Elaine St Clair have made believers of Brut absolutists with vintage Brut Cuvée ($26) racking up awards with Meyer lemon and toasty vanilla. Flights come with comp almonds, but the generous $14 cheese plate provides snacks for four.

Ⓨ ARTESA

Map p37; ☎ 877-224-8309; www.artesa winery.com; 1345 Henry Rd, Carneros; tasting $10-15; ☽ 10am-4:30pm

Minimalist Mayan temple or Bond bunker: this starkly modern winery invites creative comparisons at the friendly terrace tasting bar, with views over sculptures at neighboring di Rosa Preserve (p47). Owned by Catalan sparkling-wine producer Codorníu, Artesa has earned a strong following with its Reserve Merlot ($30), a dark-cherry beauty with a satiny mocha finish.

Ⓨ ETUDE

Map p37; ☎ 707-299-3061; www.etude wines.com; 1250 Cuttings Wharf Rd, Carneros; tasting $25; ☽ 10am-4pm Mon-Sat

Offices don't usually inspire thoughts of great wines, but call ahead for a tasting appointment, and you'll be whisked past the cubicles into a warm and private wood-paneled boardroom, Trump-style. Carneros Pinots are in top form at this Fosters-owned winery, expressing estate characteristics ranging from woodsy-incense Pinot Carneros ($42) to polished-granite Tremblor ($60).

Almond marzipan, sweet spice, white pepper and spicy anise – tastes roll off the tongue at Ceja

CEJA

Map p50; ☎ 707-226-6445; www.ceja vineyards.com; 1248 1st St, Napa; tasting $10, applicable to $50 purchase; ⏲ noon-6pm Sun-Thu, noon-10pm Fri & Sat

Former vineyard workers Felipe Moran and Pablo Ceja cultivated a following with plush, food-loving wines wine-lovers usually head to Europe to find – Vino de Casa Pinot/Syrah ($20) is a pomegranate/caramel case in point. Ceja reserve Pinot makes a three-digit splash at French Laundry, but Carneros Pinot ($40) tantalizes with wild strawberries and rooibos tea. Ceja's new tasting room features Maceo Montoya's mural celebrating winemaking's roots, from ancient Egypt through 1960s United Farm Workers labor struggles. Don't miss Ariel Ceja's free salsa lessons

at 7:30pm Saturdays, followed by Napa's best dance party.

VINTNER'S COLLECTIVE

Map p50; ☎ 707-255-7150; www .vintnerscollective.com; 1245 Main St, Napa; tasting $15-25; ⏲ 11am-6pm

The stone Pfeiffer Building was a roughhousing 1875 brewery and 1890s brothel, but mended its wild ways with its 2002 transformation into the spiffy Vintner's Collective. Twenty wineries are represented at the cozy bar, with your choice of six tastes from the daily menu.

DARIOUSH

Map p37; ☎ 707-257-2345; www .darioush.com; 4240 Silverado Trail; tasting $25; ⏲ 10:30am-5pm

Bulls balancing atop pillars mark the entry to a Persian temple of

V

THE VALLEYS

NAPA VALLEY

Hess Collection winery showcases complex Cabs and thought-provoking art

potent reds. Welcome to the American dream of Darioush Khaledi, who moved from Iran to California, turned a grocery store into a successful chain and in 2004 opened this huge monument to the history and fine reds of his native Shiraz. The Merlot ($48) is monumental too, with intensely aromatic lavender, blueberry and espresso.

HESS COLLECTION

Map p37; ☎ 707-255-8584; www.hess collection.com; 4411 Redwood Rd; tasting $10, gallery free; ⏱ 10am-5pm; Megacollectors wish they were you right now – sipping a complex Hess Cab ($60) composition of cassis and chocolate, and admiring Robert Motherwell's ink-blot abstracts. Tear yourself away from Hess' outstanding art collection for the 19 Block Cuvée ($36), a statuesque Mt Veeder Meritage presenting mission fig, blackberry and pepper on a cedar pedestal.

GIRARD WINERY

Map p37; ☎ 707-968-9297; www.girard winery.com; 6795 Washington St, Yount-ville; tasting $10-15; ⏱ 10am-6pm; Ponzi schemes offer lower returns than Artistry ($40), a Meritage with redcurrant, paprika and lilac notes that has lately tripled in value after two years of cellaring. In fruitful years, Girard produces Cab Franc

($40) as architecturally harmonious as the new tasting room, balancing light and dark, zesty blueberries and mellow sage.

STAG'S LEAP WINE CELLARS

Map p37; ☎ 707-261-6441; www .cask23.com; 5766 Silverado Trail; tasting $15-30; 10am-4:30pm
Wine-lovers buzzing about Stag's Leap could mean the AVA (growing region) or the Fosters-owned winery – but they probably mean this place, which produced the first California Cab to beat French competitors in 1976. European buyers bought the winery in 2007, but winemaker Nicolette Pruss continues the Stag's Leap legacy with Cask 23 ($195): crushed violets, Napa Cab cigar box and Sonoma figs. Definitely take the $30 tasting when they're pouring Cask 23 or Fay Estate Cab ($125).

QUIXOTE

Map p37; ☎ 707-944-2659; www .quixotewinery.com; 6126 Silverado Trail; tasting with tour $25; ☾ tours by appointment 10am, 12:30pm, 2:30pm
Veer off Silverado into another dimension, where trees wave from rooftops, a gold onion dome pops into the sky and tiled columns bulge comically under arches: this quixotic winery-dreamscape was built by pioneering green architect Friedensreich Hundertwasser. Eccentric Quixote grows Petit Sirah in the heart of Cab country, and their Quixote Estate ($60) is inky blueberry with bittersweet chocolate and tobacco.

ROBERT SINSKEY

Map p37; ☎ 707-944-9090; www.robert sinskey.com; 6320 Silverado Trail; tasting with/without food pairing $20/15, applicable to purchase; ☾ 10am-4:30pm
Winemaker Robert Sinskey and chef Maria Sinskey bring a marriage of wine and food to the tasting bar, pairing wine from organically raised grapes with seasonal bites. Sinskey's Four Vineyards Carneros Pinot Noir ($56) walks on the wild side with ferns, cedar and pepper, bringing out the nutty side of Gruyère *gougères* (cheese puffs).

GOOSECROSS CELLARS

Map p37; ☎ 800-276-9210; www.goose cross.com; 1119 State Lane, Oakville; tasting $10; ☾ by appointment 10am-4:30pm
Newbies appreciate free Wine Basics classes at 10:30am Saturdays, while aficionados book hot dates with blackberry-mocha Howell Mountain Cabernet ($69). For pre-trip wine education, Goosecross' Napa Valley Wine Radio podcast (www.napavalleywineradio.com) is the next best thing to diligent drinking.

Y GROTH

Map p37; ☎ 707-944-0290; www.groth
wines.com; 750 Oakville Cross Rd,
Oakville; ⏳ 10am-4pm Mon-Sat
This pink-stucco, family-owned
winery looks like a swanky
Southwestern mall but it's full of
surprises, from garden biodiversity projects to Sauvignon Blanc
($18.50) that's perkier than a
cheerleader, rallying taste buds
with star fruit and nectarine. Elusive Oakville Cab ($48) stacks black
cherry and pumpkin-pie on a soft
cushion of tannins – by the time
it's awarded its usual 90+ points
from critics, it's often sold out.

Y MONDAVI

Map p37; ☎ 888-766-6328; www.robert
mondaviwinery.com; 7801 Hwy 29,
Oakville; tasting $15; ⏳ 10am-5pm
'Hang a left at Mondavi,' is a handy
direction in Napa, where wineries
are oriented around Mondavi's
yellow megawinery. A pioneering
Napa vintner since 1945, Robert
Mondavi was a major supporter
of the arts, and the winery still
hosts summer concerts with
big-name groups like the B52s.
With industrial methods yielding consistent flavors, Mondavi
became a supermarket megabrand
and merged with beverage giant
Constellation in 2004. Taste mass-
produced vanilla Napa Chardonnay
($20) and chewy blackberry Cab
($28), and make up your own mind

about wine-country debates over
homogenized flavors.

Y RUBICON ESTATE

Map p37; ☎ 877-697-8242; www.rubicon
estate.com; 1991 Hwy 29, Rutherford;
tasting $25, tour $45-55; ⏳ 10am-5pm
This a Hollywood version of a winery, meticulously stage-managed
by director/vintner Francis Ford
Coppola. Fun but overproduced
estate tours convene on the red
carpet; indie tasters head into the
ivy-covered stone chateau, where
displays chronicle the Coppolas'
history, films (The Godfather,
Apocalypse Now, Virgin Suicides)
and wine ventures. Tasting bars
are overshadowed by spot-lit
racks of Godfather-worthy fedoras,
but the Rubicon Estate Cask Cab
($75) brings you back to the plot-
line with vanilla-scented cherries
and long tannins.

Y HONIG

Map p37; ☎ 707-963-5618; www
.honigwine.com; 850 Rutherford Rd,
Rutherford; tasting $10, applicable to
purchase; ⏳ 10am-4pm; 🐾 👪
Like a Disney heroine, winemaker
Kristin Belair gets help from
birds and beasts to produce
wines sustainably at this 100%
solar-powered winery: owls keep
rodents under control and trained
dogs nose out mealybugs to
eliminate the need for pesticides.
This unusual teamwork pays off in

acclaimed Rutherford Sauvignon Blanc ($25) with hints of Asian pear, almond and white pepper, and Bartolucci Napa Cab ($75) with red plum and burnt sugar. The resident animals add appeal for kids, who are welcome with their parents in the cozy tasting room by appointment.

ROUND POND
Map p37; ☎ 888-302-2575; www .roundpond.com; 875 Rutherford Rd, Rutherford; tasting with food pairing $25; ⏲ by appointment

From fruit to juice at Mondavi

Foodies, designated drivers and wine aficionados find common ground at this sustainable producer of Rutherford Cabs and artisan olive oil. At the winery, snag a table by the fireplace on the upstairs patio for wines and small bites made with local ingredients. Vertical tastings of estate Cab ($60) reveal how growing conditions tease out cassis, chocolate, leather and gun smoke. Across the street, the olive oil mill tour ($25) includes tasting estate olive oil and vinegars with rustic bread, fruit and cheese.

FROG'S LEAP
Map p37; ☎ 707-963-4704; www .frogsleap.com; 8815 Conn Creek Rd, Rutherford; tour with tasting $25; ⏲ by appointment 10am-4pm Mon-Thu; 🚶
When a burly biker found a hippie camping out on his property, what happened next was, um, unexpected. Together they pioneered organic growing practices and earned a following with Frog's Leap Sauvignon Blanc ($18), quenching thirsts for something different with clementines and mountain wildflowers. Their Napa Cab ($42) is not 'cough-and-hack', but cocoa-cherry-cola mellow with no funny faces on the finish. Limber up for free throws after touring their LEED Gold-certified barn winery and tasting room; you might win some wine.

THE VALLEYS

NAPA VALLEY

Castello Di Amorosa (p46) – if only this were your cellar at home

☿ PIÑA

Map p37; ☎ 707-738-9328; 8060 Silverado Trail; tasting $15; ⏰ by appointment

'What's our total production? You're looking at it,' says the assistant winemaker, nodding at Piña's single wall of barrels. The Piña family cultivated Napa vineyards for three generations, and it shows in Buckeye Howell Mountain Cab ($72): pure blackcurrant and lava rock after a thunderstorm.

☿ MUMM NAPA

Map p37; ☎ 800-686-6272; www.mumm napa.com; 8445 Silverado Trail; glass $6-10, tasting $25-30; ⏰ 10am-5pm; 🐾

The fabled French Champagne–maker began applying traditional methods to Napa grapes in 1986, resulting in Mumm Brut Prestige ($20) and DVX Napa Sparkling ($60), bubbling over with Queen Anne cherries and vanilla-bean ice cream. Stop by the gallery for Ansel Adams' sublime California landscape photography, and in summer dodge the crowds on the new reserve-tasting terrace ($5 extra, optional food pairing $20).

☿ GRGICH HILLS

Map p37; ☎ 707-963-2784; www .grgich.com; 1829 Hwy 29, Rutherford; tasting $10; ⏰ 10am-5pm

'Do something better every day,' was the credo that led winemaker Mike Grgich from his native Croatia to Napa and on to international fame in 1976, when his Chardonnay for Chateau Montelena (p47) humbled France's best. Today Grgich is championing biodynamic farming at his 366-acre estate, the largest certified organic and biodynamic grape grower in the US. Grgich Fumé Blanc ($30) is the wine seafood aspires to, with grapefruit and fresh apricots, and 'Cabernet lover's Merlot' ($42) hints at chocolate, tea and plum.

☒ HALL
Map p37; ☎ 707-967-0700; www.hall wines.com; 401 Hwy 29, St Helena; tasting $10-20; ⏰ 10am-5:30pm; ♿ ❀ ❀
Northern Californians are impatient for Hall's Frank Gehry–designed tasting room so they can finally one-up Southern California's Gehry-designed Disney Concert Hall over a glass of wine. Meanwhile, inspect Gehry's models of the billowing building with warped wooden-trellis roof while sipping Hall's Rosé Syrah ($24), with its own undulating layers of kiwi and rose petals, or Kathryn Hall Cab ($75), with its taste of summer barbecue and olallieberry pie.

☒ JOSEPH PHELPS
Map p37; ☎ 800-707-5789; www.jpvwines.com; 200 Taplin Rd, off

Silverado Trail; tasting $15-25; ⏰ 9am-5pm Mon-Fri, 10am-4pm Sat & Sun
Save this one for last. Phelps' Insignia ($200) has been the reigning Napa Meritage since 1974, taking the chill off spring mists outside Phelps' hillside tasting room. 'Five grapes, no rules,' is the guiding principle behind a blend reimagined with each harvest, recently featuring violet, ebony, black, white and pink pepper, and tannins with a long tail and a distinct purr. Don't skip Phelps' Sauvignon Blanc ($32), a botanical beauty of Kaffir lime, acacia and cypress.

☒ CASA NUESTRA
Map p37; ☎ 866-844-9463; www.casanuestra.com; 3451 Silverado Trail; ⏰ 10am-4:30pm Mon-Sat; ♿ ❀
Perpetually munching pet goats at Casa Nuestra seem unimpressed by the outdoor bulletin board overflowing with faded ribbons for past vintages – clearly they haven't tried the Two Goats Cab/Merlot blend ($20), a buoyant boysenberryish red easily paired with vegetarian pastas. With an organic, solar-powered winery, fundraising peace concerts, cork peace messages, a shaded picnic area and apricot-dessert Late Harvest French Colombard ($20), Casa Nuestra certainly bottles its good vibes.

🍷 SCHRAMSBERG

Map p37; ☎ 707-942-2401; www.schrams
berg.com; 1400 Schramsberg Rd, Calistoga; tour with tasting $35; ⏰ tours 10am,
11:30am, 12:30pm, 1:30pm, 2:30pm
The enchanting 1862 winery
Robert Louis Stevenson covered
in *Silverado Squatters* convinced
Jack and Jamie Davies to drop
everything in 1965 and reopen it –
and you'll see why on a lengthy
tour that'll leave you almost sorry
to adjourn to the tasting room...al-
most. Four Cuvées and a Cab later,
most visitors leave with the Blanc
de Noirs ($38) brimming with Fuji
apple and cinnamon bun.

🍷 CASTELLO DI AMOROSA

Map p37; ☎ 707-967-6272; www.castello
diamorosa.com; 4045 Hwy 29, Calistoga;
tasting $10-15; ⏰ 9:30am-6pm
Who hasn't wanted to build a
grand castle in their backyard?
Winemaker Dario Sattui built his
121,000-sq-ft Tuscan stronghold
with cross-vaulted ceilings and
Siena-inspired Great Hall murals.
After touring through wine cellars and a dungeon with torture
equipment (tour $25, ages five
and up), tastings are anticlimactic,
though late-harvest Gewürztraminer ($39) offers grace notes
of tangerine and honeysuckle.

Ninety-nine bottles of wine in the (Schramsberg) cellar, 99 bottles of wine, take one down, and pass it around...

Check the website for jousting matches.

WINE GARAGE

Map p37; ☎ 707-942-5332; www.wine garage.net; 1020 Foothill Blvd, Calistoga; ⏰ 10am-7pm

Napa's best deals come from Todd Miller's selection of 250 wines under $25, including rising-star winemakers and famous vintners with excess inventory. Staff offer tasting notes, though rarely tastings – but then, most Napa tastings cost more than a bottle here.

VINCENT ARROYO

Map p37; ☎ 707-942-6995; www.vincent arroyo.com; 2361 Greenwood Ave; ⏰ by appointment 10am-4:30pm

Bond with JJ the black Labrador retriever over Entrada ($60), a burly Syrah/Cab/Petit Sirah blend of pomegranate, spiced plums and smoke. Tastings are free, fun and slightly dangerous, with additional tastes of single-vineyard Petit Sirahs ($45 to $50) often offered to enthusiasts. The best value shall remain Nameless ($22), a Cab/Cab Franc/Merlot blend with rhubarb flavors that dissipate into a fog of white pepper.

CHATEAU MONTELENA WINERY

Map p37; ☎ 707-942-5105; www.monte lena.com; 1429 Tubbs Lane, Calistoga; tastings $20-25; ⏰ 9:30am-4pm

Their 1973 vintage popped the cork of French Chardonnay domination, and although winemaker Mike Grgich moved on to his own winery (p44), winemaker Bo Barrett's Napa Valley Chardonnay ($50) remains a standard-bearer with green apple, honey-tangerine, and kiwi. Zin has been planted locally since 1882, and Montelena's claret-style, clarion cranberry Estate Zin ($30) is dry-farmed and picked at 3am for peak flavor. Montelena continues decades-long sustainability commitments with solar operations and ladybugs guarding vineyards against pests.

NAPA – CARNEROS

A misty stretch of marshland, Napa Carneros has no downtown – but you'll find noteworthy cool-climate Pinots, bubblies, spas and sculpture among the vineyards.

DI ROSA PRESERVE

Map p37; ☎ 707-226-5991; www.di rosapreserve.org; 5200 Carneros Hwy 121; ⏰ gallery 9:30am-3pm Wed-Fri, tours depart 10am, 11am, 1pm Wed-Fri, 10am, 11am, noon Sat

No boundaries divide California's outlandish art, freakish nature and mind-blown viewers at di Rosa Preserve. Here you might bump into classes of fifth graders

Kathryn Reasoner
Executive Director, di Rosa Preserve (p47)

Shock therapy On the Preserve, art isn't safely behind a velvet rope. You'll encounter letters across a valley, video art in the basement, installations in a cramped bathroom – it's a series of shocks to the system poking the imagination awake. **How priceless** A lot of the collection is site-specific work that can't be sold or pulled off walls. Rene [di Rosa] served on the boards of the Whitney and SFMoMa, but he didn't look to Europe or New York for direction; he related to Northern California's spirit of nonconformity. He knew that uncomfortable, even dangerous, ideas tell us who we are. **Art & Nature & Food** Hess (p40) has an astonishing art collection, from Anselm Kiefer to Lynn Hershman. Artesa (p3 offers views over the valley and the backsides of Preserve sculptures, and Nest (p50) puts on exciting shows. For lunch, Boonfly Café (opposite) is a great gourmet diner, but sunny days call for fish and chips at Moore's Landing (opposite).

lying on the floor discussing million-dollar Robert Bechtel paintings on the ceiling, notice peacocks striking poses on David Ireland's fallen-angel statues or confront Ray Beldner's poignant truism spelled out in rusted metal letters across the golden valley floor: *NATURE REMAINS*. The house, wine cellar and shed gallery show landmark California contemporary art, from far-out Beat collages to interactive wall art telling you to go away, then begging you to come back. Only the Gateway Gallery can be visited without a tour, so book your tour ticket ahead.

🧖 SPA AT CARNEROS INN
Map p37; ☎ 707-299-4850; www.the carnerosinn.com; 4048 Sonoma Hwy; ⌚ 8am-8pm
Unwind in your element at the Spa, where treatments come in Carneros themes: the Cellars feature Chardonnay-apricot pedicures ($80 for one hour); the Farms include goat-butter body wraps ($145 for one hour) and the Creeks Huicha Bath offers a pebble-lined tub-treatment overlooking rolling vineyards ($75 for 30 minutes).

🍴 BOON FLY CAFÉ
New American $$
Map p37; ☎ 707-299-4870; www.the carnerosinn.com; 4048 Sonoma Hwy; ⌚ 7am-9pm

A local lunch crowd throngs this Carneros hotel, and when the wood-fired oven opens, you'll smell why: Point Reyes blue-cheese flatbread, sizzling with caramelized onions, bacon, mushrooms and thyme. Cobb salad with lip-smacking Carneros-wine vinaigrette today balances out brunch tomorrow: green eggs and ham, with leek-lemon zest cream and crispy hash browns.

🍴 MOORE'S LANDING
New American $
Map p37; ☎ 707-253-2439; www .mooreslandingnapa.com; 6 Cuttings Wharf Rd; ⌚ 11am-3pm Wed, Thu & Sun, 11am-8pm Fri & Sat
When you're convinced you're heading nowhere, keep going, and you'll find this big red shed along the Napa River. Half the local crowd is probably ditching work midweek or blowing off household chores on weekends, which is why the beer taps are flowing by noon and no one's rushing to finish thick sausages and plump tuna melts. On sunny days, head for the patio or fishing dock, and rethink ambitious afternoon plans.

NAPA

This Victorian boomtown is booming again with notable restaurants, tasting rooms, boutique shops and historic B&Bs.

SEE

NEST

Map p37; ☎ 707-255-7484; www.napa nest.com; 1019 Atlas Peak Rd; ⏱ 10am-6pm Thu-Sun

Feather your nest with inspired works by NorCal artists – Kana

Tanaka's glass raindrop installations, or Linda Kramer's American Carnival Portrait of pink-haired Ashley, who ran away with the circus. Events are more fun than you thought possible in a gallery: a show called 'Decorum' involved raucous tiara-making workshops, while an art exhibit celebrating

NAPA

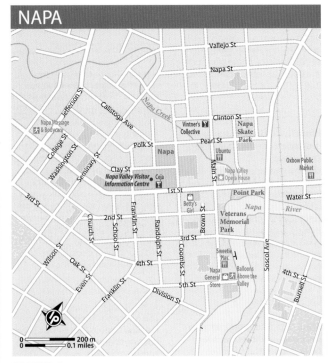

meat and potatoes offered locally made charcuterie.

DO

BALLOONS ABOVE THE VALLEY

Map p50; ☎ 707-253-2222; www .balloonrides.com; 540 Main St; $210 (specials online); ⏲ 5:30-7am departure
Grip that basket and channel your inner Jules Verne: prepare for balloon views hundreds of feet over Napa vineyards. Takeoffs and landings are gentle and the scenery may move you to sing '80s soft-rock ballads. Eager risers can arrive a half-hour early for coffee and muffins, but all passengers should be ready for takeoff around dawn (weather permitting). Flights are followed by complimentary brunch and bubbly at the Napa General Store (p52).

NAPA MASSAGE & BODYCARE

Map p50; ☎ 707-252-7079; www.napa massage.com; 1834 1st St; ⏲ 8am-8pm
Feeling light-headed after wine tasting? Come back down to earth in this cozy Arts and Crafts–style cottage, where trained professionals provide massages ($85 for one hour) and hot-stone treatments ($65 for 30 minutes). Aromatherapy is complimentary with every treatment, and specially blended without chemical additives.

Coming back down to earth in the Napa Valley

SHOP

BETTY'S GIRL *Women's Clothing – Local Designer*

Map p50; ☎ 707-254-7560; www .bettysboutique.com; 1239 1st St
Fabulousness comes made to order at Betty's Girl, where vintage cocktail numbers ($40 and up) can be altered to hug every curve, with no charge for alterations or shipping. Hollywood costume-designer Kim Northrup named her store after her stylishly resourceful mom, and you'll have déjà vu when you see her cutaway-collared jacket on the runways next season.

🏠 NAPA GENERAL STORE *Gifts*
Map p50; ☎ 707-259-0762; www.napa generalstore.com; 540 Main St
Finally, Wine Country souvenirs that are clever and reasonably priced: tubs of Napa-grapeseed sugar scrubs ($25), bangle bracelets made from recycled wine bottles ($38) and, for the secret agent who has everything, an armored wine carrier ($69). Gourmet salads and a well-stocked wine bar on-site make convenient shopping pit stops.

🏠 NAPA PREMIUM OUTLETS
Clothing
Map p37; 🕙 707-226-9876; www.pre miumoutlets.com; 629 Factory Stores Dr
Michelle Obama might shop here if she knew Napa – but shhh, keep those 40% off J Crew sleeveless dresses to yourself. American Apparel offers a rainbow of soft tees under $15, alongside Gap, Kenneth Cole, Levi's and Gymboree Kids. Fashionistas brave stiletto stampedes at Calvin Klein and Barney's New York, where prices on last season's runway looks frequently drop a digit.

🍴 EAT & DRINK
🍴 OXBOW PUBLIC MARKET
Gourmet Foods $
Map p50; ☎ 707-226-6529; www.oxbow publicmarket.com; 610 & 644 1st St; 🕙 9am-7pm Mon-Sat, 10am-5pm Sun

Other downtowns may have grim food courts, but Napa houses local food artisans under one lofty roof. Let loose on free samples of Napa olive oil and Sonoma cheese, but save room for dinner: Hog Island's sustainably harvested Sonoma oysters (six for $15); *arepas* (Venezuelan corn flatbread) with spicy tomato, black bean and creamy avocado ($6.99) from Pica Pica; and Three Twins seasonal lemon-ginger cookie ice cream ($3.65 for a single waffle cone).

🍴 SWEETIE PIES *Bakery* $
Map p50; ☎ 707-257-7280; www .sweetiepies.com; 520 Main St; 🕙 11am-2pm Mon-Sat
Designated drivers deserve infinite gratitude in Napa, or failing that, top-notch baked goods. Give the gift of a carrot, apple and zucchini morning glory muffin, pear-berry pie with flaky crusts that blow apart in stiff winds, or cupcakes with dollops of chocolate-dipped marshmallow not to be casually left in the car with a friend (ahem).

🍴 UBUNTU
Farm-to-Table Vegetarian $$$
Map p50; ☎ 707-251-5656; www.ubuntu napa.com; 1140 Main St; 🕙 5:30-9pm Mon-Thu, 11:30am-2:30pm & 5:30-10pm Fri & Sat, 11:30am-2:30pm & 5:30-9pm Sun
Fine vegetarian dining downstairs, yoga upstairs, 100 or more

Dinner's ready Initially Ad Hoc was a temporary restaurant serving affordable, tasty dinners, but people enjoyed the concept so much, Thomas Keller kept it open. The set menu is how most of us grew up eating at home: when your mom calls you in from playing outside, whatever she's cooked is what you're eating, right? **No do-overs** We've been creating new meals daily for two and a half years, and I like to honor Napa history with traditional ingredients like quince, mustard and Tempranillo. Occasionally we hit a creative wall, but then I listen to stories of people who grew up in the Valley, maybe stop for a drink at Groth (p42), and the ideas start flowing. **Gourmet playground** Whenever I can, I'll eat whatever's cooking at French Laundry (p56), and it almost makes me jealous what Jeremy Fox does with vegetables at Ubuntu (opposite).

sustainably produced wines at the bar and a biodynamic kitchen garden: welcome to NorCal, in its all-natural glory. The seasonal menu creates permanent vegetable cravings, especially crisped trumpet mushroom and truffled pecorino atop tender mustard greens and grilled *calçots* (Catalan sweet spring onions) with red-pepper-almond dipping sauce. Carrot gnocchi and kale-pesto pizza are heartier fare, and can be prepared for vegans too.

★ PLAY
NAPA VALLEY OPERA HOUSE *Performances*
Map p50; ☎ 707-226-7372; www .nvoh.org; 1000 Main St

Divas have belted their best here since 1879, but since the Opera House's restoration and reopening in 2003, the house is just as likely to be brought down by Grammy winner Béla Fleck banjo-dueling with Mali's Toumani Diabaté. Most performances are $30 to $50, and since the main theater seats 500 maximum, book ahead.

YOUNTVILLE

This onetime stagecoach stop is now a major foodie destination, with more Michelin stars per capita than any other US town.

👁 SEE
👁 MA(I)SONRY
Map p37; ☎ 707-944-0889; www.maisonry .com; 6711 Washington St; ⏱ 9am-10pm

In the blink of an (i), this 1904 stone building was transformed in 2008 into a rustic-modern showplace for furniture design and wine. Visitors sip free tastes of perfumey Arriviste Blackbird Rosé as they wander past worn Eames chairs, dodge tangled chandeliers and hang out by the fire pit in the garden.

👁 NAPA VALLEY MUSEUM
Map p37; 707-944-0500; www.napa valleymuseum.org; 55 Presidents Circle; adult/senior/child 7-17yr $4.50/ $3.50/$2.50; ⏱ 10am-5pm Wed-Mon

Art gallery, science museum, Napa history crash course: this barn-style museum covers fascinating territory. Permanent collection highlights include 19th-century California wildflower paintings by Napa's pioneering women botanical artists, and 160 years of photographs of people who put Napa on the map, from Native Wappos and Mexican ranchers to silver speculators and forward-thinking vintners.

🍴 EAT & DRINK
🍴 AD HOC
Locavore Californian $$
Map p37; ☎ 707-944-2487; www.adhoc restaurant.com; 6476 Washington St;

🕙 **5-9pm Mon, Wed, Thu-Sun, plus 10:30am-2pm Sun**

Don't bother asking for a menu at Thomas Keller's most innovative restaurant since French Laundry: you'll have whatever chef de cuisine Dave Cruz (p53) is cooking today, and be glad you did. Cruz and his kitchen brain trust invent the four-course, $48 set menu daily, serving seasonal delights in Pyrex baking dishes. Recently, sensational pickled fennel salad was only narrowly topped by Wagyu beef (of $100 steak notoriety) with the tooth-resistance of butter, followed by nutty cheeses and silky chestnut panna cotta. No substitutions are offered unless you have a dietary restriction; reserve well ahead, and pray for fennel.

🍴 **BOUCHON** *Cal-French* $$$

Map p37; ☎ 707-944-8037; www .bouchonbistro.com; 6543 Washington St; 🕙 **11:30am-12:30am**

Banter and steak frites fill the main room at Thomas Keller's ode to a Parisian bistro. But the real action is at the bar, where the lighter bar menu and cocktails poured to perfection yield conversational free-for-alls. A celebrity winemaker reminisced over oysters and martinis, while a starlet inhaling endive-watercress salad with Roquefort and Fuji apple detailed her TV pilot to a lone Texan

No menu? No worries. Let the experts make the decisions at Ad Hoc

enjoying duck-fat fries. Bouchon's bakery across the brick path offers morning-after brioche.

FRENCH LAUNDRY
Farm-to-Table Californian $$$

Map p37; ☎ 707-944-2380; www.french laundry.com; 6640 Washington St; ⏱ 11am-1pm & 5:30-9pm by reservation 1-6 months ahead
Critics call French Laundry the most important restaurant in America, and this could well be the most pleasurable meal you've ever eaten. Once you've begged for a table two to four months from now and swallowed the $240 set-menu price (service included), everything else goes down like a dream. Nine courses commence with a glass of bubbles and artful amuse-bouche, such as buttery kampachi sashimi with an astonishingly succulent, miniscule romaine leaf, followed by vegetarian or omnivore menus with classic or adventurous course options, plus optional foie gras ($35) and wine pairing ($150). Dodging the 1997 Screaming Eagle Cab ($10,075), sommelier consultations yield inspired pairings by the half-bottle ($41 plus) and glass ($18 plus) – think satiny white Burgundy matched to unctuous Spanish mackerel with blood orange and black sesame crumble. The parade of desserts includes classic 'doughnuts and coffee' (cappuccino *semifreddo*), shortbread and chocolates. Most diners depart audibly vowing to return for French Laundry–worthy achievements – the Nobel Peace Prize, perhaps.

PANINOTECA OTTIMO
Sandwiches $

Map p37; ☎ 707-945-1229; www.napa styleottimocafe.com; 6525 Washington St; ⏱ 10am-6pm Mon-Sat, 10am-5pm Sun
'The Best Sandwich Shop!' is a bold name for Napa's Italian-American celebrity chef Michael Chiarello to give his new sandwich shop, situated across the street from Thomas Keller's Bouchon Bakery. Chiarello's judicious use of organic local veggies, Italian cured meats and rustic breads does make Paninoteca the clear Napa picnic winner. Panzanella salad and slow-roasted Duroc pork panino are hits with Chiarello's organically produced wines.

REDD *Californian* $$$

Map p37; ☎ 707-944-2222; www.reddnapa valley.com; 6480 Washington St; ⏱ 5:30-9:30pm Mon-Thu, 11:30am-2.30pm & 5:30-9:30pm Fri & Sat, 11am-2:30pm Sun
Let nature take its four courses with voluptuous Napa reds, sensational NorCal ingredients and a sleek setting of tawny wood and indirect lighting. Richard Reddington wins foodie affection over glazed pork

WORTH THE TRIP: WET & WILD

> **Harbin Hot Springs** (Off map p37; ☎ 707-987-0422; www.harbin.org; 18424 Harbin Springs Rd; ⏰ front office 24hr) NorCal's legendary clothing-optional retreat offers natural-springs waterfalls, hot (113°F), warm and cold mineral-water pools, co-ed changing rooms, free yoga classes, hiking trails over 1100 acres, campgrounds, domed guest rooms, organic restaurants, natural food market and even a New Age temple. Prices for six-hour day use/camping/dorm/dome room are from $30/35/45/70.

> **Wilbur Hot Springs** (Off map p37; ☎ 530-473-2306; www.wilburhotsprings .com; Bear Valley Rd, off Hwy 20; ⏰ 10am-8pm) An 1800-acre preserve with rustic Victorian-era lodge and indoor/outdoor mineral water spa (per person day use/dorm stay/private room $47/87/from $139). Clothing is optional in pools, and silence is encouraged; students with ID get 25% off from Monday to Thursday.

> **Safari West** (Map p37; ☎ 707-579-2551, 800-616-2695; www.safariwest.com; 3115 Porter Creek Rd; adult/child $68/30) Giraffes, zebras, and flamingos roam this private wildlife preserve outside Calistoga. Take a 2 ½-hour Jeep safari (departing three times daily from mid-March to October and twice daily at other times) or stay overnight in luxury platform tents (from $170) or two-bedroom cottages ($350) to see lemurs' eyes light up and hear the purr of...wait, was that a cheetah?

belly with savory soy caramel and a kind of ménage à foie gras: foie gras served as mousse, *au torchon* (compressed loaf) and pâté. Come early for sunny tables outside by the fountain and the four-course lunch ($50 or $75 with wine pairings).

⭐ PLAY
⭐ LINCOLN THEATER
Performances
Map p37; ☎ 707-944-1300, 866-944-9199; www.lincolntheater.org; 100 California Dr
Thanks to the $22 million 2005 renovation of this 1200-seat auditorium, Napa can do what comes naturally: relax with a glass of wine and wait for Broadway shows, ma-

jor comedians, ballet performances and main-stage acts like the Indigo Girls to come to them. The theater is in the Veterans' complex across Rte 29, but the Yountville shuttle (p197) provides free rides return from Yountville for performances.

⭐ PANCHA'S *Dive Bar*
Map p37; ☎ 707-944-2125; 6764 Washington St; ⏰ noon-2am
When you cross Pancha's threshold, there's a tacit understanding that you are never to mention what goes on here once squadrons of hottie servers get off work. Singles scope out their options on sketchy couches, chefs chain-smoke through tales that would make

Up close and personal at Safari West (boxed text, p57)

Anthony Bourdain blush, scuffles break out by the pool tables and are quickly forgotten over margaritas – just don't let on we told you.

OAKVILLE

There's not really a 'ville' in Oakville, just a market and a whole lot of tasting rooms offering sensational Sauvignon Blancs and Meritages.

🍴 OAKVILLE GROCERY
Café & Sandwiches $

Map p37; ☎ 707-944-8802; www.oakville grocery.com; 7856 Hwy 29; ⏰ 8am-6pm

Gourmet specialties are good to go here: grab a ready-made roast-beef and blue cheese sandwich on fresh crusty bread, or pear salad with Rosé vinaigrette. For mid-tasting pick-me-ups, there's top-notch espresso and the Cupa Cupa, a dark-chocolate cup filled with chocolate cake and tiramisu.

RUTHERFORD

The destination of choice for Cab connoisseurs, this hot, dusty stretch of Napa is prime tasting-room territory.

THE VALLEYS

NAPA VALLEY

⊞ LA LUNA TAQUERIA
Mexican $

Map p37; ☎ 707-963-3211; 1153 Rutherford Rd; ⏱ 9am-5pm May-Nov
Cab tasters and growers scorch Rutherford dust right off their tongues with La Luna's *carne asada* (grilled beef) tacos piled with jalapenos, onions and hot salsa. Fair warning: do not attempt wine tasting or farm-machinery operation after consuming forearm-sized burritos at the ramshackle picnic table.

⊞ LONG MEADOW RANCH
Organic Produce $

Map p37; ☎ 707-963-4555; www.long meadowranch.com; 1796 Hwy 29; ⏱ 9am-5pm May-Nov
When urban foodies dream of starting a farm, this is the one they mean: certified organic and 100% solar-powered in Napa Valley, offering heirloom veggies, honey, olive oil ($20 for 375ml), peppery Ranch House Red table wine ($19) and grass-fed beef hot dogs (around $5 a pound). Browse the produce, wander the gardens and visit chickens pecking at organic fruit like supermodels.

ST HELENA

Don't be fooled by the quaint historic downtown – St Helena has cosmopolitan flair, with indie movies at the Cameo, artsy boutiques, sleek California-cuisine restaurants, and the Culinary Institute of America.

SEE

⊙ ST HELENA FARMERS MARKET

Map p37; ☎ 707-486-2662; www.st helenafarmersmkt.org; Crane Park, off Grayson Ave; ⏱ 7:30am-noon Fri May-Oct
Heirloom tomatoes are just the beginning at this farmers market, where Culinary Institute of America (CIA) chefs-in-training troll for pheasant from Clucky Plucky Poultry and for Hamada farms' apriums (apricot-plums). Picky eaters turn into budding foodies at 'Taste Exploration' events, which double-dare kids to taste weird fruit and help cook farm-fresh veggies.

🚶 DO

🚶 BALE GRIST MILL PARK

Map p37; ⏱ 707-942-4575; www.parks .ca.gov; 3369 Hwy 29; mill entry adult/child $2/free; ⏱ sunrise-sunset, call for weekend mill demos; ♿
The floorboards of Dr Edward Turner Beale's 1846 mill creak underfoot, but the 36ft waterwheel still grinds into action on weekends. Visitors can help grind polenta ($3 for 5lb), available at the museum shop. Picnicking is possible under shady trees, or hike uphill 1.1 miles to Bothe-Napa

THE VALLEYS

NAPA VALLEY

Valley State Park for your pick of tables. Goths, photographers and other fans of crumbling gravestones should take the 0.1 mile detour to Napa's Pioneer Cemetery.

SHOP

LOLO'S
Vintage Clothing
Map p37; ☎ 707-963-7922; www.lolos consignment.com; 1120 Main St; ☽ 10:30am-4pm Mon, 10:30am-5:30pm Tue-Sat, 11am-4pm Sun
Outfit your inner Wine Country eccentric with Tory Burch tunics for chic picnics and swinging '60s dresses for a groovy night at the Napa Opera. Cashmere clotheshorses will score vintage beaded cardigans and trendy numbers like Tse color-blocked tops.

NAPA SOAP COMPANY
Body & Bath Products –
Local Maker
Map p37; ☎ 707-963-5010; www.napa soap.com; 651 Main St; ☽ 10am-5pm
Wine-sniffing is fine for tasting rooms, but at home you might prefer a refreshing whiff of mandarin blossom from your Napa Soap kitchen-counter cleaner – though Cabernet Soapignon is good for a chuckle. Sheila Rock-

Cured meats or a modern-art installation? You decide at Napa Valley Olive Oil

wood handcrafts her concoctions with the environment and community in mind, using locally produced, biodegradable ingredients and donating some proceeds to the local Boys and Girls Club.

NAPA VALLEY OLIVE OIL
Gourmet Foods – Local Maker
Map p37; ☎ 707-963-4173; 835 Charter Oak Ave; ☺ 10am-6pm
At this ramshackle house with picnic tables in the overgrown yard, you may doubt you're in the right place for fine Napa olive oil. But inside note the wall covered with business cards of regular customers: it's a who's who of Napa. Wooden crates display Napa Valley Olive Oil soaps and lotions, and the extra-virgin, cold-pressed oil is distilled Napa sunshine, available by the liter or jug. In narrow aisles, mind the salami overhead and try not to elbow the macaroni.

WOODHOUSE CHOCOLATE
Chocolates – Local Maker
Map p37; ☎ 800-966-3468; www.woodhousechocolate.com; 1367 Main St; ☺ 10:30am-5:30pm
Dark-chocolate purists and vending-machine loyalists abandon past snack habits for Woodhouse's scrumptious milk chocolate Butterfly Bars with currants, almonds and Moroccan *ras el hanout* spice mix. The toffee would make

English grandmothers envious, but owners Tracy and John Anderson make every morsel in St Helena. Prices are Napa-precious, but the quality's beyond reproach.

EAT & DRINK

COOK *Cal-Italian* $$
Map p37; ☎ 707-963-7088; 1310 Main St; ☺ 7pm-10pm Tue-Sat, 11:30am-2pm Sat & Sun
No one gets seated immediately in this corridor of a restaurant, even with reservations – but no one wants to miss out on such tasty, honestly priced food, either. The seasonal menu nods to Northern Italy, focusing taste buds on three star ingredients per dish: oven-roasted greens with blood orange and toasted almonds, housemade gnocchi with sage brown butter and obligatory flourless chocolate cake with caramel and grey salt.

GO FISH *Seafood* $$
Map p37; ☎ 707-963-0700; www.gofishrestaurant.net; 641 Main St; ☺ 11:30am-9pm Sun-Thu, 11:30am-10pm Fri & Sat
Sea-foodies get schooled at Go Fish, where top-notch chefs dish ultrafresh sushi and Pacific dishes with French panache. Sample Ken Tominaga's freestyle *omokase* (sushi tasting menu) or Cindy Pawlcyn and Victor Scargle's clever Californian surf-and-turf: Pacific grouper with bacon-roasted

TOP FIVE WALLOWS IN THE MUD

> **Indian Springs** (Map p37; ☎ 707-942-4913; www.indianspringscalistoga.com; 1712 Lincoln Ave; ⏲ office hours 8am-8pm) The spa dates from 1861, with a vast hot mineral-water pool and Zen-chic cottages. Private baths in sludgy volcanic mud ($85) or mineral water ($70) with eucalyptus and lavender come with free pool access.

> **Lavender Hill Spa** (Map p37; ☎ 707-942-4495; www.lavenderhillspa.com; 1015 Foothill Blvd; ⏲ 10am-6pm Sun-Thu, 10am-8pm Fri-Sat) In private cottages, side-by-side claw-foot Jacuzzi tubs offer slippery lavender mud baths solo or as a couple ($70 per person), with 60-minute restorative therapeutic massage for $145. Visitors center 20%-off coupons make this the sweetest deal in town.

> **Dr Wilkinson's Hot Springs** (Map p37; ☎ 707-942-4102; www.drwilkinson.com; 1507 Lincoln Ave; ⏲ 8:30am-5:30pm) The 1952 motel-spa founded by John 'Doc' Wilkinson offers separate spas for men and women with wallows in volcanic mud and peat moss followed by mineral whirlpool, steam room and blanket wrap ($89 for one hour), with optional 60-minute massage ($169 for 2¼ hours).

> **Spa Solage** (Map p37; ☎ 707-226-0850; www.solagecalistoga.com; 755 Silverado Trail; ⏲ 8am-8pm) Step up to Solage's sleek Mud Bar for a custom-blended 'Mudslide' slathering of volcanic mud with your choice of essential oils, then bake in the Mud Lounge before your mineral-water soaking tub ($89). An extra $25 grants access to geothermal pools and steam rooms.

> **Golden Haven Hot Springs** (Map p37; ☎ 707-942-6793; www.goldenhaven.com; 1713 Lake St; ⏲ 9am-9pm) The tubs aren't glamorous and the volcanic mud gets reheated and reused, but these inexpensive wallows come with mineral Jacuzzi, blanket wrap and pool access (per person midweek/weekend $54/59). Go early (8am to 8:30am by appointment) or late (7pm to 8pm) for $49. Accommodations and spa packages start at $89 per person.

brussels sprouts or Monterey Bay calamari with woodsy-tart ancho-apple jus. Check the website for family sushi-rolling classes and $40 three-course feasts midweek.

🍴 **MARKET** *New American* $$
Map p37; ☎ 707-963-3799; www.market sthelena.com; 1347 Main St; ⏲ 11:30am-9pm Sun-Thu, 11am-10pm Fri & Sat
Share plates and California-style comfort with buttermilk-fried chicken and jalapeño cornbread; tuna tartare with fried capers; and macaroni and cheese with aged cheddar, bacon and herbs. Save room for gourmet s'mores with chocolate ganache and house-made marshmallows, toasted over a mini-campfire at your table.

🍴 **MODEL BAKERY** *Bakery* $
Map p37; ☎ 707-963-8192; www.the modelbakery.com; 1357 Main St; ⏲ 7am-6pm Tue-Sat, 8am-4pm Sun

Savvy foodies time Model breakfasts around 10am, before the Vahlrona *pain au chocolat* sells out, and when staff start making sandwiches with Niman Ranch meats, local cheeses and caramelized onions. Wine and cheese demand organic whole-wheat *pain du vin* with winegrape sourdough starter, fresh from the 1920s brick oven.

NAPA VALLEY COFFEE ROASTING COMPANY *Café* $
Map p37; ☎ 707-963-4491; www.napavalleycoffee.com; 1400 Oak Ave; ⏰ 7am-6pm Mon-Fri, 7:30am-6pm Sat & Sun
A lifesaver before, after and midway through wine tasting, this local roaster serves the best specialty coffee in Napa in a big, sunny café. The cappuccino foam is stiff but the prices aren't, and upbeat staff and responsible owners make this a sweet spot to read a paper, donate to local charities and recycle used batteries.

SILVERADO BREWING COMPANY *Brewpub* $
Map p37; ☎ 707-967-9876; www.silveradobrewingcompany.com; 3020 Hwy 29; ⏰ 11:30am-1am
After making wine all day, 'Napkins' crave a beer – and Silverado produces microbrews up to local standards. Brewmaster Ken Mee's Certifiable Blonde has organic ingredients and crazy-tasty malts, and

competes for attention with the stronger and slightly bitter hopped-up Amber Ale. Food is typical pub grub, but you won't lack for Buffalo wings or local company.

TAYLOR'S AUTOMATIC REFRESHER *Burgers* $
Map p37; ☎ 707-963-3486; www.taylorsrefresher.com; 933 Main St; ⏰ 10:30am-9pm; ♿
A retro-'50s classic with 21st-century Californian sensibilities: burgers are made from Niman Ranch beef or lean ahi tuna, with chili-dusted sweet-potato fries and local Double Rainbow milkshakes in refreshing mint chip or green tea. Boont Amber ale (p152) is on tap, or BYO a Napa vintage for $5 corkage. To avoid weekend waits along the white-picket fence, arrive before midday or after 2:30pm.

WINE SPECTATOR GREYSTONE RESTAURANT AT THE CULINARY INSTITUTE OF AMERICA *Californian* $$
Map p37; ☎ 707-967-1100; www.ciachef.edu; 2555 Main St; ⏰ 11:30am-9pm Sun-Thu, 11:30am-10pm Fri & Sat
Pop quizzes are tasty at Greystone, where chefs-in-training cook under the scrutiny of chef-instructors: pâté with curried apple was an A on a cracker, while risotto was a B for excess butter. The open kitchen is a great live-action *Top Chef* episode

as students prepare 'today's temptations' (four to five microplates for $25) paired with 'lessons in wine' ($14 to $20 a flight).

⭐ PLAY

☑ CAMEO CINEMA *Cinema*

Map p37; ☎ 707-963-9779; www .cameocinema.com; 1340 Main St; ⏱ check website or call
Bringing Hollywood glamour to Napa dates since 1915. Local owners Cathy Buck and Shawn LaRue stock the snack bar with artisan ge-

lato and organic coffee, and have added state-of-the-art digital and Dolby 3-D systems to this vintage single-screen movie house. Check the website for first-run and 3-D movies, Wednesday art films and Saturday late-night horror flicks.

CALISTOGA

This is the down-to-earth end of Napa, with the mud baths, tractor parades and farm-to-table dining to prove it.

An Old Faithful erupts, faithfully

○ SEE
○ OLD FAITHFUL GEYSER
Map p37; ☎ 707-942-6463; www.old
faithfulgeyser.com; 1299 Tubbs Lane;
adult/senior/child $8/7/3; ⏰ 9am-5pm
'Many Notable People Have Come
to SEE, HEAR, and LEARN the mys-
teries of this "Wonder of Nature"
that captivates the imagination –
IT'S AMAZING,' brags the old
sign at this historic landmark.
Scientists gush about this squirter,
one of only three active Old
Faithful geysers, with the plumes
that erupt up to 60ft high every
20 to 40 minutes monitored by
the Carnegie Institute to possibly
predict California earthquakes.
Visitors await spurts picnicking,
petting guard llamas, inspecting
antique seismographs and brows-
ing kitschy souvenirs.

○ PETRIFIED FOREST
Map p37; ☎ 707-942-6667; www
.petrifiedforest.org; 4100 Petrified
Forest Rd; adults/senior & child 12-17yr/
child 6-11yr $7/6/3; ⏰ 9am-5pm
Over three million years ago,
these redwoods were toppled by
a volcano eruption and buried
in ash, gradually crystallizing
into stone. Local cowboy Charles
Evans noticed a very hard stump
in 1871, and the world's largest
petrified trees were excavated
along what is today a historic
0.4-mile trail.

○ DO
○ CALISTOGA BIKESHOP
Map p37; ☎ 707-942-9687; www
.coolwinetour.com; 1318 Lincoln Ave;
⏰ 10am-6pm
Discover great whites and super-
charged reds the green way, by
bike (rental per hour/day $10/35).
Self-guided Cool Wine Tours
($79.99) come with wristband for
free tastings, itinerary consultations
to suit your skill level and wine
tastes, bike and helmet rental, and
complimentary wine-delivery service of tasting-room purchases.

○ CALISTOGA SPA HOT SPRINGS
Map p37; ☎ 707-942-6269; www
.calistogaspa.com; 1006 Washington St;
mineral pools $25; ⏰ 10am-9pm
Wellness spas are all the rage,
but Calistoga Spa offers pleasant
plunges without aromatherapy
and faddish facials. Four mineral-
water pools range from 80°F to
104°F: the coolest is big enough
for swimming, and the hottest has
Jacuzzi jets. Come after 7pm, when
the crowd is local and access is $10.

○ ROBERT LOUIS STEVENSON STATE PARK
Off map p37; ☎ 707-942-4575; www
.parks.ca.gov; 3801 Hwy 29; ⏰ dawn-dusk
The adventurous author of
Treasure Island and *Kidnapped*

Cry uncle to caffeine cravings at Yo El Rey coffee house

honeymooned in 1880 at an abandoned mine here, and the park named after him remains rugged, with hikes through evergreen forests and rock faces beloved by local climbers. Parking, picnic tables and trailheads are at the 45.4-mile marker. Posted signs about frequent smash-and-grabs suggest taking valuables with you.

🛍 SHOP

🏠 CALISTOGA POTTERY
Housewares – Local Maker
Map p37; ☎ 707-942-0216; www .calistogapottery.com; 1001 Foothill Blvd; 🕐 **11am-5pm**

Sally and Jeff Manfredi make pottery that feels good and does justice to home cooking, with simple shapes in earth tones or cheerful shades of buttery yellow, cobalt blue and oxidized-copper green.

🏠 MUDD HENS *Body & Bath Products – Local Makers*
Map p37; ☎ 707-942-0210; www.mudd hens.com; 1348 Lincoln Ave; 🕐 **10am-6pm**
Unless you live under a volcano, Mudd Hens is the best way to recreate Calistoga volcanic mud baths at home. Calistoga's dried mineral-rich volcanic mud is sold for home use for $21 per pound – half the price of any spa mud treatment, though you'll have to handle hose-down duty yourself.

🍴 EAT & DRINK

🍴 BUSTER'S *Barbecue* $

Map p37; ☎ 707-942-5605; www.busters
southernbbq.com; 1207 Foothill Blvd;
🕑 11am-8pm

When Buster's in the parking lot
grilling, that's your cue to pull over
for smoky sirloin tri-tip, hot sauced
pork ribs and hot links, whether
it's technically mealtime or not.
Sides are teensy, but you're here
for the meat, washed down at
picnic tables with Syrah from the
Wine Garage (p47).

🍴 ENGLISH
GARDEN TEA ROOMS
Tea House $

Map p37; ☎ 707-942-4262;
1107 Cedar St; 🕑 11am-6pm Thu-Mon

Teacakes and old-world graces
make a welcome break between
wildlife, wines and mud baths.
Pop by post-hike for elevenses
complete with vintage tea service,
scones, jam and clotted cream,
and return mid–wine tasting for
fortifying tea with a ploughman's
platter of salads, cheeses and
Branston pickle. High tea hits the
spot after spas with flaky homemade pastries of apricot, blue
cheese and walnut.

🍴 JOLÉ
Farm-to-Table Californian $$

Map p37; ☎ 707-942-5938; www.jole
restaurant.com; 1457 Lincoln Ave; 🕑 5-
10pm Sun & Tue-Thu, 5-11pm Fri & Sat

Jolé's organic, local flavors leap off
small plates, from local sole with
tangy Napa grapes to five-spice
duck breast with cherry reduction
over wilted mizuna and sweet-
potato puree. Sides are showstop-
pers, especially peas with roasted
artichokes and smoked ham and
crispy brussels sprouts with capers
drizzled with aged balsamic.
Seasonal desserts are unskippa-
ble, including Baldwin apple and
cranberry strudel with housemade
caramel ice cream.

🍴 YO EL REY *Café* $

Map p37; ☎ 707-942-1180; www.yoel
rey.com; 1217 Washington St; 🕑 6:30am-
3pm Mon & Wed-Sat, 7:30am-3pm Sun

Purveyor of fine organic Fair Trade
coffee, free wi-fi and inspiration,
owner J Kirk Feiereisen covered the
walls of his café with poetry and
drawings and donates proceeds
from every cup to coffee-growing
communities. BYO mug and this
surfer/environmentalist/barista
congratulates you: 'Right on!'

>SONOMA VALLEY

When you drive past a quirky white-picket fence that twists out of the ground and curls up like a toothy grin, you've officially arrived in Sonoma. Expect the unexpected here: sweet country cottages lined with Polynesian war clubs, a pajama-patchwork flag of the rogue Bear Flag nation that once ruled downtown Sonoma, bubbly Sonoma water rumored to cure rheumatism and bubbly Sonoma wine known to cure sobriety.

Now that you're in Sonoma, conventions need not apply. This rebel region attracts outliers: arena rockers who enjoy a mellow Merlot, hard-core foodies who drizzle olive oil on their ice cream, and toddlers who ride boxcars like pro hobos. Hey, don't knock it till you try it at BR Cohn Winery (p72), El Dorado Kitchen (p86) and Traintown (p83). Whether unwinding for you means riding horses, strolling through fields of

SONOMA VALLEY

🍷 WINERIES

Bartholomew Park Winery	1	D4
Benziger	2	B3
BR Cohn Winery	3	B3
Chateau St Jean	4	A1
Cline Cellars & California Missions Museum	5	C6
Eric Ross	6	D2
Gloria Ferrer	7	C6
Gundlach Bundschu	8	D5
Imagery Estate Winery	9	B3
Kaz Winery	10	A1
Ledson Winery	11	A1
Muscardini Cellars & Ty Caton	12	A1
Roshambo	(see 19)	
Schug Carneros Estate	13	C6
St Francis Winery	14	A1
Valley of the Moon Winery	15	B3
VJB Cellars	16	A1
Wellington	17	B2
Wine Room	18	A1

👁 SEE

Cornerstone Sonoma	19	C6
Jack London State Historic Park	20	A3
Sugarloaf Ridge State Park	21	B1
Wildwood Farm Nursery & Sculpture Garden	22	B2

🏃 DO

Fairmont Sonoma Mission Inn & Spa	23	C4
Garden Spa at MacArthur Place	24	C5
Kenwood Inn & Spa	25	B2
Morton's Warm Springs	26	A2
Sonoma Valley Cyclery	27	C5
Traintown	28	C5
Triple Creek Horse Outfit	29	A3

🛍 SHOP

Artefact Design & Salvage	(see 19)	
Kenwood Farmhouse	30	A1
Wine Country Chocolates	31	D2
Zipper	(see 19)	

🍴 EAT & DRINK

Artisan Bakers	32	C4
Fig Café	33	D2
Garden Court Cafe	34	D2
Glen Ellen Inn Oyster Grill & Martini Bar	35	D2
Glen Ellen Village Market	36	D2
Mondo	37	C4
Oak Hill Farm	38	B3
Olive & Vine	39	D2
Sage Fine Food & Provisions	(see 19)	
Vineyards Inn Bar & Grill	40	A1

lavender, tasting wine, or luxuriating in a natural hot springs after a day of trawling local boutiques, Sonomans can totally relate – and they've got you covered. Just beyond that twisted white picket fence, your niche awaits.

WINERIES

▼ CLINE CELLARS & CALIFORNIA MISSIONS MUSEUM

Map p69; ☎ 707-939-8051; www
.californiamissionsmuseum.com;
24737 Arnold Dr; tasting reserves/current
releases $1/free, museum free; ☯ tast-
ing 10am-6pm, museum 9:30am-4pm
fall-spring, 11am-4pm summer; ♿
Balmy days call for plummy Mourvédre Rosé ($14) at pond-side
picnics, and rainy ones for fire-
place-worthy old-vine Zinfandels
($18 to $34) and a peek at 1939
scale miniatures of California's 21
missions. Don't be fooled by the
1850s farmhouse tasting room:
this family-owned winery is large
scale and surprisingly forward-
thinking, with solar panels on the
roof, vines cultivated with composting teas and hungry sheep
keeping weeds in check.

▼ GLORIA FERRER

Map p69; ☎ 707-996-7256; www.gloria
ferrer.com; 23555 Arnold Dr; per 2oz
taste $2; ☯ 10am-5pm
Celebrate your escape from SF with
a splash of bubbly at this Mission-
style tasting room. Views over the

sprawling estate are Hitchcock-
worthy, as swirling mists infuse
Pinot Noir grapes with dewy Meyer
lemon peel and sneaky cherry-cola
flavors for GF's bargain Blanc de
Noir ($18). Bottles run up to $50 for
vintage Carneros Cuvée.

▼ ROSHAMBO

Map p69; ☎ 707-431-2051; www.rosham
bowinery.com; Cornerstone Sonoma, 23570
Arnold Dr; tasting $5; ☯ 10am-5pm
Cross an airplane hangar with an
all-ages punk club, and you have
Roshambo's new tasting room.
With beat-up yellow school lockers
used as wine racks, this isn't your
grandma's idea of Wine Country –
and neither is the wine. Bacon isn't
the first thing sippers expect from
Syrah, but Roshambo's Justice
($30) has it, and their Reverend Zin-
fandel ($25) delivers fire, brimstone
and brambleberries as promised.

▼ SCHUG CARNEROS ESTATE

Map p69; ☎ 707-939-9365; www.schug
winery.com; 602 Bonneau Rd off Arnold
Dr; tasting $5-10; ☯ 10am-5pm
Old World savvy and California
dreaming make a heady, ticklish
Rouge de Noir sparkling Pinot
($30) ideal for picnics at this grand

German Tudor-style winery. Schug is family-owned, with clever UC Davis–educated winemakers mixing specific blocks of grapes into versatile wines: Carneros Chardonnay ($28) has the poached-pear flair of White Burgundy, while well-priced Sonoma Coast Pinot Noir ($24) has a bright raspberry start and a brooding, mesquite finish.

GUNDLACH BUNDSCHU

Map p69; ☎ 707-938-5277; www.gunbun.com; 2000 Denmark St; tasting $5-10, tour $20; ⏰ tasting 11:30am-4:30pm, cave tours 1:30pm Fri-Sun

Six generations after the Bundschu family started making wines here in 1868, they've got their sustainably farmed, estate Gewürztraminer ($30) and Merlot ($30) down to a signature – and they generate 60% of their power with solar panels and recycle 70% of their water. You can sample straight from the barrel on tours of their 2000-barrel cave, but don't miss Gun Bun's mature Tempranillo ($33) with pomegranate and orange-blossom notes.

WINE EXCHANGE OF SONOMA

Map p80; ☎ 800-938-1794; www.wineexsonoma.com; 452 1st St E, Sonoma; ⏰ 10am-6pm Mon, Wed & Thu, 10am-7pm Tue, Fri & Sat, 11am-6pm Sun

Come for the wine, stay for the beer. You heard that right: while championing the new, the weird and the wow in Sonoma wines, Dan Noreen offers six beers on draft in the speakeasy-style rear tasting bar, plus another 250 bottled varieties 'at last count.' Stop by to try obscure local vintages and potent Pliny the Elder on draft (see p105) and get the new-release lowdown from informed, passionate staff.

BARTHOLOMEW PARK WINERY

Map p69; ☎ 707-939-3026; www.bartpark.com; 1000 Vineyard Lane; tasting $5-10, museum & park free; ⏰ tasting room & museum 11am-4:30pm, Palladian Villa 10am-3pm Sat & Sun; ♿

Shaggy manzanita and rampant wildflowers make this 400-acre preserve so postcard-perfect, you might forget you're here for the hooch. The vineyards were cultivated by flamboyant Hungarian count Agoston Haraszthy, who bottled California's first-known vintage in 1857 and went bust a decade later. The plot thickens as your tasting progresses from citrus-sunshine Sauvignon Blanc ($21) to smoky-midnight Desnudos Merlot ($32). Today the Gun Bun crew cultivates the certified organic vineyards, and the Bartholomew Park Museum, picnic tables and hiking trails are open to all.

Sonoma-style sips and swigs at the Wine Exchange (p71)

VALLEY OF THE MOON WINERY

Map p69; ☎ 707-939-4510; www.vom winery.com; 777 Madrone Rd; tasting $5-10; ☽ 10am-4:30pm

Midweek the tasting-room staff cracks bottles and jokes, and won't let you leave until you've swapped life stories. Valley of the Moon doesn't believe in monogamy when it comes to varietals, and they're all priced to move. Their $22 sparkling is lemon chiffon with a pecan-pie chaser and their Cuvée de la Luna ($38) is a big-boned Meritage – and after two years in American and French oak it'll give your tongue a three-minute bear hug.

BR COHN WINERY

Map p69; ☎ 800-330-4064; www.brcohn .com; 15000 Sonoma Hwy; tasting $10, applicable to purchase; ☽ 10am-5pm

Wave your lighter in the air for Bruce Cohn, the Sonoma goat-herd who moved to San Francisco in 1968 to manage a little rock band called the Doobie Brothers – and started reading up on viticulture on the tour bus. Stop by to try his ultrarich organic olive oil and laid-back Doobie Red Bordeaux blend ($32) with proceeds supporting the National Veterans Association, and rock your favorite tattered concert tee at the annual benefit concert in November.

IMAGERY ESTATE WINERY

Map p69; ☎ 877-550-4278; www.imagerywinery.com; 14335 Sonoma Hwy; tasting $10-15; 10am-4:30pm Sun-Thu, 10am-5pm Fri & Sat

High-impact biodynamic wines make a statement with original-art labels, including pretty-in-pink explosions by pop-provocateur Kara Maria and liquid landscapes by performance artist Tom Marioni. Tastings cover six wines, and like any group show, the results are mixed: Dragonsleaf Red ($38) tears across the tongue like a fume-spewing dragster, while Pallas Estate ($75) is a statuesque Cab on a Malbec pedestal dissolving into vanilla-orange creamsicle.

TOP FIVE WINE COUNTRY HOTSPOTS FOR HIPSTERS

- di Rosa Preserve: peacocks and art students preen in surreal sculpture gardens (p47)
- Roshambo: indie rockers avoid tans, play Ms PacMan and sip Syrah (p70)
- Hess Collection: post-punk Cab tasters slip on their horn-rims to inspect Anselm Keifers (p40)
- Stryker Sonoma: *Dwell* subscribers discover old vine Zins in a deconstructed Frank Lloyd Wright tasting room (p139)
- Imagery: art collectors load up on obscure varietals with artist-designed wine labels (above)

ERIC ROSS WINERY

Map p69; ☎ 707-939-8525; www.ericross.com; 14300 Arnold Dr, Glen Ellen; tasting $5; 11am-5pm Thu-Mon

Self-taught winemaker Eric Luce turns grapes from choice lots along the Russian River into small-production wines that often sell out. Robust Feeny Ranch Old Vine Zin ($30) makes a feast of tandoori takeout, and Wine Country Chocolate truffles (p91) are best enjoyed with the brandy-tinged Zin-Syrah port ($40) by the tasting room's wood-burning stove.

BENZIGER

Map p69; ☎ 800-989-8890; www.benziger.com; 1883 London Ranch Rd; tasting $10-15, tram tour adult (with tasting)/under 21yr $15/5; 10am-5pm;

Pastoral and ambitious, this family-run winery merged with megacorp Glen Ellen in 1993 to become a Demeter-certified biodynamic behemoth. Wines range from pleasant mass-market $13 to $19 Sauvignon Blancs to ostentatious $80-plus library reds. Certain reserves compare to triple-figure Napa vintages – the black-truffle-and-cranberry Gordenker Vineyard Cabernet Sauvignon ($45), for instance, turns turkey sandwiches into Thanksgiving. For explanations of biodynamics, wander through displays by the parking lot or take the 45-minute tram tour.

▼ WELLINGTON

Map p69; ☎ 800-816-9463; www .wellingtonvineyards.com; 11600 Dunbar Rd, Glen Ellen; tasting $5, applicable to purchase; ⏱ 10am-5pm

'What a looooong, strange trip it's been…' wail the Grateful Dead as you walk into Wellington's pine-paneled tasting room – but you already guessed that from

Tour the gardens of Chateau St Jean

gnarled vines out front that miraculously survived Prohibition. Eight acres of vines averaging 100 years old grow a whopping 24 kinds of grapes, supplemented by rebellious teenage Merlot, Syrah and rare Rhône Marsanne, all sustainably dry-farmed and mostly organic. Wellington offers many of Sonoma's best buys: $30 gets you a hazelnutty white port or the clove-accented Karren Vineyard Cab that landed Double Gold in the 2008 SF Chronicle Wine Competition.

▼ WINE ROOM

Map p69; ☎ 707-833-6131; www .the-wine-room.com; 9575 Sonoma Hwy; tasting $5; ⏱ 11am-4pm Mon-Thu, 11am-5pm Fri-Sun; 🐾

Talk about a block party: this co-op offers 20 tastes from five neighborhood wineries. Look for Orchard Station's green-apple Sauvignon Blanc ($18), bottled Napa sunshine Moondance Merlot ($24) and Sonoma Portworks' figgy Aris Petite Sirah Port ($30). Since Friendly Dog Winery is featured here, dogs are welcome indoors and at outdoor picnic tables.

▼ VJB CELLARS

Map p69; ☎ 707-833-2300; www.vjb cellars.com; 9077 Sonoma Hwy, Kenwood; tasting $5; ⏱ 10am-5pm

The impeccable dark-roast espresso at the bar and welcoming toast of grassy, fizzy Prosecco are worthy Italian imports, but VJB's zero-oak Gabriella Ranch Chardonnay ($18) and shortbread-rich Baci di Famiglia Chardonnay Port ($28) are small-production Sonoma specialties. The Belmonte family owners give their tasting room the look and warmth of a Venetian café, complete with toasts in Italian. *Cin-cin!*

☑ MUSCARDINI CELLARS & TY CATON

Map p69; ☎ 707-833-0526; www .muscardinicellars.com, www.tycaton .com; 8910 Sonoma Hwy; tasting $10, applicable to purchase; ⏰ 11am-6pm
Double up with tastings from two upstart wineries, featuring radically limited 33- to 250-case new releases that regularly rack up West Coast awards. Check out Muscardini Barbera ($49), a stand-out Stateside vintage of this food-championing Italian red, and the Muscardini Gracie Creek Syrah ($42), hitting low berry notes and trailing silk in its wake like Billie Holliday. If it's open, try Ty Caton Estate Tytanium ($75), a blend of Cab, Petit Sirah, Syrah and Merlot that wraps your tongue in black cherry, cocoa and leather.

☑ CHATEAU ST JEAN

Map p69; ☎ 707-833-4134; www .chateaustjean.com; 8555 Sonoma Hwy; tasting $10-15; ⏰ 10am-5pm
The gardens outside this photo-op faux-chateau have seen their share

WORTH THE TRIP: LAVENDER FIELDS FOREVER

Between the wine tasting and the heady aroma of 4500 lavender plants, you can almost hear your blood pressure drop at **Matanzas Creek Winery** (☎ 800-590-6464, ext 19; www.matanzascreek .com; 6097 Bennett Valley Rd; tasting $5, applicable to purchase; ⏰ tasting 10am-4:30pm, tours 10:30am & 2:30pm Mon-Fri, 10:30am Sat). In late June and late September, rolling purple fields in bloom add airborne floral notes to Matanzas Creek's crisp crimson Sonoma County Rosé of Merlot ($17). Take a self-guided tour of the lavender fields or follow a prebooked guided tour of the six California native gardens.

of Hollywood weddings, but the romance kicks off indoors for lovers of vanilla-rich Chardonnays ($20 to $45) and spa-ready, salted-cantaloupe Alexander Valley Fumé Blanc ($20). Their highly rated Cabernets are worth a taste, but at $130 to $180 a pop, they're not exactly wallet-friendly.

☑ KAZ WINERY

Map p69; ☎ 707-833-2536; www .kazwinery.com; 233 Adobe Canyon Rd, Kenwood; tasting $5-10, applicable to purchase; ⏰ 11am-5pm Fri- Mon; 🐾
With quirky, organically grown, California-to-the-core wines, the Kasmier family doesn't need

elaborate enticements to sell out their microproduction of 1500 cases. Kristin lines up offbeat varietals on the barrel-top bar: rough, ready, redcurrant Hooligans Grenache ($36), blackberry-velvet Outbound Cab Franc ($40) and strawberry-and-violets Nebbiolo Blush Port ($32).

ST FRANCIS WINERY
Map p69; ☎ 888-675-9463; www.stfranciswinery.com; 100 Pythian Rd; tasting $10-15, food & wine pairing $30, tour $20, workshops $25-65; ⏰ 10am-5pm
Dinner parties are plotted over Artisan Wines Flight pairings with two-bite amuse-bouche by Chef David Bush. A recent highlight was the cocoa-rich Wild Oak Merlot ($38) with chicken mole. One-hour tours of the solar-powered winery are available and the hands-on Aroma Workshop ($25) or Blending Seminar ($65, including custom-blended bottle) offer takeaway skills.

LEDSON WINERY
Map p69; ☎ 707-537-3810; www.ledson.com; 7335 Sonoma Hwy; tasting $5-15; ⏰ 10am-5pm
Turrets and a steep black-slate roof make this castle ideal for Ozzy Osbourne or Tim Burton – but beyond the Hollywood Goth glamour is a family-owned winery that takes its varietals dead seriously. Nine massive Merlots

($30 to $85), three noteworthy Sauvignon Blancs ($24 to $26) and no less than 17 distinct California Zins ($32 to $48) make choosing five tastes a challenge – but don't miss Lodi Old Vine Zin ($36) for strawberry dusted with pink pepper. If the Zins sneak up on you, there's an in-house deli with panini and other snacks.

SONOMA – CARNEROS

Emerging from the swirling mists along this surreal stretch of highway are sculpture gardens, a sunny Nascar racetrack, sparkling wineries, and rebel reds served in what looks like a fall-out shelter.

CORNERSTONE SONOMA
Map p69; ☎ 707-933-9474, 707-933-3010; www.cornerstonesonoma.com; 23570 Arnold Dr; admission free; ⏰ 10am-5pm
Sixteen noted landscape designers were each given 1800 sq ft to let their imaginations take root, turning an ordinary lawn into a living gallery. Contenders for best of show are Andrea Cochran's meditative willow-twig version of a corn maze and Andy Cao's dreamy 'Lullaby Garden,' an undulating golden field punctuated with a black whirlpool.

INFINEON RACEWAY

Off map p69; ☎ **800-870-7223; www .infineonraceway.com; 29355 Arnold Dr**
Who says designated drivers must be bored in Wine Country? Go, speed racers, go, to Infineon's website to book tickets to the Nascar Cup, NHRA Drag Racing, the Superbike Showdown and other events. To get behind the wheel of a Formula 3–model FJR-50 yourself, consider a workshop at the Jim Russell Racing School (☎ 800-733-0345; www.jimrussell usa.com). At about $2000 a day, classes aren't cheap – but that's $9,998,000 less than a Formula 1 racecar.

ARTEFACT DESIGN & SALVAGE

Gardening Supplies & Home Decor
Map p69; ☎ **707-933-0660; www.artefact designsalvage.com; Cornerstone Sonoma, 23562 Arnold Dr;** ⏱ **10am-5pm**
Backyards become miniature Wine Countries with the right props: mortar and pestles for culinary herb gardens, mossy bird baths for the overgrown-vineyard effect and the obligatory barrels repurposed as tables. For that Sonoma-spa look, they also sell Buddha statues in every size and your choice of pose: cross-legged, reclining or laughing.

Sculpture 'Blue Tree 2' by Claude Cormier at Cornerstone Sonoma

Date tonight? Visit the farmers market first

decanters shaped like disposable water bottles. For gifts, check out the birdhouses made of school-books, cases of artisan-designed jewelry and delicate vases made from old light bulbs.

 SAGE FINE FOOD & PROVISIONS
Sustainable Californian $

Map p69; ☎ 707-935-1681; www.sage provisions.com; Cornerstone Sonoma, 23584 Arnold Dr; ☼ 9am-5pm

Fast food, Sonoma-style: flavorful, organic, and locally grown, served outdoors or inside a glammed-up galvanized-tin shed. Meaty panini trump burgers, but better still is the savory tart of the day with luscious local greens and pickled red onions.

SONOMA

The rebel heart of California since 1823 – downtown Sonoma was once ruled by drunken revelers, but is now the stomping ground for farm-to-table foodies, indie-cinema buffs and Wine Country style-setters.

ZIPPER *Gifts & Home Decor*

Map p69; ☎ 707-996-7956; www .zippergifts.com; Cornerstone Sonoma, 23592 Arnold Dr; ☼ 10am-5pm

Nope, not a single grape-cluster tile or decoupaged wine-label tray in sight – equip your home bar with a sense of humor instead, with one-of-a-kind wine glasses made of antique teacups and

SEE

ADOBE BARRACKS

Map p80; ☎ 707-935-6832; www.parks .ca.gov; 20 E Spain St; adult/child $2/free (fee covers same-day admission to Mission SF Solano); ☼ 10am-5pm;

Mexico's Comandante of Northern California, General Vallejo, built this adobe in 1840 to house his troops, but it became the capitol of a rogue nation on June 14, 1846, when American settlers of varying sobriety surprised the guards and declared an independent 'California Republc' [sic] with a homemade flag featuring a blotchy bear. The US took over the republic a month later, but abandoned the barracks during the Gold Rush, leaving Vallejo to turn them into (what else?) a winery in 1860. Today barracks displays describe the lives of soldiers: seldom paid and often bored, with pistols, cards and a mule for company. San Francisco's 1906 Earthquake destroyed the original Bear Flag, but replica T-shirts in the gift shop earn street cred in Sonoma bars.

FARMERS MARKET AT SONOMA PLAZA

Map p80; ☎ 707-538-7023; Sonoma Plaza; ☽ 5:30-8pm Tue, 9am-noon Fri Apr-Oct; Ⓥ ♿ ☺

You'll need all five senses for this market: taste local wildflower honey, sniff handmade herbal soaps, admire multicolored mounds of heirloom tomatoes, thump ripe watermelons and hear live bands and kids squealing over organic corn dogs.

LAHAYE ART CENTER

Map p80; ☎ 707-996-9665; 148 E Napa St; ☽ 11am-5pm

At this collective in a converted foundry, you can view the storefront gallery and meet the artists in their garden studios. Vines and horses are recurring themes, but standouts include Brigitte McReynolds' dreamscape encaustics (wax-pigment paintings) and Beverly Prevost's asymmetrical ceramic dinnerware, featured at Café La Haye (p86) next door.

MISSION SAN FRANCISCO SOLANO

Map p80; ☎ 707-938-9560; 114 E Spain St; adult/child $2/free (fee covers same-day admission to Adobe Barracks; ☽ 10am-5pm; ♿

The last California mission was established in 1823 and peaked around 1832, when it included a tannery, vineyard and 10,000 acres farmed by 900 conscripted Native Californian workers. But with settlers lobbying for private land ownership and Native Californian workers dying of introduced illnesses, Mexico secularized Mission San Francisco Solano in 1834. The East Spain Street wing remains largely intact, from the Bell Room and dining room hung with paintings of California's missions to the reconstructed chapel.

SONOMA VALLEY MUSEUM OF ART

Map below; ☎ 707-939-7862; www .svma.org; 551 Broadway; adult/family $5/8, Sun free; ⏰ 11am-5pm Wed-Sun
Art upstages even Sonoma wine at SVMA openings, where you might spot a David Best art car encrusted

with faux pearls and glow-in-the-dark skulls, or a table that converts into a rifle case by conceptual sculptor Gord Peterson. Join Sonoma's free spirits and fashionistas for MIX cocktail lounge nights and the museum's fabulous October Día de los Muertos exhibition.

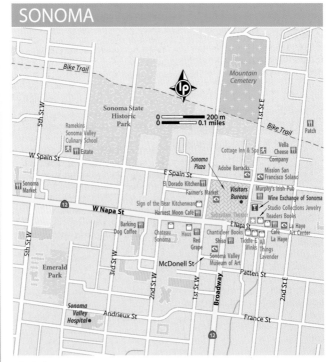

Fancy a splash? Cool down at the Fairmont Sonoma Mission Inn & Spa

🏃 DO

🏃 COTTAGE INN & SPA

Map p80; ☎ 800-944-1490; www
.cottageinnandspa.com; 310 1st St E;
⏰ 8am-10am & 2-7pm
The next best thing to having a
close friend with a weekend home
and a massage license may be a
scented deep-tissue massage in
this sunny garden spa right off
Sonoma's town square. Rates are
higher than Sonoma's average
at $125 plus per hour, but the
winter-blues treatment is a worthy
splurge involving hot stones,
warm towels and heavenly ginger
massage oil.

🏃 FAIRMONT SONOMA
MISSION INN & SPA

Map p69; ☎ 707-938-9000; www
.fairmont.com/sonoma; 100 Boyes Blvd;
bathhouse entry $39 or free with 2 treat-
ments; ☎ spa 7:30am-8:30pm, fitness
facilities 6am-8:30pm
Cure hangovers Sonoma-style
with a full day in the Jacuzzi tubs,
herbal steam room, dry sauna and
thundering showers of varying in-
tensity from 'exfoliating' to 'mega'
for $39 (plus obligatory 18%

service surcharge). Entry is free with two treatments, ranging from Sonoma lavender facials ($169 for one hour) to more esoteric therapies including chakra readings and 'subtle energy balancing' ($139 for one hour).

🏋 GARDEN SPA AT MACARTHUR PLACE
Map p69; ☎ 707-933-3193; www.mac arthurplace.com; 29 E MacArthur St; 🕙 9am-8pm

Get that healthy, wine-soaked glow with 'Sonoma Wine Therapy': a Chardonnay bath, Chardonnay sugar scrub and massage with essential oils ($225 for 100 minutes). If you'd rather save time and cash for wine tasting, the 50-minute Red Wine Grapeseed Massage ($118) leaves the skin soft and slightly buzzed. Access to the hotel pool and fitness facilities is free with treatments.

🏋 RAMEKINS SONOMA VALLEY CULINARY SCHOOL
Map p80; ☎ 707-933-0450; www .ramekins.com; 450 W Spain St

Wine Country's most famous workshop venue for home chefs brings out extraordinary *Top Chef* ambitions in everyone, with hands-on cheese-making seminars and knife-skills boot camps. Reserve well ahead for delectable winemaker dinners and demonstrations by Sonoma's legendary

globe-trotting cookbook author Paula Wolfert.

🏋 SONOMA VALLEY CYCLERY
Map p69; ☎ 707-935-3377; www.sonoma cyclery.com; 20091 Broadway; town/road/mountain bike hire per day $25/45/65; 🕙 10am-6pm Mon-Sat, 10am-4pm Sun

Hit the hills on rental wheels, with maps and helmets helpfully supplied upon request. For a more scenic, easygoing route,

TOP FIVE WINE COUNTRY GADGETS
> Vinturi: Aerates aged wine faster than decanting, so you can drink it sooner – $39 at Oxbow Market (p52).
> Two-prong wine-bottle opener: Low-tech and less likely to leave cork in the bottle – $6 at Sign of the Bear (p85).
> Oak staves wine rack: Seasoned oak recycled into one-of-a-kind storage, signed on the back by the artisan – $89 and up at Napa General Store (p52).
> Vac-u-Vin: The vacuum pump and stopper slow down oxidization, buying a couple of extra days to enjoy opened wine – $14 at Sign of the Bear (p85).
> Wine-barrel cheese board: Reclaimed wine-stained oak makes a dramatic backdrop for Sonoma cheeses – $39 and up at Kenwood Farmhouse (p95).

head up Arnold Dr, away from cars suddenly swerving into winery driveways.

TRAINTOWN
Map p69; ☎ 707-938-3912; www.train
town.com; 20264 Broadway; park entry
free, most rides $2-5; ☻ 10am-5pm sum-
mer, 10am-5pm Fri-Sun Sep-May; ♿
Aaaaaaaaall aboard! Kids hop onto quarter-scale boxcars and adults squeeze in alongside them for a 1.25-mile trip through delightfully narrow tunnels and shrunken towns. Families pose for holiday-card photos waving presidentially from three full-size cabooses, with babies gamely sporting engineering caps. The carousel, Chatanooga Choo-Choo Chairs and most other rides involve spinning and whirling, best enjoyed before any food or wine tasting.

SHOP
ALL THINGS LAVENDER
Body & Bath Products – Local Maker
Map p80; ☎ 707-938-1080; www
.sonomalavender.com; 115 E Napa St;
☻ 10:30am-6pm
Lingering inside this boutique could induce narcolepsy, what with the lingerie sachets and teddy bears stuffed with lavender grown on a local farm. The farm opens to

the public for a Lavender Festival in June, offering facials, lavender brownies, aromatherapy lectures and other surefire insomnia cures.

CHANTICLEER BOOKS
Antiques & Books
Map p80; ☎ 707-996-7613; www
.chanticleerbooks.com; 127 E Napa St;
☻ 11am-5:30pm Wed-Sun
Collectors troll this antiquarian dealer for vintage lithographs of California wildflowers and rare books by authors who kicked off their careers in California. Recent finds include illustrated editions of Jack London's Wild West classics and first editions of Robert Louis Stevenson's 1886 *Kidnapped* and Mark Twain's 1885 *Huckleberry Finn*.

CHATEAU SONOMA
Home Decor & Gifts
Map p80; ☎ 707-935-8553; www.chateau
sonoma.com; 153 W Napa St; ☻ 10:30am-
6pm Mon-Sat, 11am-5pm Sun
French whimsy meets the Wild West in true Wine Country style – think crystal candelabras in rusted birdcages, a wine rack that appears to be made from twigs, and birds' nests perched atop linen-bound books. Owner Sarah Anderson combs the Provence and Sonoma countryside so you can score perfume atomizers, handmade beeswax candles

Browsers, bookworms and bibliophiles come together at Readers Books

and decorative balls of hemp twine without getting your shoes muddy.

🏠 HAUS *Clothing*

Map p80; ☎ 707-939-6460; 135 W Napa St; ⏱ 10am-6pm Mon-Sat & noon-5pm Sun; ♿
Svelte Sonomans have an unfair advantage, and it's not the farm-fresh salads or miracle-working spas: it's this supplier of sleek raw-silk dresses, expensive dark jeans and artfully cut jackets. Walls papered with handwritten ledger sheets show owner Zanita Zody's preference for timeless, creatively

reused and one-of-a-kind items, including baby clothes made from recycled rock T-shirts.

🏠 READERS BOOKS *Books*

Map p80; ☎ 707-939-1779; www.readers books.com; 130 E Napa St; ⏱ 10am-9pm Mon-Sat, 10am-8pm Sun; ♿
Upgrade from airport paperbacks with gripping thrillers by first-time authors, cheese-making how-tos by Sonoma *fromagers*, fascinating Jack London biographies and memoirs of a Russian River garlic-grower. Don't miss readings here to get your books signed by the author.

SONOMA VALLEY > SONOMA

THE VALLEYS

SONOMA VALLEY

SIGN OF THE BEAR
KITCHENWARE *Housewares*
Map p80; ☎ **707-996-3722;**
435 1st St W; ⏱ **10am-6pm**
All the gourmet supplies you
never knew you needed are here:
a Bundt pan shaped like an octo-
pus, wine aerators and iconoclas-
tic measuring spoons that dole
out 'a smidge' or 'a tad.' Narrow
aisles teeter with fragile culinary
must-haves – watch your bag and
your step.

STUDIO COLLECTIONS
JEWELRY *Jewelry – Local Maker*
Map p80; ☎ **707-935-6772; 126 E Napa St**
Nothing says, 'I missed you,' like
souvenir Wine Country corkscrews
bought at the airport, right?
When in doubt, opt for one-of-
a-kind pendants of embroidered
silk framed in silver by Sausalito
designer Presh, Bakelite buttons
fashioned into cocktail-ready silver
rings by Sonoma designer Sally
Bass, or cascading tourmaline earrings by jeweler and store owner
Bess Nathan Rice.

TIDDLE E WINKS
Gifts & Candy
Map p80; ☎ **707-939-6933; www.tiddle
ewinks.com; 115 E Napa St;** ⏱ **11am-
5pm Sun-Thu, 11am-6pm Fri & Sat;** ♿
Adults regularly embarrass their
kids squealing over all this nostalgic candy and old-fashioned fun:

Pixie Stix, Abba-Zabba, Silly Putty,
Slinkys and more. Original gift
options include vintage Japanese
tin robots and souvenir Wine
Country tea towels embroidered
in Sonoma.

🍴 EAT & DRINK
🍴 ARTISAN BAKERS *Bakery* $
Map p69; ☎ **707-939-1765; www.artisan
bakers.com; 750 W Napa St;** ⏱ **6:30am-
3pm Mon-Sat, 7am-2pm Sun;** Ⓥ ♿
Burly construction workers talk
shop over cappuccinos and
cranberry-walnut pumpkin tea-
cake, shoppers gossip over quiche
with hazelnut Romesco sauce and
sommeliers argue over wine pairings for Artisan's gooey brownies,
while wine-tasting picnickers grab
the signature baguettes.

🍴 BARKING DOG COFFEE
Café $
Map p80; ☎ **707-996-7446; www
.barkingdogcoffee.com; 201 W Napa St;**
⏱ **6am-8pm Mon-Fri, 7am-8pm
Sat & Sun;** 📶 ♿
Directions are hardly necessary
because you can smell the beans
roasting down the block. Rush
hour hits twice daily: late morning,
when wine-tasters cure hangovers
with lattes made from local Clover
Stornetta milk, and midafternoon,
when gaggles of high schoolers
update Facebook profiles using
free wi-fi over Ghirardelli cocoa. >

🍴 CAFÉ LA HAYE
Locavore New American $$

**Map p80; ☎ 707-935-5994; www
.cafelahaye.com; 140 E Napa St;
⏰ 7-10pm Tue-Sat**
Only three dozen people can
squeeze in, and the luckiest are
seated near the tiny kitchen
watching Chef Norman Owens'
team dish out New American
classics: salads featuring produce
grown within a 60-mile radius,
pork loin with cherry-pistachio
stuffing and to-die-for berry-
studded Meyer lemon cheesecake.
Make sure you reserve well ahead.

🍴 EL DORADO KITCHEN
Sustainable Californian $$

**Map p80; ☎ 707-996-3030; www
.eldoradosonoma.com; 405 1st St W;
⏰ 11:30am-2:30pm & 5:30-9pm**
Wild Western roots and sustainable bounty are the secrets to Chef
Justin Everett's Sonoma signa-
tures, including huevos rancheros
flatbread with housemade chorizo
and local Liberty Farms duck

Color-coordinated crocks and pots at Sign of the Bear Kitchenware (p85)

TOP FIVE SONOMA CHEESES

> Vella Romanella: Hard cow's milk cheese with the savory flavor of Parmigiano Romano from Vella Cheese (p90), ideal with assertive Napa Cabernet Franc.
> Andante Acapella Ashed Round: Delicate goat's milk in a volcanic, ashy rind – a velvet fist in an iron glove that pairs with like-minded Carneros bubbly. Made by Sonoma's Soyoung Scanlan and available at Oxbow Market (p52).
> Bellwether Carmody: Quintessentially NorCal — easygoing and a little nutty. Made by Cindy and Liam Callahan on the Sonoma coast and available at Boont Berry Farm (p153); enjoy with Anderson Valley Rosé of Pinot Noir.
> Redwood Hill Farm California Crottin: pungent French-style goat cheese with California earthiness that amps up Dry Creek Syrahs. Made on America's first certified Grade A Humane goat farm in Sebastopol by the eco-smart Bice family. Get yours at Oakville Grocery (p58).
> Pug's Leap Buche: Soft goat cheese aromatic with lemongrass, made by Pascal Destandau and Eric Smith in a solar-powered Dry Creek dairy. Pick up yours at Preston Vineyards (p126), and devour sun-warmed with chilled Chardonnay.

breast with organic huckleberry sauce. Dinner is a major production, with all eyes on the open kitchen from the 21ft communal table. Lunch is more relaxed, with friends splitting biodynamic salads, gargantuan pastrami sandwiches and parmesan-dusted truffle fries, but get your own soft-serve ice cream topped with BR Cohn olive oil and sea salt.

ESTATE
Locavore Cal-Italian $$

Map p80; ☎ 707-933-3663; www
.estate-sonoma.com; 400 W Spain St;
⏱ noon-3pm & 7-10pm Wed-Sun
Sonoma's landmark mansion features a modern menu with a Tuscan edge, pleasing vegetarians with produce from the restaurant garden and committed carnivores

with sensational tripe in rich tomato sauce. The best deal is served at the bar or on the porch: $10 for a 10in pizza with a glass of Pinot Noir. Try the reinvented capricciosa with meaty mushrooms, house-cured pancetta, fontal and a farm egg.

HARVEST MOON CAFÉ
Locavore Californian $$

Map p80; ☎ 707-933-8160; www.harvest
mooncafesonoma.com; 487 1st St W;
⏱ 5:30-9pm Sun-Thu, to 9:30pm Fri & Sat
Simple, casual, heartwarming fare served indoors or on the patio, with ingredients you'll recognize from farms up the road, and menu staples easily described in 10 words or less: beet salad with smoked salmon and avocado, housemade garlic sausage with

green-bean casserole and carrot cake with cream-cheese frosting and caramel.

🍴 MONDO *Beer Bar* $
Map p69; ☎ 707-938-8013; www.mondo sonoma.com; 875 W Napa St; 🕑 lunch & dinner

Meet your new favorite local brew: creamy Anderson Valley oatmeal stout, undefeated Racer 5 IPA from Bear Republic, or expletive-worthy Russian River Damnation, all for $4.50 a pint. When the munchies kick in, get the housemade sausage with a side of onion rings dredged in buttermilk and Panko crumbs.

🍴 MURPHY'S IRISH PUB
Pub $
Map p80; ☎ 707-935-0660; 464 1st St E; 🕑 11am-11pm Sun-Thu, 11am-midnight Fri & Sat; 🕭

Outdoor tables fill up fast with chatty regulars. Emerald-Isle-philes stick to well-poured Guinness, but a vocal splinter group prefers Boddington's on tap. The pub grub is standard, though the fish and chips are helpfully absorbent.

🍴 PATCH *Organic Produce* $
Map p80; ☎ 707-939-8125; 260 2nd St E; 🕑 9am-3pm'ish' Mon-Sat May-Nov; V 🕭 🕭

It's not quite old Eire, but the Guinness is still good for you at Murphy's

Score picnic supplies and gardening tips at this historic patch of community farmland, preserved from developers for over 130 years. Generations of Sonomans swear by the Patch's bounty of salad greens, strawberries and heirloom tomatoes. If no one's staffing the stall, weigh your produce and leave payment in the box.

🍴 RED GRAPE *Pizza* $$
Map p80; ☎ 707-996-4103; www.thered grape.com; 529 1st St W; **V** **♿**
Choose red or white wine and red or white toppings for thin-crust pizza: either way you win here. The prosciutto with goat cheese and arugula is a sauce-less wonder and, despite the extra-cheesy name, 'Under the Tuscan Sun' balances rich tomato sauce with roasted garlic, sun-dried tomato, olives, spinach and feta. Settle into your booth with a half-bottle of 300-case vintages you won't find elsewhere, and eavesdrop on promising first dates and teens greeting their track coaches.

🍴 SHISO *Sushi* $$
Map p80; ☎ 707-933-9331; www.shiso restaurant.com; 522 Broadway; ☎ 12:30-2pm & 4:30-9pm Wed-Sat, 4:30-9pm Sun-Mon; **V**
Roll in from the wineries for specialty rolls named after NorCal American Viticultural Areas (AVAs),

> **TOP FIVE WINE COUNTRY STOPS FOR GARDENERS**
> > Patch: Sustainable produce from a historic urban garden (opposite).
> > Cornerstone Sonoma: Wild ideas for high-concept backyards (p76).
> > Wildwood Farm Nursery & Sculpture Garden: Major drama with Japanese maples and contemporary sculpture (p93).
> > Matanzas Creek Winery: Lavender fields and wild-looking California native gardens (p75).
> > Philo Apple Farm: Biodynamic-certified orchards, heirloom produce and a glorious backyard arbor (p156).

especially the multifaceted Howell Mountain (truffled ponzu sauce, tempura shrimp, cucumber and avo with spicy tuna) and mellow Mendocino (albacore, asparagus and green onions with aioli and sweet eel sauce). The sushi menu isn't strictly sustainable, but local organic veggie rolls are a plus for vegetarians and non-vegos alike.

🍴 SONOMA MARKET
Deli & Groceries $
Map p80; ☎ 707-996-3411; 500 W Napa St; **V** **♿**
The deli counter competes with restaurants charging three times the price, with seasonal panini and tortas pressed until piping hot and gooey with Sonoma cheese

invented by chef Chris Mazzanti, who recently ran the CIA's kitchen. Thirty kinds of baked goods cover every craving and dietary restriction from crusty olive breads to gluten-free brownies, and even the salad offerings seem obscenely decadent.

🧀 VELLA CHEESE COMPANY
Cheeses – Local Maker $
Map p80; ☎ 800-848-0505; www.vellacheese.com; 315 2nd St E; ⏱ 9:30am-6pm Mon-Sat
Massaged with cocoa and pepper and aged for two years, the decadent Dry Jack has been the Vella family's claim to fame for 75 years – but have you tried their savory, nutty Romanella? Don't be shy about asking for samples, and assemble your own gift packs of vacuum-sealed artisanal cheeses for the hopeful foodies back home.

⭐ PLAY
🎬 SEBASTIANI THEATRE
Cinema
Map p80; ☎ 707-996-9756; www.sebastianitheatre.com; 476 1st St E; adult/senior & child under 12yr $9/6; ⏱ 7pm Mon-Thu, 6:30pm & 8pm Fri & Sat, 1pm & 8.30pm Sun; 🧑‍🦽
Keeping Sonoma's single-screen deco movie palace up and running is a labor of love for owner Roger Rhoten, who tears your

ticket at the door and runs the vacuum as you leave. Major releases occasionally get bumped for film festivals, concerts and Sonoma High School musicals, but the Sebastiani spots Oscar contenders early and runs them for weeks longer than multiplexes.

GLEN ELLEN

This hidden valley was adventure-author Jack London's favorite discovery, and it's still full of surprises, from first-rate dining in the local supermarket and bombastic Cabs from biodynamic vineyards to London's collection of 600 rejection letters.

👁 SEE
🏛 JACK LONDON STATE HISTORIC PARK
Map p69; ☎ 707-938-5216; www.jacklondonpark.com; 2400 London Ranch Rd; admission per vehicle $6; ⏱ 9:30am-7pm daylight savings, 10am-5pm non-daylight savings
He wrote *The Call of the Wild* and traveled the world over – much of it in a rowboat – but Jack London's greatest satisfaction was the 129-acre estate of sunny meadows, storied oaks and gnarled vineyards he rescued from slash-and-burn deforestation, and farmed sustainably. The historic farmstead is only open on weekends, but you

can peek inside the library to see London's cowboy hat hanging alongside his typewriter and Dictaphone. After her husband's death, Charmain London moved to the stone House of Happy Walls, where today you can climb stairs lined with Polynesian war clubs to learn of Jack's checkered career as a pirate, cannery worker, gold prospector, Marxist labor leader and Meiji war correspondent – all before age 24. Hike uphill toward the lake and 'Pig Palace' or down-hill past the fire-destroyed 'Wolf House' (London's dream home).

DO

⛷ MORTON'S WARM SPRINGS

Map p69; ☎ 707-833-5511; 1651 Warm Springs Rd; adult/senior & child $8/7, reserved picnic/BBQ sites per person $11; 10am-6pm Sat & Sun May, Sep & Oct, 10am-6pm Tue-Sun Jun-Aug; ♿

Long before Ethel and Harold Morton bought these 20 acres back in 1938, native Wappo considered its natural springs to have healing properties – and its soporific effect is undeniable. Even hyperactive kids mellow out in three geothermal mineral pools, especially after creek hikes, volleyball marathons, horseshoe grudge matches and sweaty soccer games on the grounds. Rates for picnic sites and BBQ pits may seem steep, but proceeds benefit the local teen center.

⛷ TRIPLE CREEK HORSE OUTFIT

Map p69; ☎ 707-887-8700; www.triple creekhorseoutfit.com; 2400 London Ranch Rd; group rides 1/2hr $60/90, 3 hr incl lunch $250; ⏰ by reservation

No Wild West trip is complete without riding off into the sunset with Chardonnay in the saddle-bag. Triple Creek offers one- to three-hour guided rides along the sunny slopes and fragrant redwood groves of Jack London and Sugarloaf Parks, for scenic splendor without the foot blisters.

SHOP

⬡ WINE COUNTRY CHOCOLATES
Chocolates – Local Maker

Map p69; ☎ 707-996-1010; www.wine countrychocolates.com; 14301 Arnold Dr; ⏰ 10am-5pm

Wine and dine at the same time with Vintners Blend artisanal truffles in signature Sonoma flavors: Port, Zinfandel, Cabernet Sauvignon and Champagne. Wine aficionados get dark-chocolate sour-cherry bark for Pinot tastings, and pair Cabs with dark-chocolate *mendiants* topped with pistachios and apricots. Wave through the kitchen window at mother-daughter chocolatiers Betty and Caroline Kelly, who'll offer you samples personally if they're not up to their elbows in scrumptiousness.

🍴 EAT & DRINK

🍴 FIG CAFÉ

Locavore Californian $$

Map p69; ☎ 707-938-2130; www.thefig
cafe.com; 13690 Arnold Dr; 🕑 5:30pm-
late daily, also 10am-2:30pm Sat & Sun
This ranch-house bistro isn't afraid
to bare it all, from the exposed
beams and open kitchen to Julie
Higgins' paintings of bodacious
nudes frolicking in the vineyards.

Cheese-in-production at Vella (p90)

Sonoma's best seasonal ingredi-
ents are presented here in all their
glory: arugula salad with pancetta,
goat cheese and fig vinaigrette, an
exemplary duck and sausage cas-
soulet, and your choice of Sonoma
wines or complimentary corkage.

🍴 GARDEN COURT CAFÉ

Diner $

Map p69; ☎ 707-935-1565; www
.gardencourtcafe.com; 13647 Arnold Dr;
🕑 7:30am-2pm Wed-Mon; 👶
Fresh-baked sticky buns are the
obvious order, but the Garden
Court's claims to fame among wine
tasters are stomach-steadying,
palate-awakening egg dishes. Their
Benedicts come with housemade
Hollandaise, your choice of one to
three eggs and a boggling choice
of toppings, including the 'Wild'
combo in honor of Jack London:
green chilies, housemade turkey
chorizo and Jack cheese.

🍴 GLEN ELLEN INN OYSTER GRILL AND MARTINI BAR

Seafood $$

Map p69; ☎ 707-996-6409; www.glenellen
inn.com; 13670 Arnold Dr; 🕑 11:30am-9pm
Fri-Tue, 5:30-9pm Wed & Thu
Advanced hedonists graduate
from wine tasting to martinis
and oysters here. Classic raw
scores a passing grade, baked
with Meyer lemon garlic butter
earns extra credit, and fried
crispy with Tabasco butter and

chased with a dirty martini is an automatic A-plus. After one of each with complimentary dill scones, you'll want to split or skip ultrarich mains like stuffed duck breast or mussels in white wine. Attendance isn't mandatory at dessert, but miss the espresso martini and your hedonist license is revoked.

🍴 GLEN ELLEN VILLAGE MARKET *Deli & Groceries* $

Map p69; ☎ 707-996-6728; www .sonoma-glenellenmkt.com; 13751 Arnold Dr; Ⓥ ♿

A fantasy supermarket, with organic local produce, small-production wines, artisanal goat cheeses, plus biodegradable sunblock, all at fair prices. The divine deli counter wraps around the back of the store, serving hot, fresh panini and sustainably raised meats for barbecuing.

🍴 OAK HILL FARM *Organic Produce* $

Map p69; ☎ 707-996-6643; www.oak hillfarm.net; 15101 Sonoma Hwy, Glen Ellen; Ⓨ 11am-6pm Wed-Sun Apr-Dec; Ⓥ ♿ 🐾

An ecosystem unto itself, bountiful Oak Hill farm packs 200 varieties of produce and flowers into 45 acres bounded by California oaks and manzanita. Spring offers greens galore, summer brings sunflower fields, watermelon and

tomatoes, and herb garlands and edible squash are available in the Red Barn well into December.

🍴 OLIVE & VINE *Cal-Mediterranean* $

Map p69; ☎ 707-996-9150; www .oliveandvine.com; 14301 Arnold Dr; Ⓨ 10am-3pm Tue-Sat

This gourmet and housewares emporium features a catering kitchen that offers a limited daily menu of seasonal salads, a sandwich of the day, and Mediterranean-style dishes. Take yours to go or enjoy here with a glass or flight from the 'Unwined' wine bar. Service is secondary and slow, since catering staff are usually busy preparing for some event, but the flavors are first-rate.

KENWOOD

Whether you prefer your nature wild or tame, Kenwood delivers: bonsai groves, a rugged hilltop park, a ranch hotel and a spa that puts local grapes to work in pampering treatments.

🔲 WILDWOOD FARM NURSERY & SCULPTURE GARDEN

Map p69; ☎ 707-833-1161, 888-833-4181; www.wildwoodmaples.com; 10300 Sonoma Hwy; Ⓨ 9am-4pm Wed-Sun, to 2pm Tue
Japanese maples and dogwood trees blush red in fall and pink

in spring, summer brings heady whiffs of spicy heirloom tomatoes and exotic vegetables, and winter adds stark drama to dwarf conifers and gingko bonsai. Abstract sculptures complete the fantastical scenery, including Kazuko Matthews' whimsical 'Garden teapot' and Mary Fuller's moon balancing a moon on her head.

☉ SUGARLOAF RIDGE STATE PARK
Map p69; ☎ 707-833-5712; www.parks.ca.gov; Adobe Canyon Rd; parking/camping/firewood $6/20/5.50
Deer can hardly be bothered to dash away when you approach on this 25-mile network of trails. Along the summit trail up Bald

Mountain (2729ft), you might even glimpse a shy fox, coyote or bobcat before it flees – to avoid chase scenes, no dogs are allowed in the park. Wildflowers carpet this stretch of hills in spring, and a 25ft waterfall and spawning steelhead trout appear after winter rains. On clear August nights, take the 0.25-mile trail to the Robert Ferguson Observatory to watch meteor showers.

⚑ KENWOOD INN & SPA
Map p69; ☎ 707-833-1293; www.kenwoodinn.com; 10400 Sonoma Hwy; ⏱ by appointment
Never mind the rustic waterwheel out front: this spa brings

Fresh produce and chefs on show offer dramatic flair at the Fig Café (p92)

on the Wine Country glam, from pomegranate-infused Champagne body scrubs ($125 for 50 minutes) to complimentary sparkling wine accompanying many treatments. The Kenwood specializes in 'vinotherapy' (wait, isn't that what you've been doing at tasting rooms?) with Riesling grapeseed oil in sugar scrubs ($125 for 50 minutes) and antioxidant red-wine body wraps that go straight to your head ($175 for 80 minutes).

☐ KENWOOD FARMHOUSE
Gifts – Local Maker
Map p69; ☎ 707-833-1212; 9255 Sonoma Hwy; ☼ 10:30am-7pm
Laid-back Sonomans seem to have all the time in the world, yet somehow they produce this broad range of artisanal lavender soaps, beeswax candles, hand-crocheted baby clothes and cheese boards made from reclaimed wine barrels. Prices run the gamut at this co-op,

but are often below the expected retail elsewhere.

▦ VINEYARDS INN BAR & GRILL *Sustainable Cal-Basque* $$
Map p69; ☎ 707-833-4500; www.vineyardsinn.com; 8445 Sonoma Hwy; ☼ 11:30am-9:30pm Mon, Wed & Thu, 11:30am-10pm Fri & Sat, 11:30am-9pm Sun
Beyond certain separatist instincts, Sonoma and Basque Country have one thing in common: a passion for pristine seafood and seasonal ingredients. All meat and dairy here are certified organic, the seafood is line-caught, and most of the produce comes from Chef Esteban's certified organic and biodynamic Rose Ranch. If you try only one burger in Wine Country, let it be the Jake Steak: a half-pound of succulent grilled chuck on ciabatta. Over 25 years, Vineyards has reduced their landfill waste by 90%, composting everything from placemats to oyster shells, and grinding bottles into garden gravel.

>RUSSIAN RIVER VALLEY

True to form, Russian River Valley history is full of twists. While local prospectors were finding ways to strike it rich – lumber, quicksilver, railroads and Christmas wreaths – a Freestone innkeeper was torching bridges across the river to boost business. Russian River always brimmed with outlandish ideas: lumber baron Colonel Armstrong ended up

RUSSIAN RIVER VALLEY

▼ WINERIES
Arista 1 C2
Bottle Barn 2 E2
Dutton Estate &
  Sebastopol Vineyards
  Tasting Room 3 C3
Dutton-Goldfield &
  Balletto Tasting Room ...4 D3
Freestone Vineyards 5 C4
Gary Farrell 6 C2
Hartford Family Winery ...7 C2
Hop Kiln Winery 8 C1
Iron Horse 9 C3
J Vineyards & Winery ...10 D1
Korbel Champagne
  Cellars 11 B2
Marimar 12 C3
Martinelli 13 D2
Moshin 14 C2
Porter Creek 15 C2
Rochioli 16 C1
Sophie's Cellars 17 A2

● SEE
Armstrong Woods 18 A1
California Carnivores ...19 E4
Florence Ave 20 E1
Funeria 21 C3
Graton Gallery 22 C3
Luther Burbank
  Home & Gardens 23 F3
Quicksilver Mine Co ...24 C2
Schulz Museum 25 E3

Sebastopol Center
  for the Arts 26 F1
Sonoma County
  Museum 27 E3

大 DO
Armstrong Woods Trail
  Rides & Pack Trips.....(see 18)
Burke's Canoe Trips 28 C2
Johnson's Beach 29 A4
King's Sport & Tackle ...30 A4
Monte Rio Community
  Beach 31 A3
Osmosis 32 C4
Pee Wee Golf & Arcade ...33 B4
Sumbody &
  Sumtime Spa 34 F1

🛍 SHOP
Beekind 35 D4
Guerneville 5 & 10 ......36 A4
Guerneville Farmers
  Market 37 A4
Hand Goods 38 B4
Midgley's Country
  Flea Market 39 D4
Mr Ryder & Co 40 C3
Occidental Farmers
  Market 41 B4
People's Music 42 F1
Renga Arts ....(see 38)
Santa Rosa
  Downtown Market 43 F3

Sebastopol Farmers
  Market 44 F1
Sonoma Antique Society ...45 D4

🍴 EAT & DRINK
Ace-in-the-Hole
  Cider Pub 46 C3
Barley & Hops Tavern ...47 B4
Bistro des Copains 48 B4
Bohemian Market ......(see 47)
Café les Jumelles 49 A2
Dawn Ranch Roadhouse ...50 A4
East-West Café 51 F1
Farmhouse Inn &
  Restaurant 52 C2
Food for Humans 53 A4
Jhanthong Banbua 54 F3
Mom's Apple Pie 55 C3
Mosaic 56 C2
Pat's Diner 57 A4
Roasters Espresso 58 C3
Russian River
  Brewing Co 59 F3
Saint Rose 60 C4
Underwood Bar & Bistro ...61 C3
Wild Flour Bread 62 C4
Zazu 63 D3

⭐ PLAY
Hopmonk Tavern 64 F1
Rainbow Cattle Co 65 A4
Rio Theater 66 A3
Wells Fargo Center
  for the Arts 67 E2

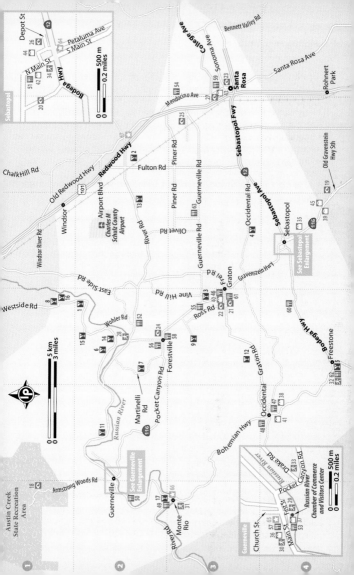

protecting old-growth redwoods; Czech political refugee Francis Korbel started growing French grapes in California soil; and socialites shed starchy Victorian conventions for free love by the riverside.

In the 20th century, summer resorts and apple orchards displaced lumber camps and mercury mines, and hippies hitched here to farm organically and create funky folk art. The valley's risk-taking mindset has also proved useful in growing thin-skinned Pinot Noir grapes – an easily damaged variety that turns to raisins in strong sun and rots in the rain – not recommended for the faint of heart.

For prize Pinot, redwood grandeur and free thinking look no further than around the next Russian River bend.

WINERIES

� BOTTLE BARN

☎ 707-528-1161; www.bottlebarn .com; 3331-A Industrial Dr, Santa Rosa; ⏱ 9:30am-6:30pm Mon-Sat, to 5pm Sun

Bargain hunters hit Bottle Barn for Sonoma County Fair winners and other rising vine stars below tasting-room prices. Recent finds include Quivira Grenache ($21.99; p123), Hartford Russian River Valley Zin ($29.99; opposite) and Trentadue Old Patch Red ($9.99; p139). Check out Ben's Bargains for deals under $10.

� DUTTON-GOLDFIELD & BALLETTO TASTING ROOM

☎ 707-568-2455; www.duttongoldfield .com, www.ballettovineyards.com; 5700 Occidental Rd, Santa Rosa; tasting $5-10; ⏱ 10am-4pm

One tasting room, two celebrated wineries, 10 worthwhile tastes. Balletto's latest value-priced Estate Zin ($21) features hints of fresh fig laced with cinnamon and begs for BBQ chicken. Don't miss the Devil's Gulch Vineyard Pinot ($55), which unfolds on the tongue like a bolt of cherry-red ombré silk gradually fading into violet and sage.

☓Y FREESTONE VINEYARDS

☎ 707-874-1010; www.jpvfreestone .com; 12747 El Camino Bodega; ⏱ 11am-5pm Fri-Sun

Only a brave vintner plants misty coastal dairy pastures with persnickety Pinot grapes, which have a love–hate relationship with fog. But Phelps (p45) compounded the challenges: its Freestone grapes would be cultivated biodynamically, yielding unfined, unfiltered wine flowing from fermentation tanks to barrels in an innovative gravity-flow facility. Winemaker Theresa Heredia (p103) takes to the task with gusto, creating Fogdog Pinot ($40) that hints at truffle salt, redwood and anardana (Indian pomegranate-seed spice).

MARIMAR

☎ 707-823-4365; www.marimarestate
.com; 11400 Graton Rd; tasting $10, wine
& tapas pairing $20; ⏰ 11am-4pm
Scrap-metal dog sculptures
among dense, 70% certified–
organic vines signal a worthy
detour from ordinary tastings.
Vintner/chef Marimar Torres
pairs four quixotic California
Chardonnays and Pinots with her
Cal-Catalan tapas, including fava-
bean stew that teases out bacon-
fattiness in the estate Pinot Noir
($42). Marimar's steel-tank-
fermented Acero Chardonnay
($29) brings on Mediterranean
summer with hints of tarragon
and lemon cologne.

DUTTON ESTATE & SEBASTOPOL VINEYARDS TASTING ROOM

☎ 707-829-9463; www.duttonranch
.com, www.sebastopolvineyards.com;
8757 Green Valley Rd; tasting $10, wine &
cheese pairing $20; ⏰ 10am-4pm
Steve Dutton has been growing
grapes in the Russian River Valley
since 1964. His experience is evi-
dent in the pristine flavors of his
estate-grown Manzana Pinot Noir
($45): pomegranate, rosebuds
and clementine. Featured cheese
pairings and bottle bargains are
irresistible, especially the Sonoma
chèvre- and mandarin-tinged Late
Harvest Colombard ($18).

IRON HORSE

☎ 707-887-1507; www.ironhorsevine
yards.com; 9786 Ross Station Rd; tasting
$10-15; ⏰ 10am-3:30pm
Drink the way nature intended,
at an outdoor tasting bar sipping
superior bubbly and distinctive
reds overlooking rolling vineyards
and redwood ridges. The Blanc des
Blancs ($38) drifts across the palate
like frothy fog and puts a sparkle in
the eyes of Champagne connoisseurs – it's easily worth twice the
price. BDX-3 ($38) is a fireworks-
display Meritage, trailing cassis,
cedar and mesquite embers. Also
check out their memorable Friday-
morning winemaker tours.

HARTFORD FAMILY WINERY

☎ 800-588-0234; www.hartfordwines
.com; 8075 Martinelli Rd; tasting $5-15,
applicable to purchase;
⏰ 10am-4:30pm
Don't let Hartford's swanky tasting room, reputation for Chardonnays, and Kendall-Jackson family
ties throw you off the scent of
seven of Russian River's most
daring Pinots and radical-fringe
Zins. Land's Edge Pinot ($45) is
the California coast in a bottle:
wildflowers run off rocky cliffs
into mineral-rich tide pools. Dina's
Vineyard Zin ($50) could easily go
Zincognito, with its sneaky Syrah-
style spices and gravel-voiced Cab
tannins.

THE VALLEYS

RUSSIAN RIVER VALLEY

Pines in the distance and wine in the glass – Russian River Valley contentment at Gary Farrell

MARTINELLI

☎ 707-525-0570; www. martinelli winery.com; 3360 River Rd, Windsor; tasting $5-15, applicable to purchase; ⏱ 10am-5pm

Scandal rocked a Tuscan village around1887, when a local wine-maker eloped to California – and all these years later, the Martinelli family's unfined, unfiltered Bella Vigna Pinot ($43) delivers cocoa-cherry flavors as juicy as small-town gossip. Tastings are served in the century-old barn, but celebrity winemaker Helen Turley keeps Martinelli ahead of the creative curve with Blue Slide Ridge Pinot ($125), a collage of blueberries, violets and orange chanterelles.

SOPHIE'S CELLARS

☎ 707-865-1122; www.sophiescellars .com; 20293 Hwy 116; ⏱ 11am-7pm Thu-Mon

Name your go-to wine, favorite food or ideal date night, and owner/connoisseur John Hag-gard will sketch you a tasting itinerary and supply free tasting passes. Sophie's stocks many wines that aren't often sold to the public, including cultish Flowers Perennial Sonoma Coast Pinot blend ($40) and collector's-trophy William Selyem Precious Mountain Pinot ($149), plus select Sonoma cheeses. Bonus: Bistro des Copains (p112), Dawn Ranch Roadhouse (p116) and Mosaic (p118) don't charge corkage on wine bought here.

☎ KORBEL CHAMPAGNE CELLARS

☎ 707-887-2294; www.korbel.com; 13250 River Rd; ☷ 10am-5pm

The name dimly recalls New Years past – Korbel shipped 1.6 million cases for millennium celebrations – but don't hold that against America's megaproducer of budget bubbly (nonvintage $12). Munch deli sandwiches and sniff your way through 250 kinds of roses on the historic estate of Francis Korbel, the escaped Austro-Hungarian political-prisoner-turned-vintner who pioneered California's Champagne-style sparklers. Free tastings feature award-winning XS brandy ($14), which packs quite a punch spiked with Madagascar vanilla and orange peel.

☎ GARY FARRELL

☎ 707-473-2900; www.garyfarrell wines.com; 10701 Westside Rd; tasting $10-15; ☷ 11am-4pm

High on a hilltop overlooking the Russian River is a flock of drinkers gurgling their way through the long finish of their Gary Farrell wines. Cab drinkers who judge by the numbers will be impressed by the aromatic Hallberg Pinot ($50), a luxury cascade of blueberries and cinnamon that lingers for two minutes.

☎ MOSHIN

☎ 707-433-5499; www.moshin vineyards.com; 10295 Westside Rd; ☷ 11am-4:30pm

Pinot made in small batches by a winery full of big ideas: organic farming, solar power and an energy-saving gravity-flow facility. Free tastings feature Russian River Valley Pinot Noir ($34), complete with blackcurrants and its own autumn spice rack. Moshin Potion ($32) is a musky dessert wine with cucumber and honeysuckle – mix one part to two parts vodka for martinis with Bond-worthy mojo.

☎ PORTER CREEK VINEYARDS

☎ 707-433-6321; www.portercreek vineyards.com; 8735 Westside Rd; ☷ 10:30am-4:30pm

'We like to start in the gutter and drink our way out,' wisecracks the pourer, lining up free tastes on the reclaimed bowling-alley lane that serves as a bar. Porter Creek's Demeter-certified biodynamic vineyards yield top-notch Fiona Hill Vineyard Pinot Noir ($36) with hints of redcurrant and walnuts. Watch out for Timbervine Ranch Syrah ($36), with cocktail-hour flavors of martini olives and bacon-wrapped fig.

☿ ARISTA

☎ 707-473-0606; www.aristawinery
.com; 7015 Westside Rd; tasting $5;
⏱ 11am-5pm daily

Small is beautiful at this family-owned winery with bonsai gardens, miniature waterfalls and an Anderson Valley Gewürztraminer ($25) with traces of lime, lychee and coconut. Enjoy the view from a picnic table and drink it, too: Russian River Pinot ($40) is as buoyant and lazy as its namesake, with undercurrents of raspberry, orange zest and nasturtium petals.

☿ ROCHIOLI

☎ 707-433-2305; www.rochioliwinery
.com; 6192 Westside Rd; ⏱ by appointment 11am-4pm Thu-Mon mid-Jan–mid-Dec

Three generations of Rochiolis have tended these prestigious 168-acre vineyards, and their estate wines score top marks from critics – and are priced accordingly. Russian River Valley Estate Pinot ($60) tastes of tart cherry melting into cinnamon saltwater taffy, while the Estate Chardonnay ($55) is like Clint Eastwood: mellowed with age, but still flinty.

☿ HOP KILN VINEYARDS

☎ 707-433-6491; www.hopkilnwinery
.com; 6050 Westside Rd; tasting $5-7;
⏱ 10am-5pm

Triple chimneys to dry hops for beer grace this century-old stone structure, built by 25 devoted Italian masons in just 35 days. Step into the redwood-beamed tasting room of this historic landmark for Rushin' River Red ($23), a Syrah-Grenache blend brimming with strawberry, leather and redwood bark. But the real steals here are artisan vinegars, including balsamic ($11) comparable to aged Modena imports at thrice the price.

☿ J VINEYARDS & WINERY

☎ 707-431-3646; www.jwine.com;
11447 Old Redwood Hwy; tasting with/without oysters $25/10, food & wine pairing on terrace/in Bubble Room $35/60; ⏱ 11am-5pm

Giddiness comes naturally in the lofty Gordon Heuther–designed tasting room with such heady choices: all-sparkling flights with oysters, bubbly and Pinot with hors d'oeuvres on the terrace, or Bubble Room flights of six wines with organic small plates. J's main claim to fame is lemon-zested-wedding-cake Cuvée Brut ($28), but limited-production Brut Rosé ($40) features lemongrass and blood oranges. Owner Judy Jordan adds green twists to conventional sparkling-wine production, eliminating chlorine, recycling corks for handicrafts and using ground cover for pest control.

Theresa Heredia
Winemaker, Freestone Vineyards (p98)

Peptides and Pinots I was studying peptide synthesis at the University of California when I heard about some bizarre peptide behavior over in the viticulture department – and that was it, I was hooked on the science of wine. When Phelps (p45) invited me to work on Freestone, they didn't need to ask twice. **Daredevil Chardonnay** We have the luxury of being backed by a family-owned winery that takes risks to produce stellar wines. Not many wineries would attempt to produce Chardonnay in this damp, cold coastal. **Pairing Pinot with oysters, and enology with ecology** Fogdog Pinot has an earthy character that works with barbecued oysters and, of course, salmon. California's wild salmon is at a low point now, but we hope to bring them back. We recycle our wastewater through beneficial bioreactor microbes, so none of it goes into Salmon Creek downstream. There's more to a good glass of biodynamic wine than you'd think.

SANTA ROSA

The biggest town in Wine Country is the home of Snoopy, Santa Rosa plums, Damnation beer and the Sonoma County Fair.

☉ LUTHER BURBANK HOME & GARDENS

☎ 707-524-5445; www.lutherburbank .org; cnr Santa Rosa & Sonoma Aves; admission free, guided tour adult/senior/ child $5/4/free; ☾ gardens 8am-dusk, home 10am-3:30pm Tue-Sun Apr-Oct

Thumbs don't get greener than those of pioneering horticulturalist Luther Burbank, who from 1871 to 1926 developed 800 hybrid plants – including the nectarine and Russet potato – for maximum nutrition, flavor, sustainability and beauty. Burbank's estate show-cases his superaromatic roses, a fast-growing walnut tree intended as a renewable furniture resource, and spineless cacti to feed animals.

☉ SCHULZ MUSEUM

☎ 707-579-4452; www.schulzmuseum .org; 2301 Hardies Lane; adult/senior & child $8/5; ☾ 11am-5pm Mon-Fri, from 10am Sat & Sun, closed Tue Sep-May

Calling all Charlie Brown softies, bossy Lucys and multitalented Snoopys: this museum shows how *Peanuts* creator Charles M Schulz pinpointed your personalities in print and created now-classic animations of squawking adults, the Great Pumpkin and the joyous Snoopy dance. Second Saturdays every month feature emerging cartoonists-in-residence, and Mondays from 10am to noon bring flocks of tot-towing moms for Mommy and Me activities.

☉ SONOMA COUNTY MUSEUM

☎ 707-579-1500; www.sonomacounty museum.org; 425 7th St; ☾ 11am-5pm Tue-Sun

Killer robots, running fences and rocking accordionists: you never know what's next at this converted post office. Explore Sonoma history from the Gold Rush through the installation of Christo's 1976 *Running Fence* and George Lucas–inspired interactive design. Highlights include 19th-century photos of local China-towns, and midcentury pottery from Pond Farm, the Guerneville studio started by Bauhaus-trained artists who fled Nazi Germany. First Fridays feature free live music.

🍴 JHANTHONG BANBUA
Thai $$

☎ 707-528-8048; 2400 Mendocino Ave; ☾ 11am-10pm Mon-Fri, 5-10pm Sat

When tasting-room pourers suggest cool-climate whites with Thai food, Jhanthong Banbua is what they have in mind. Aromatic

Rediscover Lucy and poor ol' Charlie Brown at the Schulz Museum

lemongrass, roasted peanuts and chili *sriracha* sing on the palate. Lunch specials offer three dishes for $10 – try lime shrimp lettuce wraps, tapioca balls with chicken and peanuts, and the spicy papaya salad.

🍴 RUSSIAN RIVER BREWING CO *Brewpub* $
☎ 707-545-2337; www.russianriver brewing.com; 729 4th St; ⏱ 11am-midnight Sun-Thu, to 1am Fri & Sat
While these taps are flowing, bar talk is all about Consecration, Damnation and Pliny the Elder. Consecration is a winemaker's favorite

beer aged six months in Cab barrels with currants, Damnation is aged with oak chips for that steady, slow burn, and Pliny's an easy-drinking IPA honoring the Roman thinker who named hops. Only the brave attempt Mortification, a Belgian-style barley wine with 11% alcohol.

🍴 ZAZU *Farm-to-Table Cal-Italian* $$
☎ 707-523-4814; www.zazurestaurant .com; 3535 Guerneville Rd
Other restaurants have organic-produce suppliers, sous-chef squadrons and recipe books – Zazu

has an organic garden, three talented chefs (including *Top Chef* contestant Zoi Antonitsas), an in-house salumist and actual soul. Go nouveau with Liberty duck breast atop housemade spaetzle, or get medieval with a whole roasted pig and heaps of polenta and rapini. Dessert is Sonoma on a platter: Andante's herbed Pastoral cheese with tender local honeycomb.

☆ WELLS FARGO CENTER FOR THE ARTS
Performances
☎ 707-546-3600; www.wellsfargo centerarts.org; 50 Mark West Spring Rd

Watch this space for performances reflecting Sonoma's wildly eclectic tastes, from American Ballet Theater and Ladysmith Black Mambazo's soulful acappella to Cheech & Chong's stoner comedy and philosopher-punk Henry Rollins' rapid-fire spoken word. Management discourages dancing in the aisles during American Philharmonic and Santa Rosa Symphony concerts – but Sonomans can't be dissuaded from head-banging to Dweezil Zappa or flailing to Grateful-Deadly Dark Star Orchestra.

Salts, soaks, scrubs, melts, milks and fizzers – an organic cornucopia at Sumbody & Sumtime Spa (p108)

TOP FIVE RUSSIAN RIVER OUTDOOR MARKETS

> **Midgley's Country Flea Market** (☎ 707-823-7874; 2200 Gravenstein Hwy S; 🕑 6:30am-4:30pm Sat & Sun weather permitting, closed Dec) Finds include art-deco brooches, an original Doors album and psychedelic jumpsuit.
> **Occidental Farmers Market** (☎ 707-793-2159; www.occidentalfarmersmarket .com; 🕑 4pm-dusk Fri Jun-Oct) Organic and biodynamic produce, Gerard's paella hot off the skillet, and tiny tots rocking out to Sonoma County Taiko's drum line.
> **Sebastopol Farmers Market** (cnr Petaluma & McKinley Aves; 🕑 10am-1:30pm Sun Apr–mid-Dec) Down-home and worldly-wise: apple pies, African beats, locally crafted teapots and Mayan herbal cold remedies.
> **Santa Rosa Downtown Market** (☎ 707-524-2123; www.srdowntownmarket.com; cnr 4th and B Sts; 🕑 5-8:30pm Wed mid-May–Aug) Artisan cheeses, three stages of live music, picture-perfect produce and killer tamales.
> **Guerneville Farmers Market** (☎ 707-869-8079; 16201 First St; 🕑 4-7pm Wed mid-May–Oct) Nature's bounty – from sweet peas in spring and watermelons in summer through fall apples and pumpkins – spills out of pickups .

SEBASTOPOL

Americana with a hippie twist sets Sebastopol apart: head here for Gravenstein apple pie and conceptual art, tidy lawns dotted with salvaged-junk sculptures and impromptu music jams at outdoor markets.

SEE

CALIFORNIA CARNIVORES

☎ 707-824-0433; www.california carnivores.com; 2833 Old Gravenstein Hwy S; 🕑 10am-4pm Thu-Mon

Even vegans can't help admiring these savage beauties with colorful dewy leaves and deadly grips on houseflies. It's survival of the fabulous among these carnivorous plants, from classic red-toothed Venus flytraps to deceptively innocent pink butterwort rosettes. Many specimens from Australia and Latin America flourish in Sonoma's freakish climate, but don't overlook Californian hybrids like Godzuki, named for what it looks like: the son of Godzilla.

FLORENCE AVE

☎ 707-824-9388

What do you do when neighbors plunk a 15ft fisherman made of junk in their front yard? If you're a resident of Florence Ave, you ask Montreal transplants Patrick Amiot and Brigitte Laurent for one of your own. Their sculptures dot the Sonoma landscape, but FloAve remains their definitive outdoor gallery, with a skeleton on a motorcycle salvaged from auto parts, Elvis appearances enshrined in a 10ft jukebox, and a giant duck made from a recycled RV.

ⓒ SEBASTOPOL CENTER FOR THE ARTS

☎ 707-829-4797; www.sebarts.org; 6780 Depot St; ☯ 10am-5pm Mon-Fri, 1-4pm Sat & Sun

Tucked behind the mini-mart, this gallery overflows with outlandish art. The Center for the Arts draws international entries for its

annual documentary film festival in March, but its signature shows reveal wide-ranging local talents in extreme choppers (custom-built motorcycles), conceptual art exploring the fourth dimension and quilts made of fragrant local beeswax.

DO

SUMBODY & SUMTIME SPA

☎ 707-823-2053; www.sumbody.com; 118 N Main St; ☯ 10am-7pm Tue-Sun

Get the good stuff in the buff. Sumbody makes ecofriendly organic bath products such as

Feel the rhythm in People's Music

Satsuma Cardamom sea-salt scrub and the aptly named Knock Out Bath Melt of cocoa butter, kava kava, lavender and valerian. Head through the storefront to spa-retreat rooms for circulation-enhancing Swedish massage ($75 for one hour) or facials ($39 for 30 minutes) promising to 'expel gunk' from your skin.

SHOP

SONOMA ANTIQUE SOCIETY *Antiques*
☎ 707-829-1733; www.antiquesociety .com; 2661 Gravenstein Hwy S; ◷ 10am-5pm

Clear your morning schedule for 20,000 sq ft of finds from 100 local dealers. Treasures unearthed here include a vintage *Playboy Gourmet* cookbook for seducing dates with booze-soaked meats, perversely cheerful dimpled-glass candy dishes from the Great Depression and lithographed 1960s Sonoma wine labels.

BEEKIND
Gourmet Foods & Skincare
☎ 707-824-2905; www.beekind.com; 921 Gravenstein Hwy S; ◷ 10am-6pm

Honey is Sonoma's next artisanal food star – have it pure or infused with local lavender, creamed or atop honeycomb slabs, from bees bingeing on wildflowers or redwood forests. If you'd rather

mind your own beeswax, Beekind will set you up with supplies to start your own hive and to hand-craft candles.

PEOPLE'S MUSIC
Musical Instruments
☎ 707823-7664; www.peoples musicontheweb.com; 122 N Main St; ◷ 10am-6pm Mon-Fri, to 5pm Sat, 11am-4pm Sun

Summer in Sebastopol is one big, BBQ-fuelled jam session stretching from street corners to back patios, aided and abetted by People's Music since 1973. People's provides bongos, ukuleles, hemlock-root flutes, didjeridoos, harps, guitars and other instruments; you supply the natural talent – or sign up for a quickie lesson at the shop.

EAT & DRINK

ACE-IN-THE-HOLE CIDER PUB
Cider & Barbecue $
☎ 707-829-1101; www.acecider.com; 3100 Gravenstein Hwy N; ◷ 11:30am-9:30pm Sun-Thu, to 10pm Fri & Sat

Pre-Pinot, hard cider was the toast of Sebastopol – and Ace is staging its comeback. Try the signature microbrew and Brut-style Joker Cider with Ace's berry-, pear- and honey-infused ciders in a bar sampler, or pair pints

V

THE VALLEYS

RUSSIAN RIVER VALLEY

with barbecued oysters and fish and chips from Ace's BBQ shack. Score $1 off pints weekdays from 3pm to 6pm, and stick around for local bands.

EAST-WEST CAFÉ
Cal-Mediterranean $

☎ 707-829-2822; www.eastwestcafe sebastopol.com; 128 N Main St; 8am-9pm; V

Middle East goes Wild West: think grilled eggplant and feta cheese on pesto-slathered organic bread, or falafel with housemade hummus wrapped in warm tortillas. Standouts are anything with tahini or off the breakfast menu – organic Sonoma pancakes in a short or full stack with real maple syrup are served all day.

MOM'S APPLE PIE
Pie $

☎ 707-823-8330; www.momsapple pieusa.com; 4550 Gravenstein Hwy N; 10am-6pm; V

The all-American classic is alive and well thanks to 'Mom' Betty Carr, who moved to California from her native Japan to study home economics and became Sonoma's pie-making legend. The secret to Mom's success: flaky crusts that bubble over with cinnamon-sprinkled local Gravenstein apples (at peak tartness August to November).

SAINT ROSE
Californian $$

☎ 707-829-5898; www.cafesaintrose .blogspot.com; 9890 Bodega Hwy; 5-9pm Wed-Fri, 9am-2pm & 5-9pm Sat & Sun

Eclectic small plates change with the pick of the day from next-door Bohemian Groove farm. Inspirations blow in from the Mediterranean and Pacific, resulting in white peaches with Serrano ham and almonds and a nouveau sloppy Joe: curried pulled pork and crabmeat cooked in a banana leaf. Call ahead for $28 prix-fixe Thursday dinners with movie screenings and live music Wednesdays.

⭐ PLAY

⭐ HOPMONK TAVERN
Live Music

☎ 707-829-7300; www.hopmonk.com; 230 Petaluma Ave

World beats, home brews and local mussels with garlic fries – Sonoma pulls out all the stops in this stone-walled tavern and beer garden. Open-mic Tuesday draws out shy folks for rocking acoustic jams, Thursday is bust out breakbeats and b-boying, and salsa is served *muy caliente* every other Wednesday. Get tickets in advance for Sonoma's Django-gypsy dance band Dgin, Bay Area brass funkmasters Monophonics and '70s blues rockers Little Feat.

FREESTONE

The first stop on the Bohemian Hwy is a town straight out of an old Western movie, only with organic bread, cedarwood spa treatments and biodynamic Pinot.

🗾 OSMOSIS

☎ 707-823-8231; www.osmosis.com; 209 Bohemian Hwy; ☀ 9am-8pm daily
Buried in wood chips to the neck – this is the life. Osmosis' Cedar Enzyme Bath ($85 for 45 minutes) is a redwood tub filled with soft, slow-fermenting cedar chips and rice bran to warm tired muscles. Revive as needed with the essential-oil Zen Harmony Facial ($155 for 75 minutes) or Connective Tissue Massage ($135 for one hour).

🍞 WILD FLOUR BREAD

Sustainable Bakery $
☎ 707-874-2938; www.wildflourbread .com; 140 Bohemian Hwy; ☀ 8:30am-6pm Fri-Mon
Watch artisan bakers ply their craft around a massive table, and hear stomachs growl as organic, crusty loaves emerge from the wood-fired brick oven. Dedicated breakfasts arrive before 10:30am for whipping-cream scones and sticky buns, but afternoon is time for cheesy flatbread snacks in the garden amid towering sunflowers and tubby goats.

OCCIDENTAL

This bend in the Bohemian Hwy is ahead of the curve with organic food, sustainable souvenirs and historic B&Bs.

🏠 HAND GOODS

Arts & Crafts – Local Makers
☎ 707-874-2161; 3627 Main St; ☀ 10am-6pm
'We were just a bunch of hippies,' says a ceramist at the counter, recalling Hand Goods in the '70s. 'Now we're just a bunch of hippies whose work gets seen all over the world.' Today 200 Sonoma artisans line the shelves, from Anthony Powers' scrap-wood marquetry vases to Anita Peery's speckled stoneware. Don't miss locally authored books, including a historical walking tour of Occidental.

🏠 RENGA ARTS

Sustainable Arts & Crafts – Local Makers
☎ 707-874-9407; www.rengaarts.com; 3605 Main St; ☀ 11am-5pm Fri-Mon
Renew, reuse and rejoice at Renga Arts, an eco-boutique packed with clever, well-priced gifts hand-crafted from reclaimed materials. Get green-fabulous with cocktail rings made from billiard balls, birdhouses constructed from vintage yardsticks and a winsome button-eyed, stuffed 'socktopus.'

Occidental's Barley and Hops Tavern is keepin' it real for Wine Country beer drinkers

🍴 BARLEY AND HOPS TAVERN
Pub & Californian $

☎ 707-874-9037; www.barleyandhops
tavern.blogspot.com; 3688 Bohemian Hwy;
🕑 4-9pm Mon & Wed-Sat, noon-9pm Sun
New in 2008, this clapboard pub is
already rolling with regulars who
trust owner–barkeep Noah Bolmer
to suss out their next favorite brew,
supply hearty bites involving
Sonoma sausages, and keep the
choc-Guinness mousse coming.

🍴 BISTRO DES COPAINS
Cal-French $$

☎ 707-874-2436; www.bistrodescopains
.com; 3782 Bohemian Hwy; 🕑 5-9pm
Sun-Thu, to 10pm Fri & Sat
Pinot tasting generates primal
urges for French fare, and Bistro

des Copains delivers Gruyère-
gooey onion soup and charcuterie
plates featuring rabbit terrine
and cornichons galore. Signature
mains come in sizzling iron pots,
including braised short ribs and
Coquilles San Jacques brimming
with scallops, local mushrooms
and creamy goodness. Come
weekdays for bargain three-course
menus, Tuesday for free corkage
and Wednesday for $1 oysters.

🍴 BOHEMIAN MARKET
Market & Deli $

☎ 707-874-3312; 3691 Main St; Ⓥ ♿
Go Boho for granola-gourmet
picnic needs: Fair Trade chocolate,
tangy kombucha (fermented
mushroom tea), vegan potato

chips, certified humane Redwood Hill Sonoma cheese and pasture-raised deli meat. The squishy deli bread is nothing special, so some sandwich assembly may be required at Wild Flour Breads (p111).

MONTE RIO

This retro resort boasts a vintage movie theater, gourmet hot dogs, and families and fishing enthusiasts making the most of beach days under the bridge.

☆ MONTE RIO COMMUNITY BEACH

☎ 707-865-2487; www.mrrpd.org/facilities.html; under the Monte Rio Bridge
Leave the 21st century behind as you pass under the bridge and onto a beach straight out of a Norman Rockwell painting. Flannel-clad teens skip stones, parents teach kids to dog-paddle and toddlers brandish rocket-shaped popsicles from summer boardwalk concession stands. For maximum Americana, don't miss the July 4 Water Carnival and fireworks here.

⊞ CAFÉ LES JUMELLES
New American $$
☎ 707-865-9500; 20391 Bohemian Hwy; ☽ 7:30am-10pm, closed for dinner Mon; Ⓥ ♿
Comfort food just got smarter: brunches feature poached eggs

instead of fried, and crispy potato-apple griddle cakes rather than soggy pancakes. Salads tempt with house-marinated red onions and sirloin steak, but chilly Russian River nights demand chef–owner Rob Holmes' wine-braised chicken, Oysters Rockefeller and house-made vegan burgers on just-baked potato-sourdough buns.

☆ RIO THEATER   *Cinema*
☎ 707-865-0913; www.riotheater.com; 20396 Bohemian Hwy; adult/child & matinee $8/6; ☽ Wed-Sun
Dinner and a movie go retro at the Rio, a vintage Army Quonset hut converted to a movie theater in 1950, complete with a concession stand serving gourmet hot dogs ($7). Instead of showing ads before Oscar winners and family favorites, owners Don and Susi Schaffert run slideshows of 1970s family vacations. The corrugated-metal bunker is spruced up with 1970s save-the-whales murals outside and *Star Wars* murals inside – but it's c-c-cold in here fall to spring, so bring a blanket or a hot date.

GUERNEVILLE

Don't call it a hideaway – the rainbow flag flies proudly over Guerneville's historic resorts, attracting GLBT travelers, bikers and families down to the river and out to the redwoods.

 SEE

ARMSTRONG WOODS

☎ 707-869-2015; www.parks.ca.gov; 17000 Armstrong Woods Rd; parking $6, overnight camping $20; ⏲ 8am–1hr after sunset

The oldest redwood here is a true survivor: 308ft high, 1400 years old and named for a lumber baron. Colonel James Boydston Armstrong bought these 440 acres in 1874 to make his fortune in lumber, but was utterly stumped by an old-growth grove he couldn't bear to chop down. With help from Luther Burbank (p104), Armstrong and his plucky daughters lobbied tirelessly to preserve the grove as a state park in 1917. In 2008 budget cuts threatened closure of Armstrong Woods but popular uproar preserved this spectacular park, with its 1-mile forest-floor Pioneer Trail and 10-mile back-country ridgeline hikes to rustic Bullfrog Pond camping facilities.

🚶 **DO**

ARMSTRONG WOODS TRAIL RIDES & PACK TRIPS

☎ 707-887-2939; www.redwood horses.com; 17000 Armstrong Woods Rd; ⏲ 7am-9pm

Glimpse redwood irises, meet deer and hear nothing but bullfrogs on Armstrong Woods Trail rides. Overnights with tents and showers ($380 per person for two to four riders) and full-day excursions ($140 per person) include meals, and are led by experienced naturalist Laura Ayers. Shorter trail rides (adult/child $75/65) run 2½ hours in the morning or afternoon, with 1½ hours of horseback riding and pauses for rest and awe.

JOHNSON'S BEACH

☎ 707-869-2022; www.johnsonsbeach .com; end of Church St; 🕙 10am-6pm May-Oct

Inner tubes, beer concessions and a sandy kiddies pool mean good times for all at Johnson's Beach. This isn't some fancy-schmantzy resort where everyone tiptoes around: there's squealing and splashing all summer from biker dudes with toddlers and Speedo-clad bankers tossing beach balls.

KING'S SPORT & TACKLE

☎ 707-869-2156; www.guerneville sport.com; 16258 Main St

King's offers kayaks, canoes, fishing gear and guides as needed for Russian River outings, plus free boating instruction, along with pickup and drop-off. The current is slow year-round, so count on three hours of paddling from Guerneville to Monte Rio. Steelhead trout are fair game November through March, catfish are caught in spring and bass abound in summer, but endangered Chinook salmon are no-go until further notice.

One regular at the Rio (p113) goes so far as to claim it boasts the 'BEST snack bar EVER'

☗ PEE WEE GOLF & ARCADE

☎ 707-869-9321; 16155 Drake Rd; 18 holes $6; ⏲ 11am-11pm daily Jun-Aug, to 10pm Sat, to 6pm Sun mid-Apr & Sep

Four generations of Guernevillans have attempted holes-in-one at this course built by mini-golf pioneer Bill Koplin. The course closes winter to spring, when it's often flooded by the Russian River – once local volunteers repaint Pee Wee's concrete cannibals stirring their pot of people stew, summer has officially arrived.

🛍 SHOP

🏠 GUERNEVILLE 5 & 10

Gifts

☎ 707-869-3404; www.guerneville 5and10.com; 16252 Main St

Everything you'd expect from a classic American dime store – bubble-gum cigars, Wiffle balls, Whoopee cushions – plus board games, knitting needles and other essential supplies for rainy days along the Russian River. You can't buy much for a nickel or a dime, but you'll get more than your money's worth of nostalgia.

🍴 EAT & DRINK

🍴 DAWN RANCH ROADHOUSE

New American $$

☎ 707-869-0656; www.dawnranch.com; 16467 River Rd; ⏲ from 5:30pm; 👶

This cozy place dates back 100 years, with the vintage photos to prove it. The menu adds organic twists to roadhouse classics: fish and chips means Panko-crusted cod with sweet-potato fries, calamari gets gussied up with a chili-orange glaze and roast chicken comes with local mushrooms. The bar serves specialty cocktails – the Sidekick with Korbel brandy and lime is a star.

🍴 FOOD FOR HUMANS

Sustainable Market – Local Makers $

☎ 707-869-3612; 16385 First St; Ⓥ 👶

All the organic produce, sea vegetables and other natural foods staples are here, but pastries, cheeses, honeycomb and fruit-juice popsicles keep regulars coming back for more. After 20 years, this plucky hippie grocery still holds its own against the Safeway across the street, even though it doesn't serve alcohol, meat or fish.

🍴 PAT'S DINER *Diner* $

☎ 707-869-9904; www.pats-restaurant .com; 16236 Main St; ⏲ 6am-3pm

Run by the Hines family since 1945, Pat's has cured hangovers with restorative powers that start working the moment diners step inside and get a whiff of eggs, hash browns and the signature garlic salsa. Pat's serves hotcakes, waffles and flaky Danishes, too.

Farmhouse Inn & Restaurant (p118) – rustic on the outside, gastronomic genius within

⭐ PLAY

⭐ RAINBOW CATTLE CO
GLBT Entertainment

☎ 707-869-0206; www.queersteer.com; 16220 Main St; ☽ 6am-2am

Steer yourself to the Rainbow Cattle Co for men, music and Mason jars of Long Island iced tea. The nightly roundup includes bartenders quick with a quip, gay bears ranging from macho to cuddly, plus sundry grrrrls, gal pals and bikers. Summer brings gay Russian River out to play with Sunday backdoor BBQs and color-coded Steer Tag parties: red means taken, yellow means persuadable and green means good to go.

FORESTVILLE

This former mercury-mining boomtown has recently struck a creative vein with galleries, loca-vore restaurants and innovative wineries.

◉ QUICKSILVER MINE CO

☎ 707-887-0799; www.quicksilver mineco.com; 6671 Front St; admission free; ☽ 11am-6pm Thu-Mon

Prospectors once headed to Russian River to mine for quicksilver (a form of mercury) – but for the past 25 years, Quicksilver Mine Co has been a mother lode of Northern California arts and crafts. All media, styles and sizes are represented, from tiny bug-eyed blown-glass fish by Freestone's John Rizzi to huge, dreamy DNA-shaped sculptures woven from monofilament by Sonoma County's Tari Kerss.

🛶 BURKE'S CANOE TRIPS
☎ 707-887-1222; www.burkescanoe trips.com; 8600 River Rd; per person $59; ☎ daily by reservation
Paddle downriver past sunbathing turtles, otters doing backstroke and Great Blue Herons. In calm currents May to October, canoeists should count on early start times and late-afternoon pickups, pack a picnic and drinks, and make a day of the 10-mile route downstream. Life jackets are provided but passengers must be at least five years old, able to swim and willing to pack out trash.

🍴 FARMHOUSE INN & RESTAURANT
Californian $$$
☎ 707-887-3300; www.farmhouseinn .com; 7871 River Rd; ☺ 5:30-9:30pm Thu-Mon
Not your average farmhouse, unless you know farmers who regularly serve foie gras and Kurobota pork (the porcine Kobe beef equivalent) with pairings from a certified master sommelier. The menu is fresh and seasonal, though not strictly local – Chef Steve Litke reaches

out to Japan for silken *hamachi* and Maryland for soft-shell crabs. Consider his signature 'Rabbit Rabbit Rabbit,' with the eponymous ingredient variously roasted, bacon-wrapped and confit with mustard.

🍴 MOSAIC
Sustainable Locavore Californian $$
☎ 707-887-7503; www.mosaiceats.com; 6675 Front St; ☺ 11:30am-2:30pm & 5:30-9:30pm Mon-Fri, 10:30am-2:30pm & 5:30-9:30pm Sat & Sun
Discover dishes more pampered than a Hilton sister: lunchtime quail arrives wrapped in translucent prosciutto, while filet mignon gets massaged with coffee and dressed with cocoa-cabernet demi-glace and truffle oil for dinner. Ingredients arrive on your plate ultrafresh, directly from the restaurant's farm and other producers.

🍴 ROASTERS ESPRESSO
Coffee $
☎ 707-887-1632; www.roastersespresso bar.com; 6656 Front St; ☺ 6am-6pm Mon-Fri, from 7am Sat & Sun
Roasters serves the best cappuccino for miles around, made with locally roasted Fair Trade coffee. Only two treats can top that after a morning of wine tasting: a cookie hot out of Roasters' solar-powered oven or an espresso milkshake.

GRATON

Look out for cutting-edge cuisine in the local saloon, trendsetting home decor in the old post office and clapboard cottages jammed with eye-opening arts and crafts.

FUNERIA

☎ 707-829-1966; www.arthonorslife.com; 2860 Bowen St; admission free; ☽ 'by appointment & chance'

The dead get their due in this unusual gallery of memorial art, ranging from Richard Serra–style steel monoliths to the Urn-a-Matic, a vacuum cleaner for ashes with a screen showing home movies in an infinite loop. Funeria annually hosts arguably the world's best (and only) juried show of artist-made cremation urns.

GRATON GALLERY

☎ 707-829-8912; www.gratongallery.com; 9048 Graton Rd; ☽ 11am-6pm Mon, Wed & Thu, 10:30am-7pm Fri & Sat, 10am-5pm Sun

Dinky Graton packs a creative wallop with 30 local artists packed into this skinny gallery. Recent standouts include linocut prints of gnarled oaks crowning a Russian River ridgeline by Sebastopol's Rik Olson and green vases with Japanese basket-weave patterns from Sebastopol's Nichibei Pottery Studio.

MR RYDER AND CO
Antiques

☎ 707-824-8221; www.mrryderantiques.com; 9040 Graton Rd; ☽ 11am-5pm Mon-Sat, 10am-4pm Sun

You might have to elbow Martha Stewart aside to snag those 1920s carved-wood egg cups – she recently raved about the selective collective of antiques dealers inside this former post office. Recent scores include a Victorian brooch, gently worn Steiff teddy bears and 1920s bottles with faded labels promising miracle cures.

UNDERWOOD BAR & BISTRO *Californian* $$

☎ 707-823-7023; www.underwoodgraton.com; 9113 Graton Rd; ☽ 11:30am-2:30pm & 5-10pm Tue-Thu & Sun, 11:30am-2:30pm & 5-11pm Fri & Sat

The sexiest saloon in the West has the low mirrors and red-leather booths of a genteel French bistro, but the long, boisterous bar of a Wild West watering hole. The globe-trekking small-plates menu brings choruses of 'Ooh, you've got to try this,' especially tuna tartare with Moroccan preserved lemon and Hong Kong hoisin-sauced ribs with mango slaw.

>DRY CREEK VALLEY

Healdsburg is a dream date worthy of a hit R&B song: it's out to wine and dine you, rub you with hot stones and serve you espresso tomorrow morning. But when it's not busy seducing visitors, there's another side to Healdsburg. Graze the farmers market, rent a bike and cruise past historic homes on Grove St, hang out at El Sombrero until you finish that mondo burrito, or catch air at the skate park.

Just over Hwy 101 from downtown Healdsburg is Dry Creek Valley, a dreamscape of lazily grazing sheep, fish leaping from glistening streams and gnarled old vineyards. Dry Creek Valley wineries offer glorious reds in glorified sheds, preferring to make their presence known with award-winning wines rather than fancy tasting rooms. Bikers wave to bio-dynamic farmers sputtering past on tractors fueled with used cooking oil, creating cravings for french fries. But since there are no restaurants in Dry Creek, come prepared: bring picnic provisions and stop by the Healdsburg Visitors Bureau (p200) to pillage their free-tasting passes.

DRY CREEK VALLEY

🍷 WINERIES

Amphora	1	C2
Bella Vineyards	2	C1
Kokomo Winery	(see 1)	
La Crema	3	B5
Longboard Vineyards	4	C5
Peterson Winery	(see 1)	
Preston of Dry Creek	5	C1
Quivira	6	C2
Seghesio Family Winery	7	A2
Topel Winery	8	B4
Truett-Hurst	9	C2
Unti	10	C2

💿 SEE

Hand Fan Museum	(see 18)	
Healdsburg Farmers Market	11	A4

🏃 DO

Healdsburg Farmers Market	12	B4
Lake Sonoma Fish Hatchery	13	C1
Akoia Day Spa	14	B4
Carson Warner Skate Park	15	A1
Relish Culinary Adventures	16	B5
Russian River Adventures	17	D6
Spa at Hotel Healdsburg	18	B4
Spoke Folk Cyclery	19	B5

🛍 SHOP

Arboretum	20	B4
Artists & Farmers	21	B5
Baksheesh	22	B5
Cheese Shop	23	B4

🍴 EAT & DRINK

Barndiva	24	B5
Bear Republic Brewing Co	25	B4
Bovolo	26	B5
Cyrus	27	B4
Dry Creek General Store & Bar	28	D2
Flying Goat Coffee	29	B4
Oakville Grocery	30	B5
Ravenous	31	B4
Scopa	32	B4
Taqueria El Sombrero	33	B5

⭐ PLAY

Raven Film Center	34	B4

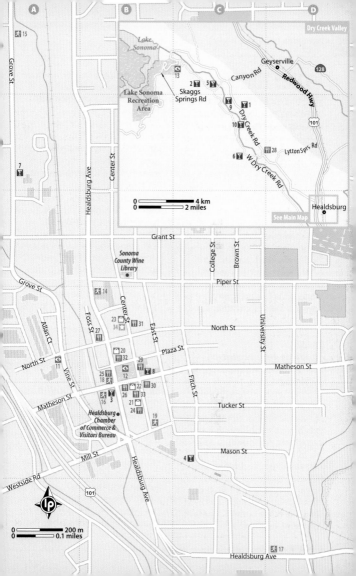

Dry Creek Valley

Lake
Sonoma

13

2 5

Canyon Rd

Geyserville

128

Redwood Hwy

Lake Sonoma
Recreation
Area

Skaggs
Springs Rd

9

1

Dry Creek Rd

10

28

Lytton Sprs Rd

101

6

W Dry Creek Rd

0 ————— 4 km
0 ————— 2 miles

See Main Map

Healdsburg

Grove St

15

7

Healdsburg Ave

Center St

Grant St

Sonoma
County Wine
Library

College St

Brown St

Piper St

Grove St

14

Center St

Foss St

North St

University St

Allan Ct

23
34

27

31

East St

Plaza St

North St

20
32

Vine St

11

25
18

12

29

8

Matheson St

North St

16

26

22

21

33

30

Fitch St

Matheson St

3

24

19

Tucker St

Healdsburg
Chamber
of Commerce &
Visitors Bureau

Mason St

4

Mill St

Westside Rd

101

Healdsburg Ave

0 ————— 200 m
0 ————— 0.1 miles

17

Healdsburg Ave

WINERIES

☑ LONGBOARD VINEYARDS
☎ 707-433-3473; www.longboard vineyards.com; 5 Fitch St; tasting $5, applicable to purchase; ⏱ 11am-6pm Mon & Wed-Sat, to 5pm Sun

'Howzit, bra? You know I need DaKine…' You too may turn surfer with Longboard's signature Merlot ($24), a wave of juicy redcurrant that lingers long with 9% Malbec ('da kine' means 'choice stuff'). The surf theme is an obvious market-ing scheme, but surfer–winemaker Odded Shakked (formerly at J, p102) has the skills to back it up: DaKine Vineyard Syrah ($34) field blend is Malbec blueberry Zen in a swirl of Petit Sirah tannins and cinnamon Zin.

☑ LA CREMA
☎ 707-431-9400; www.lacrema .com; 235 Healdsburg Ave; tasting free; ⏱ 10:30am-5:30pm

The Jackson family made their fortune with megabrand Kendall-Jackson, and now with La Crema they've got something to prove: can they make smaller-production wines without sacrificing value? Free tastings reveal winemaker Melissa Stackhouse's talents in an Anderson Valley Pinot ($34) ripe with blueberry intrigue and Earl Grey tea. While better Sonoma whites are available at similar

prices, the Sonoma County Syrah ($20) is good value, stacking up redcurrant, cinnamon and tobacco.

☑ TOPEL WINERY
☎ 707-433-4116; www.topelwines .com; 125 Matheson St; tasting 4/6/9 wines $5/8/11, $5 applicable to purchase; ⏱ 11am-7pm

The inviting California Arts and Crafts tasting room sets the mood for Meritage le Mariage ($32), a happily-ever-after Cab blend with Cab Franc, Petit Verdot and Merlot matching cherry and red licorice. To spice things up after le Mariage, try Syrah Cuvée Donis ($25), a zing of white pepper, a hint of cherries and a silky finish. Topel was founded by a lawyer-turned-winemaker who makes wines without chemical pesticides and hosts frequent benefits for the animal shelter and food bank.

☑ SEGHESIO FAMILY WINERY
☎ 707-433-7764; www.seghesio.com; 14730 Grove St; ⏱ 10am-5pm

Behind the tasting room bar is a window into Seghesio's barrel room, where cellar masters pace the floor like anxious babysitters. This attention is a point of pride for the Seghesio family, once Son-oma's biggest producers – but in the 1980s, they decided to go for quality over quantity. White Fiano

Grab a bottle and enjoy a picnic at Quivira Winery

($20) is a Roman charmer hinting at lemon zest and muscat grape, while Home Ranch Zin ($36) adds pink-peppercorn sass to ripe fruit from 100-year-old vines. Signature Venom ($50) is a high-end Sangiovese affectionately called a 'baby Brunello': pomegranate and carnations swaddled in red velvet.

QUIVIRA
☎ 707-431-8333; www.quivirawine
.com; 4900 W Dry Creek Rd; tasting $5;
🕙 11am-5pm

Press accolades and awards keep rolling in for pioneering Quivira (Key-VEER-ah), the Dry Creek Valley landmark that's organic, Demeter-certified biodynamic and 100% solar-powered. Look out for steelhead trout making a comeback in Wine Creek, thanks to Quivera's creek clean-up efforts. Wine Creek Syrah ($28) is an illusionist, covering blueberries with a silk hanky and revealing geraniums with a flourish, while Petit Sirah ($26) packs more espresso beans and blackberries than Seattle.

UNTI
☎ 707-433-5590; www.untivine
yards.com; 4202 Dry Creek Rd;
🕙 by appointment

Unti's dedication to artisanal methods is obvious in their Demeter-certified biodynamic

AGENDA: DRY CREEK DAY OFF

> 9am: 'Sorry, don't think I can make it…cough, cough…right, I'll rest up, lots of water.'
> 10am: Roll from hotel bed into Flying Goat (p133) for coffee and gossip with strangers.
> 11am: Late start on wine tasting, panic setting in…head directly to Unti (p123) for reserve Syrah.
> Noon: All is right with the world. Maybe eating is a good idea? Swing by Dry Creek Store (p135) for provisions.
> 1pm: Over to Quivira (p123) for acclaimed Wine Creek Ranch Syrah and picnic.
> 2:30pm: West Dry Creek as the afternoon sun filters through the trees — bucolic splendor overload. Stop by Hop Kiln (p102) for a vinegar tasting with pretzels.
> 3pm: Porter Creek (p101) is famous for its Pinots, but you know the score: Timbervine Ranch Syrah.
> 4:30pm: Twilight in Armstrong Woods (p114). Breathe deeply.
> 6pm: Return to Healdsburg for the detoxifying Sauvignon Blanc wrap at the Spa at Hotel Healdsburg (p129).
> 7:30pm: Remember food. Remember water. Remember to call in late tomorrow. 'Yes, feeling much better now…no, really.'

winery, but it occasionally verges on madness: the Reserve Syrah ($50) was stomped twice underfoot to yield only five barrels. The current-release Syrah ($26) is no slouch either, aged 14 months in French oak for a redcurrant and ancho-chili finish. Unti's Italian roots run deep, as you'll gather from the vintage paintings of Italy in the barn tasting room and their cherry-mocha Sangiovese ($30).

☿ AMPHORA
☎ 707-431-7767; www.amphorawines.com; Bldg 6, 4791 Dry Creek Rd; ⏰ 11am-4:30pm
'How'd they get that in there?' is the natural response to tasting Amphora's wines. Their tasting room is a glorified shed, leaving all the frills to go in the bottle – their Jacob's Ridge Cab ($45) has the heft of buckwheat pancakes and the delight of boysenberry syrup. It's no wonder Amphora's Dry Creek Zin ($26) took top Zin honors at the 2009 SF Chronicle Wine Competition, with ripe red raspberries, white pepper and cinnamon-dusted peach in a velvet cloak.

☿ PETERSON WINERY
☎ 707-431-7568; www.petersonwinery.com; 4791 Dry Creek Rd Bldg 7; tasting $5; ⏰ 11am-4:30pm
A bunny with antlers crossed out in red marks the shed-door entry to Peterson: you are now entering Zero Manipulation territory. Peter-

son's pristine field blend Tradizionale Zin ($26) brings out prime Dry Creek Valley old-vine characteristics: sun-ripe raspberry, black pepper, pumpkin-pie spice and traces of oak. Il Granaio Sangiovese ($25) is left unfined and unfiltered, with Cab and Syrah helping to coat the mouth with espresso, chocolate-covered cranberries and a stolen puff on a cigar.

KOKOMO WINERY
☎ 707-433-0200; www.kokomowinery
.com; 4791 Dry Creek Rd; ☼ 11am-4:30pm
Some wines just don't know how to deal with food and sulk to be in the same room with anything but blue cheese – but not those from indie producer Kokomo. Behind the sliding barn door there's Greenday on the soundtrack and award-winning Dry Creek Valley Zin ($27) at the bar, with hints of cherry jam on toasted French bread. The Sonoma Bela Cuvée ($20) is a robust Meritage blend that practically orders a pizza or a BLT for you.

TRUETT-HURST
☎ 707-433-6913; www.truetthurst
.com; 5610 Dry Creek Rd; ☼ 11am-5pm Fri-Sun, by appointment Mon-Thu
The new kid on the block is already winning awards, earning bio-dynamic certification and making

Beach boys aside, Kokomo is certainly a place to take it slow

old-vine Zins to be reckoned with. Settle into creek-side Adirondack chairs with a picnic and bottle of Three Vineyards Old Vine Zin ($25), bright raspberry with a puff of BBQ smoke on the finish. Technically the acronym in Dark Horse GPS ($40) stands for Grenache, Petit Sirah and Syrah, but this wine has built-in Dry Creek flavor geo positioning: woodsy chanterelles, sunny valley strawberries and whiffs of white pepper and sea salt.

� PRESTON OF DRY CREEK
☎ 707-433-3372; www.prestonvine yards.com; 9282 West Dry Creek Rd; $5, applicable to purchase;
🕒 11am-4:30pm
Fingernails are permanently purple at Preston after years of handcrafting exciting wines from

estate-grown, certified-organic grapes. Barbera ($32) is typically a medium-bodied red, but Preston's is a mouthful of blackberry pie and roasted peaches. Preston's sustainable farming methods involve planting artichokes and radishes for pest control, so there's fresh produce here in ad- dition to Preston's own olive oil, fresh-baked bread, and neighbor- hood cheeses for noshing. Come prepared to picnic on Sundays, when the 3L jugs of Guadagni Red ($32), an old-school Zin, Car- ignane and Mourvédre Cali blend get broken out.

� BELLA VINEYARDS
☎ 707-473-9171, 866-572-3552; www .bellawinery.com; 9711 W Dry Creek Rd; tasting $5; 🕒 11am-4:30pm

TOP FIVE DRY CREEK PLAYDATES
> Winter Wineland (Jan) See p24.
> Wild Steelhead Festival (www.corpslakes.us/Sonoma; Feb) The endangered local fish is making a comeback, with help from fishy art exhibits and tours of the Lake Sonoma Fish Hatchery. Celebrations include a kiddies trout pond and (somewhat perversely) fly-fishing and cooking demos on the Healdsburg Plaza.
> Earth Day Festival (www.corpslakes.us/Sonoma; Apr) Party with the planet: plant a tree, spot a rare bird, take a ranger-led nature hike or just mellow out and watch fish eggs hatch at the Lake Sonoma Recreation Area.
> Healdsburg Jazz Festival (www.healdsburgjazzfestival.org; Jun) Big names hit small venues around Healdsburg, as talents like New Orleans' ReBirth Brass Band, legendary pianist McCoy Tyner and bossa-nova diva Leny Andrade work up winery crowds.
> Wine & Food Affair (www.wineroad.com/events; Nov) What Zin works for dessert and what cut of pork pairs with Pinot? Solve crucial dilemmas with weekend pairings throughout Dry Creek, Alexander and Russian River Valleys.

Spelunk as you taste at Bella, where the bar is burrowed right into Lilly Hill. Work your way through the estate Zins and small-production Syrahs, but return to the violets-and-ruby-grapefruit Rosé ($20) for sunny picnics aboveground. Late Harvest Zin ($30) should only be opened for dinner parties you don't want to end: guests will linger over those plum, caramel and cardamom flavors.

HEALDSBURG

Healdsburg trumps Napa style with upscale restaurants, chic hotels and trendsetting boutiques, but just a couple of blocks off the Plaza you'll find the town's mellow side, with Victorian B&Bs, taco joints and a community skate park.

Art or accoutrement? Peek behind the hand fans

SEE

HAND FAN MUSEUM

☎ 707-431-2500; www.handfan museum.com; 327A Healdsburg Ave; ⏱ 11am-4pm Wed-Sun

Unless you're an opera diva or close friend of Karl Lagerfeld, it's probably been a while since you've seen someone working a hand fan – as this tiny museum shows, it's a lost art. Before text messaging, a fan was the ultimate flirtation device, providing cover for whispers, slipped notes and rendezvous plotted with coded gestures. Fans signaled your status better than Facebook, with exquisite artistry: intricate Italian mother-of-pearl fans telegraphed high-maintenance sophistication, while painted-silk scenes of sweet shepherdesses eluding love-struck shepherds revealed a shameless flirt.

◎ HEALDSBURG FARMERS MARKET

☎ 707-431-1956; www.healdsburg
farmersmarket.org; cnr North & Vine Sts
(Sat), Healdsburg Plaza (Tue);
⏱ 9am-noon Sat May-Nov,
4-6:30pm Tue Jun-Oct

Thanksgiving comes twice a week, when Healdsburgers beam over the cornucopia of foods and hand-made goods produced by their neighbors. Most of the 50 producers arrive from within 10 miles of downtown Healdsburg. Graze your way past ripe organic produce, Yucatan tamales, Pug's Leap goat cheese (p87) and Sonoma toffee stalls, then check out souvenir options from local artisans.

🏃 DO

🏃 AKOIA DAY SPA

☎ 707-433-1270; www.akoiadayspa
.com; 452B Healdsburg Ave; ⏱ 10am-7pm

With all that Dry Creek Zin, you should already be relaxed – but Akoia is determined to leave you glowing and more worldly, too. Swedish hot-stone massages ($140 for 90 minutes) and polishing treatments involving local grape seeds and sea salt in rich cocoa butter ($85 for an hour) leave you luminous for less than other spas using lesser products. Go global with the floral Javanese body scrub ($95 for an hour) or the Thai herbal poultice

massage ($120 for 90 minutes), and everyone back home will wonder where you've been and how soon they can get there.

🏃 CARSON WARNER SKATE PARK

☎ 707-431-3301; www.carsonwarner
skate.com; ⏱ 8am-5pm

No one is going to cramp your ramp style here, so long as you brought your helmet and safety pads, or rented some from Spoke Folk (opposite). Built using donations (the band Primus held a benefit concert) as a memorial to a local teen skater, this nonprofit park provides a free venue with challenges for in-line skaters and skateboarders at all skill levels.

🏃 RELISH CULINARY ADVENTURES

☎ 707-431-9999; www.relish
culinary.com; 14 Matheson St; ⏱ by
appointment

Sooner or later at some upscale Healdsburg restaurant, you realize:

TOP FIVE BEER BARS IN WINE COUNTRY

> Anderson Valley Brewing Company (p152)
> Russian River Brewing Co (p105)
> Bear Republic Brewing Co (p132)
> Silverado Brewing Company (p63)
> Barley & Hops (p112)

'I could probably learn to cook this.' Relish is out to prove you right, supplying recipes, prep skills and an appreciation for farm-fresh and artisanal ingredients and how to highlight them on the plate. On the second Saturday of the month (May to October), Relish's participants meet local farmers, collect ingredients at the farmers market and cook up a feast. Seasonal day trips range from winter wild-mushroom forages in Dry Creek to summer searches for the perfect peach in Sonoma orchards. Check the website for winemaker dinners, absinthe tastings and all-inclusive locavore weekends.

RUSSIAN RIVER ADVENTURES
☎ 707-433-5599; www.rradventures .info; 20 Healdsburg Ave; $45 per person or dog; 🐾
California's wilderness is beyond splendid, but let's be honest: it can get uncomfortable out there. Russian River Adventures provides cushy inflatable canoes and kayaks so that modern trailblazers don't have to relive Jack London's long, hard days getting tossed around in a rowboat – but don't worry, there are tricky turns and rope swings along the three- to six-hour Russian River route to get adrenaline pumping. In late summer and fall tranquil waters require more paddling, and spring rains can bring mild rapids.

This ecotourism outfit provides drop-off and pickup, including delivering your car and gear to you.

SPA AT HOTEL HEALDSBURG
☎ 707-431-2800, 800-889-7188; www .hotelhealdsburg.com; 25 Matheson St; ⏰ 9am-8pm by appointment
Strains from wineglass-lifting are cured by massages with all the fixings: organic skincare products, herbal tea, trail mix and a hot tub. Highlights of this ultrasleek, high-end spa are the Crushed Zinfandel Body Polish ($115 for 50 minutes), an exfoliating Zin-sugar scrub followed by a liberal slathering of Zin–shea butter lotion, and the combo massage, a work over with hot stones, deep kneading and rather ticklish reflexology ($110 for 50 minutes). Spa packages and accommodations deals are available online.

SPOKE FOLK CYCLERY
☎ 707-433-7171; www.spokefolk.com; 201 Center St
No matter if you're a biathlete or your last ride was in spinning class, you're going to wish you'd rented a bike once you glimpse Westside Dr. This tree-lined country road winding through vineyards will make you eternally grateful for nature and calf muscles, and Spoke Folk will help you plan an itinerary

Smile and say 'Fromage!' at the Cheese Shop

to match your skill level. No kids' bikes, but there are trailers for toting wee ones and tandem bikes to get slacker teens in gear.

SHOP

◻ ARBORETUM
Sustainable Clothing
☎ 707-433-7033; www.arboretum apparel.com; 332 Healdsburg Ave; ⏱ 10am-6pm Wed-Mon

Ultrasoft bamboo-fiber cardigans, chic handbags made from reclaimed Camaro upholstery, and sweatshop-free hoodies: Arboretum gives fresh meaning to the expression 'fashion conscious.' This eco-boutique emphasizes Fair Trade practices and US designers – though your friends might kill for that reclaimed-wood cocktail ring. The men's section isn't an afterthought, with one-of-a kind hand-printed tees and sleek organic-cotton pants.

◻ ARTISTS & FARMERS
Gifts & Home Decor
☎ 707-431-7404; www.artistsand farmers.com; 237 Center St

Shabby chic gets real at Artist & Farmers, neighbor and partner of Barndiva (opposite). There's nothing faux about the rustic look here: those metal-banded vessels that look like old-time water jugs are exactly that, and closely

DRY CREEK VALLEY > HEALDSBURG

THE VALLEYS

DRY CREEK VALLEY

observed rooster portraits capture the comical droop in a particular cockscomb. The prices can be a little unreal (ouch, three-figure decanters) but most items are locally sourced and fairly traded, and it's cheaper than Dry Creek real estate.

🛍 BAKSHEESH *Gifts*
☎ 707-473-0880; www.baksheesh fairtrade.com; 106B Matheson Street; 🕙 10am-6pm Mon-Sat, 11am-5pm Sun
Household goods with a global outlook – how very Sonoma. Everything here is sourced from a Fair Trade collective: Vietnamese recycled-newspaper trivets, Chilean salsa dishes shaped like pigs and Fair Trade–certified chocolate. Collectives in 40 countries cover gift needs from $2 finger puppets to $90 Alpaca shawls. Look for smaller sister stores on the Sonoma Plaza and in downtown St Helena.

🛍 CHEESE SHOP
Gourmet Foods & Gifts
☎ 707-433-4998; www.doraliceimports .com; 423 Center St; 🕙 10am-6pm Mon-Sat
Once you've perfected your swish at wineries, you automatically advance to the next level of California connoisseurship: local cheese pairings. The Cheese Shop has you covered, with artisanal and sustainably produced

wonders, from the adventurously stinky aged goat Capricious to the crowd-pleasing mild Point Reyes Blue, as well as special cheese paper to keep purchases from molding or sweating. It also sells Oakland-made Cosmic chocolates featuring Snoop Dogg and President Obama, and to complete your four basic Wine Country food groups, imported Italian truffle salt.

🍴 EAT & DRINK
🍴 BARNDIVA
Locavore Californian $$
☎ 707-431-0100; www.barndiva.com; 231 Center St; 🕙 5:30-11pm Wed & Thu, noon-midnight Fri & Sat, 11am-midnight Sun
Don't hate Barndiva because it's beautiful – especially by day, when sunshine illuminates the wood bar and filters through trees by the garden waterfall. Barndiva is a little high maintenance – service can be slow even when it's near empty – but they put the local love right on the plate. 'Eggs Benny' is shorthand for Benedict with free-range eggs, house-baked brioche and Champagne hollandaise, while inventive salads like Liberty Farms duck confit with pomegranate, satsuma and pickled ginger will make you want to bear-hug the chef. Don't forget to try one of the specialty cocktails, either.

NAPA & SONOMA >131

THE VALLEYS

DRY CREEK VALLEY

🍴 BEAR REPUBLIC
BREWING CO *Brewpub* $
☎ 707-433-2337; www.bearrepublic
.com; 345 Healdsburg Ave; ⏰ 11:30am-
9pm Sun-Thu, 11am-10pm Fri & Sat
Cask pours of experimental
brews, served with heads as rich
and foamy as cappuccino, are
the order of choice here. For a
signature drink, go with the crisp,
bitterly badass Racer 5 IPA, or
give the bartender some idea
what you like – stout, amber,
long walks on the beach – and
they'll let you sample a seasonal
brew or two. Go ahead and drink
your dinner – the food here is
just average.

🍴 BOVOLO
Locavore Cal-Italian $
☎ 707-431-2962; www.bovolorestau
rant.com; 106 Matheson St; ⏰ 9am-6pm
Mon, Tue, Thu & Fri, to 9pm Sat & Sun
Bovolo will slip you the pig any
chance it gets, and for that, some
of us are profoundly grateful. Bovolo uses excellent local
products and makes its own cured
meats, but pork is its passion. Its
best pizza has roasted squash,
sage leaf, ricotta salata and Black
Pig bacon. Your breakfast choice
should be clear: an egg sandwich,
with Bellwether Carmody cheese
(p87) – and more bacon.

From Hop Rod Rye to Big Bear Black, try them all at Bear Republic Brewing Co

WORTH THE TRIP

Nature lovers and nature voyeurs converge at Lake Sonoma Recreational Area's main attraction: the **Lake Sonoma Fish Hatchery** (☎ 707-431-4590; www.corpslakes.us /sonoma; 3333 Skaggs Springs Rd; ☼ visitor center 8:30am-5:30pm Wed-Sun, fishery 8:30am-3:45pm, park 8am-sundown). From January to April, fish risk death to reach this hot spot in the desperate hope of spawning (insert clubbing analogy here). Visitors scrutinizing their every move doesn't deter the inevitable ichthyic orgy. In fact, the fish seem to thrive on the attention: with the help of the hatchery, the endangered wild steelhead trout is making a comeback. Lake Sonoma also has nature hikes (maps available at the visitor center), a boat marina and an overlook with a two-story observation deck to spot local hawks (ignore that yellow eyesore of a bridge over the dam below). Camping is allowed upon request at the visitor center but due to drought conditions, potable water and showers were unavailable at the time of writing.

🍴 CYRUS

Californian $$$

☎ 707-433-3311; www.cyrus restaurant.com; 29 North St; ☼ 6-11pm Wed-Mon; **V**

Cyrus crafts cocktails with just-squeezed seasonal juices, topmost-shelf hooch and a full spice rack. Casual diners will prefer the constantly celebrating crowd in the bar, where plates are available à la carte. Dishes are often laced with truffles – a transparent culinary ploy but it works, especially the truffled red-wine risotto and gnocchi with Brussels sprouts and truffled pecorino. In the dining room, Chef Douglas Keane offers five- or eight-course seasonal tasting menus ($102 and $130, respectively), the difference being a cheese course, chilled dessert and bonus protein (succulent duck, if you're lucky). Vegetarian options are thoughtful, if not wildly adventurous, and wine pairings are worth considering at $70 for five pairings, given corkage is $35 per bottle.

🍴 FLYING GOAT COFFEE

Café $

☎ 707-433-8003; www.flyinggoatcoffee .com; 419 Center St; ☼ 6am-1pm Mon-Fri, from 7am Sat

Espresso drinks here are so rejuvenating, you'll feel capable of anything…possibly even another day of wine tasting. The secret: fresh-roasted beans and milk so rich, the fern drawn in the foam remains intact after three delicious sips. Every espresso drinker in a 5-mile radius comes here at least once a day, so you'll never lack for company in line.

Bits, bobs and beers at the Dry Creek General Store

RAVENOUS RESTAURANT
New American $$
☎ 707-431-1302; 420 Center St
When tasting-room pourers recommend burgers with their Zin and Dungeness crab cakes with Sauvignon Blanc, that's when you'll be Ravenous. Call ahead to score a seat in this cottage, and expect a wait once you're there – rushing isn't done here. The hand-written menu makes every dish sound seductive, but that burger is beyond plump, and ginger-lemon-cilantro aioli tops the crab cakes. Corkage is $10, so BYO if you're wining with your dining. In summer, hit the backyard patio bar with Healdsburg's hipper half.

SCOPA
Italian & Pizza $$
☎ 707-433-5282; www.scopahealds burg.com; 109A Plaza St; ⏰ 5:30-10pm Tue-Sun
Now that you've stocked up on Dry Creek Sangiovese, all you need is an Italian grandmother to whip you up a hearty dinner to go with it. Failing that, head to Scopa for Nonna's slow-braised chicken melting into a polenta pillow. The thin-crust Pizza Margherita has just enough mozzarella, tangy tomato sauce and oregano that it doesn't go sliding off onto your neighbor's lap (yes, you'll be sitting that close). Reservations are essential.

OAKVILLE GROCERY
Groceries $
☎ 707-433-3200; www.oakvillegrocery .com; 124 Matheson St; ⏰ 8am-6pm
You might not catch the family resemblance between Napa's innocent little country store (p58) and this snazzy food emporium, but both are out to spoil you for local choices. Do you go with the house-baked calzone, organic field-greens salad or local fruit, fresh bread and sustainably farmed local caviar? At $18, boxed lunches are pricey – you're better off assembling your own.

THE VALLEYS

DRY CREEK VALLEY

TAQUERIA EL SOMBRERO

Mexican $

☎ 707-433-3818; 245 Center St; 11am-7.30pm

When Healdsburg's tempting boutiques, tasting rooms, spas and swanky restaurants threaten to shatter budgetary resolve, El Sombrero comes to the rescue. Pastor tacos come fully loaded with plump, marinated pork. If you're planning to finish that huge burrito in one sitting, pick out some Norteño on the jukebox and settle in for the long haul.

 PLAY

RAVEN FILM CENTER

☎ 707-522-0330; www.srentertainment grp.com/raven.asp; 415 Center St; adult/child, senior & matinee $9.25/6.25; ⏲ show approximately 4:30 & 7pm daily, 9pm Sat & Sun

Though it may not seem sprawling from the outside, the Raven has four theaters screening first-run movies and Oscar contenders. Parents take note: a deal has been struck to allow alcohol sales in the back two theaters, so anyone un-

der 21 won't be allowed in those theaters. Tickets can be bought in advance online or at the cinema.

DRY CREEK ROAD

Rolling vineyards, plenty of sunshine, and not much else – farmers and wine tasters converge at the general store for picnic supplies and front-porch chats.

DRY CREEK GENERAL STORE & BAR *Cafe & Bar* $

☎ 707-433-4171; www.dcgstore.com; 3495 Dry Creek Rd; ⏲ 6am-6pm Mon-Thu, to 7pm Fri & Sat, bar 6-9pm Mon-Sat

When your stomach protests Zin before lunch, make a pit stop here for a Toscano salami and Manchego cheese sandwich or the classic BLT. Coffee is helpfully stationed by the door for a quick pick-me-up on the porch. Stick around for the bar to open, when locals roll in for a beer – you might even impress the old-timers if you can identify the farm equipment hanging from the rafters.

>ALEXANDER VALLEY

You want fries with that burger, or maybe a $100 vintage Cabernet? Alexander Valley has your order covered. At the foot of the Mendocino redwoods and just over the other side of a volcano from Napa, this is where Americana meets cosmopolitan flair. Alexander Valley has been a major thoroughfare since Wild West days, and the quaint houses that dot the landscape have seen it all: bordellos, stagecoach stickups and, of course, bootlegging.

Early Italian immigrants recognized farming potential in this rugged region. By selling Zinfandel grapes for 'sacramental wine' during Prohibition, farmers preserved some vineyards that today yield extraordinary old-vine vintages. Citrus also thrived, and Cloverdale's Citrus Fair became the pride of the West, eventually launching a wine-tasting competition that morphed into the San Francisco Chronicle Wine Competition in 2000.

The valley isn't letting all the attention change much. You'll still find vintners pouring their wine from jugs, pizza-makers preparing their own pepperoni, and farmers proudly selling fruit at the Cloverdale Farmers Market. And the fries aren't bad, either.

ALEXANDER VALLEY

☖ WINERIES

Alexander Valley
  Vineyards 1 C6
Fritz Underground
  Winery 2 A3
Hawkes 3 C5
Locals Tasting
  Room 4 D4
Meeker Vineyards 5 D3
Robert Young 6 C4
Rosso & Bianco 7 B4
Sausal Winery 8 C5
Silver Oak 9 B3

Stryker Sonoma 10 C5
Terroirs Artisan
  Wines 11 D4
Trentadue 12 B4

◎ SEE

Cloverdale Citrus
  Fair Grounds 13 C2
Cloverdale Farmers
  Market & Art Fair 14 C1
Cloverdale Museum 15 C1
Geyser Arts Gallery 16 D4

☖ SHOP

Jimtown Store 17 C5

☖ EAT & DRINK

Diavola 18 D4
La Hacienda 19 C2
Pick's Drive-In 20 C2
Santi 21 C3

☆ PLAY

Clover 22 D2

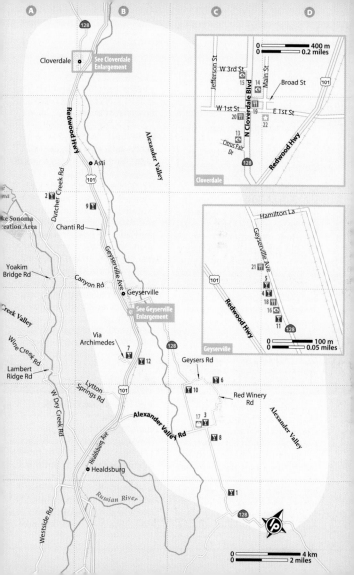

WINERIES

☈ ALEXANDER VALLEY VINEYARDS

☎ 707-433-7209; www.avvwine.com; 8644 Hwy 128; ☉ 10am-5pm
Foodies recognize this 100K-case family winery from restaurants nationwide serving their value-priced Sin Zin ($20), which isn't your stereotypical fruit bomb: expect fireworks with a long fuse, a brief blueberry burst and cascading spice from 10 months in American oak. But aficionados are inevitably here for limited-production Cyrus ($55), a monumental Meritage with unlikely flavors of Carrara marble and California poppies. Tastings are free and occasionally involve chocolate.

☈ SAUSAL WINERY

☎ 707-433-2285; www.sausalwinery .com; 7370 Hwy 128; ☉ 10am-4pm
Stubborn doesn't begin to describe the 50- to 130-year-old vines here, reaching through clay, sand and gravel to yield Zin grapes with hard-earned character. After three generations of coaxing from the Demostene family, these vines produce a top-value Family Zin ($19) with teak and cinnamon chasing wild blackberries, and a Private Reserve ($24) from 90-year-old vines that leaves the tip of the tongue velvety with

anisette and the sides tickling with green peppercorn. Tasting is free, and the fluffy black cats occasionally consent to petting.

☈ ROBERT YOUNG

707-431-4811; www.ryew.com; 4950 Red Winery Rd; tasting $5, applicable to purchase; ☉ 10am-5pm
The Gold Rush didn't work out as expected for Peter Young in 1858 – instead of gold he found sunshine and oceanic sediment. Four generations later, the pick of his family's abundant harvest is reserved for Alexander Valley Estate Chardonnay ($40), with hints of pannacotta with lemon zest; the signature Scion ($58), a Meritage that gives you a full two minutes to identify flavors from rose petals to mocha; and elusive 400-case Alexander Valley Estate Merlot ($50), with chocolate cherries and oaky Cab aspirations.

☈ HAWKES

☎ 707-433-4295; www.hawkeswine .com; 6734 Hwy 128; tasting $5; ☉ 10am-5pm
Funky teapots from Stephen Hawkes' vast personal collection grace the walls of Hawkes' tasting room: that's your first hint you're not in Napa anymore. The second is Hawkes' solid-value Cab ($40), which puts on a show of red currant and pluot and disappears in a magician's poof of smoke – not

the dragon's breath of some big Napa vintages. Father–son winemakers Stephen and Jake may joke with visitors over oolong tea, but they're serious about not over-oaking their wines, letting their Merlot ($30) bring on the spice without trouncing delicate floral notes.

☿ STRYKER SONOMA
☎ 800-433-1944; www.strykersonoma.com; 5110 Hwy 128; tasting mixed/Zin/Bordeaux varietals free/$5/10; ⏱ 10:30am-5pm

Meticulous simplicity gives modern elegance to Stryker's Frank Lloyd Wright–inspired tasting room, and its wines too. Exposed steel supports lift the roof to maximize vineyard views from the bar, where 14 distinct Zins and 13 Cabs reveal the underlying traits of those vineyards. Speedy Creek Vineyard's 100°F summer days intensify redcurrant, black pepper and basalt in Zin, while volcanic Ash Creek wines start juicy and end in ashy intrigue. Vintages are limited, with an average of about 200 cases sold only online or at the vineyard.

☿ TRENTADUE
☎ 707-433-3104, 888-332-3032; www.trentadue.com; 19170 Geyserville Ave; port & reserves tasting each $5; ⏱ 10am-5pm

After all those Alexander Valley Zins and Cabs, give your tongue CPR: Chocolate Port Resuscitation. Trentadue's acclaimed Chocolate Amore is a Merlot-based, cocoa-infused serotonin starter with the mouthfeel of chocolate frosting and 8% residual sugar. There's reserve tasting, but Trentadue's real strength is value-priced fruity reds that show their true colors on the finish. The estate Merlot ($18) starts with sugarplums but ends with blackberry and parsley, and Old Patch Red ($14) puts strawberry-pepper Zin in the spotlight.

☿ ROSSO & BIANCO
☎ 707-857-1400; www.rossobianco.com; 300 Via Archimedes; tasting table/California/Sonoma wines free/$5/8 ⏱ from 11am

Francis Ford Coppola's latest epic undertaking is this just-launched Dracula-esque castle winery with bocce courts, an amphitheater and swimming pools – the café is already generating buzz. Director's Cut reserves have dancing-devil labels that animate when you spin the bottle – oof, don't try that after potent, action-packed reds like the Dry Creek Zin ($23) or Syrah ($32). The best buy is the four-pack of Sofia Mini Blanc de Blanc ($15): bubbly, fun and stylish with traces of violets.

A WEEKEND OF PURE ZIN

Day One Start at Alexander Valley Vineyards (p138) with blockbuster Sin Zin, then discover great values on smaller productions and old-vine reserves at Sausal (p138). Grab sandwiches at Jimtown Store (p142) to enjoy with a *terroir* tasting of single-vineyard offerings at Stryker Sonoma (p139). Up the road in Geyserville, hit Geyser Arts (p143) for handmade home decor to pair with artisan wines, and brace yourself for Locals (below), where you can compare Sonoma and Lodi old-vines. Dinner awaits at Diavola (p143), and overnight in Cloverdale puts you in position to Zin-hop down Dry Creek.

Day Two Start underground with reserves at Fritz (p142), then spelunk at Bella's (p126) caves for their Late Harvest. Emerge for a picnic and organic estate Zin at Preston (p126), then go for the gold-winning options at Amphora (p124). Enjoy a leisurely coffee on the porch at Dry Creek Store (p135) before a detoxifying herbal poultice massage at Akoia (p128), dinner at Scopa (p134) and face plant on your hotel bed in Healdsburg.

TERROIRS ARTISAN WINES

☎ 707-857-4101; www.terroirsartisanwines.com; 21001 Geyserville Ave; tasting $5; 11am-5:30pm

Kerry Damskey's chic exposed-brick tasting room showcases his career as consulting winemaker for four family vineyards: Godwin, Hughes, Peña Ridge and his own Palmeri project. The tasting menu features two to four wines per vineyard, and you can sample at the sleek concrete bar or by the gas fireplace. Ones to watch are Godwin's Chardonnay ($28), with traces of clover, nasturtiums and sea salt, and Merlot ($35), with white pepper and jasmine begging for green curry.

LOCALS TASTING ROOM

☎ 707-857-4900; www.tastelocalwines.com; 21023-A Geyserville Ave; 11am-6pm Wed-Mon

'We've only got an hour – let's get cracking!' says Sharon with an enthusiastic finger snap as she lines up free varietal tasting flights (plural) on the bar. With 62 wines from 10 local wineries on the tasting menu, many of them award-winning drops, an hour only begins to do Locals' selection justice. Compare the balance of herbs and oak in Hawley's Sonoma Viognier ($23) to the steely star fruit of Praxis' Lodi Viognier ($17), and plan your order at Diavola next door around your choice of reds. Pepperoni pizza hits the mark with Dark Horse's wild blackberry–sage Zin-Syrah Gunfighter blend ($20), while succulent sweetbreads deserve Portalupi's Russian River Pinot, with all the elegance of a velvet fainting couch.

☗ MEEKER VINEYARDS
☎ 707-857-1795; 21035 Geyserville
Ave; www.meekerwine.com; tasting $5;
⏱ 10:30am-6pm Mon-Sat, noon-5pm Sun
Now that the bank has become
Meeker's tasting room, the vault is
always open and tastes are poured

for free. Charlie Meeker claims he
found the cure to the midlife crisis
back in the '70s: loud blues and
big reds, such as the Barberien
blend ($32), a stampede of
blueberry and burnt sugar. Charlie
recommends the berry upbeat

Packed to the rafters – the impressive barrel room at Stryker Sonoma (p139)

WORTH THE TRIP

A pit stop for a gourmet sandwich and soda takes a detour down memory lane at **Jimtown Store** (☎ 707-433-1212; www.jimtown.com; 6706 Hwy 128), where you'll find bottles of strawberry Crush, old tin signage, antique toys and hand-carved Mexican hot chocolate whisks while waiting for your prosciutto, fig and gorgonzola sandwich. Yes, this place knows how quaint it is – ever since Martha Stewart featured it on TV, urbanites regularly comb the place for oilcloth placemats and other rustic-chic decor. But it's been a local landmark since 1895, and Thursday nights from March to November still attract a local crowd for food and wine pairings.

Pink Elephant Rosé or the 'macho Merlot,' which muscles in with clove, cinnamon and cherry pie, as preventive therapeutic measures.

☏ SILVER OAK

☎ 800-273-8809; www.silveroak.com; 24625 Chianti Rd; tasting $20, $10 applicable to purchase; ☽ 9am-4pm Mon-Sat
'Life is a Cabernet' quips this Cab specialist – but life isn't cheap, and neither are acclaimed aged Silver Oak Cabs. A 25-year-old Balthazar Cab will run you five grand, but for a $20 tasting, you can taste both of Silver Oak's current contenders in the ongoing Alexander Valley–Napa Cab grudge match. The latest Alexander Valley Cab

($70) suggests chocolate, licorice whips and daisy chains, before an unexpected detour into dense blackberry thickets. The new-release Napa Cab ($100) is brooding and nostalgic, with hints of burnt sugar, briar rose and cedar embers giving you something to chew on once the tannins fade. In August, hit their Reserve Release party for food pairings and rare library wines.

☏ FRITZ UNDERGROUND WINERY

☎ 707-894-3389; 24691 Dutcher Creek Rd, Cloverdale; tasting $5; ☽ 10:30am-4:30pm
Hobbits with a thing for Zin would feel right at home in this cozy tasting lair built into the side of a grassy hill, with views over a pond and verdant valley. Family-owned since 1979, Fritz is a small producer of single-vineyard designate Zins ($22 to $44) with hints of blackberries, tobacco and leather that sell out each harvest, and an Estate Sauvignon Blanc ($22) that forms a conga line of citrus and tropical fruit flavors.

GEYSERVILLE

The stagecoach stop where Italian-American cowboys once hung their spurs is now a magnet for foodies and wine lovers, with

THE VALLEYS

ALEXANDER VALLEY

saloons offering homemade charcuterie and wine served on the old bank counter.

⦿ GEYSER ARTS GALLERY

☎ 707-857-9870; www.geyserarts.com; 21015 Geyserville Ave; ⏱ 11am-6pm
Add instant soul to Ikea decor with these handmade modern conversation pieces at very reasonable prices. California quilter Diane Hock lights up the room with 'Spring Fling,' a burst of Japanese cherry blossoms seen through a kaleidoscope. Michael Wisner's modern Southwest vases add handmade character to mid-century decor, with his striking burnished-graphite ceramics incised with Mata Ortiz zigzag motifs.

⦿ DIAVOLA *Italian* $$

☎ 707-814-0111; www.diavolapizzeria.com; 21021 Geyserville Ave; ⏱ 11:30am-9pm
Thin-crust, wood-fired wonders topped with housemade pepperoni and fresh arugula pesto are worth the drive up from San Francisco or even Los Angeles, and quite possibly from Chicago – and that's not even taking into consideration savory sweetbreads and the stellar charcuterie plate (just what Nonno likes). The fresh ingredients are pure California, but the flavors have been carefully calibrated to that elusive golden mean that makes food authentically Italian. Local Hawkes' house wine by the half-liter ($13) or generous jug ($50) makes a real pizza party.

⦿ SANTI *Italian* $$

☎ 707-857-1790; www.tavernasanti.com; 21047 Geyserville Ave, Geyserville; ⏱ lunch Wed-Sat, dinner nightly
Diavola's handsome big brother adds old-world seduction to new-world ingredients. The spaghetti carbonara with housemade pancetta is an easy choice, but adventurous eaters will go for the beef tripe with basil, red pepper and a farm-fresh egg. Confident handling is also the key to the gently pan-roasted local petrale sole atop oven-dried tomatoes, Romanesco broccoli and tiny chick peas, drizzled with authentic *acqua pazza,* a broth lightly infused with tomato, garlic and pepper flake.

CLOVERDALE

The old West lives on in Cloverdale, with its showpiece Victorian B&Bs, vintage movie theater, authentic '50s diners, and an all-out hootenanny of a farmers market.

Stop in for an old-school burger and float at Pick's

California grown, and local bands provide dinner music to go with your hot dogs.

CLOVERDALE MUSEUM
☎ 707-894-2067; www.cloverdale historicalsociety.org; 215 N Cloverdale Blvd; ⏱ 11am-3pm Thu-Mon Mar-Oct
The gingerbread-trimmed brick Gould-Shaw House survived Cloverdale's Wild West days, when this stagecoach pit stop featured 100 inns and brothels. Today this 1859 Gothic Revival cottage shows what domestic life was like in the Golden West, when an outdoor privy and wood-burning stove were still standard – but cutting-edge technologies like gramophones, cameras and electricity arrived early thanks to cash from mining, farming and other less legal but highly lucrative occupations.

CLOVERDALE FARMERS MARKET & ART FAIR
cnr Cloverdale Plaza & Broad St; ⏱ 5:30-7:30pm Fri Jun–mid-Sep; 👶
Bountiful citrus brought visitors from miles around to Cloverdale a century ago, and now the crowds are coming back to discover the pride of local farms. There's a genuine county-fair atmosphere at this farmers market, with displays of arts and crafts alongside stalls of homemade jam and still-warm pies. The produce is all

LA HACIENDA Mexican $$
⏱ 707-894-9365; 134 N Cloverdale Blvd; ⏱ noon-3pm & 7-10pm
Follow the '50s neon sign into this old-school Mexican restaurant, complete with antlers, murals, wrought-iron lamps and the obligatory colorful papier-mâché parrot. Diners are usually families enjoying a night out or friends celebrating birthdays with generous $5 frozen margaritas. Service is spot-on – authentic

tacos are served with sizzling marinated steak atop warm, soft tortillas and pork carnitas slowly dissolving in their own juice. Plates come with housemade chips and salsa, Spanish rice and smoky beans. At lunch, the 'small' (read: rather large) plate costs $7.50.

🍴 PICK'S DRIVE-IN
Diner $

☎ 707-894-2962; 117 S Cloverdale Blvd; 11:30am-8pm Mar-Oct

An all-American roadside classic with big burgers hot off the grill, root-beer floats and housemade lemonade served by chipper high-schoolers. Cut them some slack if your burger and choco-late malt order isn't ready in under two minutes flat – this isn't

Mickey Dees, and your food is being made to order by someone who's got algebra and prom to worry about.

⭐ CLOVER   *Cinema*

☎ 707-894-7920; www.cinemawest .com/clo.html; 121 E 1st St; adult/child & senior $8/5.50; ⏰ last show 7pm

Movie night is exciting again at the tiny Clover, a historic cinema retrofitted with stadium seating. The venue is well run by a local cinema chain that specializes in bringing big movies to small-town theaters. Mondays and Tuesdays are reserved for indie films and dark-horse Oscar contenders. Even fancy B&Bs only offer basic cable up here, and mall multiplexes can't compare to the charm of the Clover.

>ANDERSON VALLEY

So you don't usually associate fine wines with hippies? Anderson Valley, nestled in western Mendocino County, will change that. When back-to-the-land homesteaders put down roots here in the 1970s, they brought radical ideas about conservation, and now Anderson Valley has a 30-year lead over Napa in organic farming, solar power and planting lesser-known grape varietals amid gardens and orchards for biodiversity. Sunny days and foggy nights make Birkenstocks with socks actually seem logical, but they're also ideal growing conditions for heirloom apples and hardy Pinot Noir and Chardonnay grapes.

Granted, grapes and apples aren't the only cash crops in this part of Mendocino County – traipse off the redwood trails and you might stumble into someone's private pot plot. Around here, no one probes about what you do for a living, and most assume you're headed for the coast. But when mellow Mendocinoans ask how you're doing, they actually wait for the answer, and if you stick around longer than a day you'll soon be on a first-name basis with half the valley.

ANDERSON VALLEY

▼ WINERIES

Breggo	1 C4
Brutocao	2 B3
Claudia Springs Winery	3 A2
Esterlina	4 A2
Greenwood Ridge Vineyards	5 B3
Handley Cellars	6 A2
Husch Vineyards	7 A3
Lazy Creek Winery	8 B3
Meyer Family Cellars	9 D6
Navarro Vineyards	10 B3
Roederer Estate	11 A3
Scharffenberger Cellars	12 B3
Toulouse Vineyards	13 B3
Zina Hyde Cunningham	14 C2

◎ SEE

Anderson Valley Brewing Company	15 D2
Anderson Valley Museum	16 C2
Boonville Farmers Market	(see 23)
Hendy Woods State Park	17 B3

⚐ DO

Philo Apple Farm	18 B3

🏠 SHOP

Farmhouse Mercantile	19 D2
Rookie-To Gallery	20 D2

⅏ EAT & DRINK

Boont Berry Farm	21 C2
Boonville General Store	22 C2
Boonville Hotel	23 C2
Lauren's	24 D2
Lemon's Philo Market	25 B3
Mosswood Market	26 D2

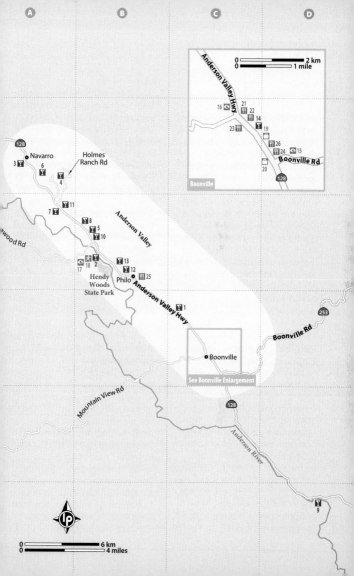

WINERIES

MEYER FAMILY CELLARS
☎ 707-895-2341; www.mfcellars.com; 19750 Hwy 128; 🕐 10am-5pm Mon-Sat

Ports and Syrahs aren't what you'd expect from cool-climate Anderson Valley, so this small-scale specialist winery from the family behind megabrand Silver Oak is a surprise – it's like spotting Meryl Streep at Sundance. But Meyer's woodsy, white-pepper Syrah ($35) is quite the character actor, and here there are no small ports: the 500ml Zin port ($35) makes a cassis entrance and memorable brandy exit. Tastings, bocce and picnics are free.

ZINA HYDE CUNNINGHAM
☎ 707-895-9462; www.zinawinery.com; 14077 Hwy 128; tasting $5, applicable to purchase; 🕐 10am-5pm

All this gingerbread-trimmed tasting room needs to take you back to 1865, when Zina Hyde Cunningham started growing grapes in Mendocino, is swinging saloon doors. Zina Hyde's great-grandson Bill now makes limited-production wines along with cousin Steve Ledson (p76), and the spiffy mirrored oak bar showcases Anderson Valley Pinot Noir ($48), big on rhubarb and juniper berries and green-tomato Mendocino Sauvignon Blanc ($18).

BREGGO
☎ 707-895-9589; www.breggo.com; 11001 Hwy 128; tasting $5, applicable to purchase; 🕐 11am-5pm

The vineyard estate is only recently planted, but already *Food & Wine* magazine has named Breggo the best new winery of 2008. Forget glorified lemonades passing themselves off as Pinot Gris: Breggo's Wiley Vineyard is a definitive version ($25), with lasting flavors of quince, wildflowers and fragrant beeswax. The Anderson Valley Pinot ($42) is like meeting a tsar, with regal impressions of black tea, cherry jam and a swirl of smoke.

SCHARFFENBERGER CELLARS
☎ 707-895-2957; www.scharffenberger cellars.com; 8501 Hwy 128; tasting $3, applicable to purchase; 🕐 11am-5pm; 👶

This sparkling winery is no longer run by the SF chocolatier (Roederer owns it), and most of these dry sparklers are better with apps than dessert – but with 100% malolactic fermentation, the $20 Brut of Pinot Noir and Chardonnay is a liquid lunch of mango and shortbread. The second fermentation produces a subtler Crémant ($25), with softer bubbles and a vanilla-lychee finish. Crayons occupy kids while you compare four bubblies.

TOULOUSE VINEYARDS
☎ 707-895-2828; www.toulouse
vineyards.com; 8001 Hwy 128;
☀ 11am-5pm; ☻

Once the yellow lab sniffs you over, you're in: step up to the barrel-top bar for a free six-wine tasting full of surprises. Toulouse plays against type with an Anderson Valley Pinot ($39) that offsets the usual cherry with exotic *ras el hanout* spice and an estate Riesling that delivers honeysuckle and carrot cake. Guys who think real men don't drink Rosé should try explaining that to owner, winemaker and fire captain Vern Boltz, who makes the meanest Rosé of Pinot Noir in the Valley, with sour-cherry outbursts and a cedarwood chip on its shoulder.

BRUTOCAO
☎ 707-895-2152; www.brutocaocellars
.com; 7000 Hwy 128; tasting free;
☀ 10am-5pm

Versatile Pinots at down-to-earth prices are the standouts at Brutocao (a Venetian name pronounced BREW-toe-coe) including a $26 Anderson Valley Pinot singing three-part harmony with white, pink and black pepper. Tasting notes call Hopland Zin ($22) 'a dusty Stetson atop a ballroom gown,' and they're not kidding: that dazzling ruby fruit kicks up some dust, and it's a surprisingly cheap date.

Bubbles are blended with local art in the Scharffenberger Cellars tasting room

Y NAVARRO VINEYARDS
☎ 707-895-3686; www.navarrowine
.com; 5601 Hwy 128; 🕐 10am-5pm
winter, 10am-6pm summer; 🐾
Local favorite and critical darling
Navarro sells feel-good, great-
value wines like a Mendo Pinot
that brings home the bacon on
toast for $19. That guy who looks
like Santa is Ted, who has owned
Navarro with his family since 1974
and couldn't be happier to pour
you their latest spiced-lychee dry
Gewürz ($19) or divulge family se-
crets for cooking with Verjus (tangy
Pinot juice, $11). Navarro farms
sustainably, provides full-time jobs
with benefits for workers and delivers handcrafted wines that rack up
awards and compliments at parties.

Y GREENWOOD RIDGE ●
VINEYARDS
☎ 707-895-2002; www.greenwoodridge
.com; 5501 Hwy 128; 🕐 10am-5pm
Flashbacks are a given here, and
not just because of the psych-
edelic stained glass. Memories of
blackcurrant jam and leather club
chairs come flooding back with the
Pinot ($30), and their Sauvignon
Blanc ($18) might remind you of
lemon pies, wheatgrass and the
days when smoking was allowed
indoors. The octagonal tasting
room made of a single fallen redwood tree is a Zen lodge featuring
a hilarious collection of canned

wines from around the world – the
'On the Road' orange-crush wine
cooler is probably the only hooch
Jack Kerouac would've refused.

Y LAZY CREEK WINERY
☎ 707-895-3623; www.lazycreek
vineyards.com; 4741 Hwy 128; 🕐 by
appointment or 'when the gate's open,
come on in'
Follow the winding lane through
weathered wooden gates and
past ancient oaks dripping with
moss, and you'll find the tidy
cottage and shaggy barns where
Lazy Creek's magic happens.
Since 1974, this microwinery has
concentrated on organic growing
methods and three wines: a grassy
old-vine dry Gewürztraminer ($26)
with happy hints of Macintosh apple; an estate Pinot ($42) with rose,
satsuma and bay leaves instead
of pepper; and a splendid woodsy
Anderson Valley Syrah ($39) that'll
remind you of the journey here.

Y ROEDERER ESTATE
☎ 707-895-2288; www.roedererestate
.com; 4501 Hwy 128; tasting $6;
🕐 11am-5pm
Opera arias and briskly professional
pours may make you wonder if
you're still in Mendocino – where's
the reggae and the love? – but the
blushing dry Brut Rosé ($29) and
the extra-fine creamy mousse on
L'Ermitage Brut ($47) could make

a rapper ditch Cristal. Though industrial growing methods now produce 75,000 cases of apple-cheeked $22 Brut MV, 5000-case productions make Rosé and L'Ermitage lucky supermarket finds.

HUSCH VINEYARDS
☎ 800-554-8724; www.huschvineyards.com; 4400 Hwy 128; ⏱ 10am-5pm
Sipping Sauvignon Blanc in a shotgun shack at Husch: how Mendocino can you get? The oldest winery in the valley is pushing 40 and well-established, but two-thirds of its 6000-case production is only available here. Picnickers pop by for melony Mendo Sauvignon Blanc ($13.50) and young Carignane-blend Mojo Red ($11), while tasters mob the bar for bold raspberry and wet redwood Mendo Cabernet Sauvignon ($21) and peachy-keen Late Harvest Gewürztraminer ($20).

HANDLEY CELLARS
☎ 800-733-3151; www.handleycellars.com; 3151 Hwy 128; ⏱ 11am-6pm
Leave the French countryside behind in Napa and enter the global village of Handley, with Salif Keita on the soundtrack and Balinese wooden elephants grazing on Persian carpets. At the carved-wood bar, tastings reveal winemaker Milla Handley's passion for versatile California blends that enhance world cuisines: the mineral-tinged, tropical Pinot Gris ($16) holds its own against green curry, while

Navarro Vineyards -- an Anderson Valley blend of vistas, vines and...miniature sheep?

the cardamom-scented Redwood Valley Zin ($20) works equally with chana masala or groundnut stew.

☕ ESTERLINA

☎ 707-895-2920; www.esterlina vineyards.com; 1200 Holmes Ranch Rd; ☺ call for appointment

Four miles past Philo, a gravel road leads the way to a *terroir*-rich vineyard with sweeping valley views. Esterlina's Cole Ranch microappellation yields an Estate Dry Riesling ($19) that's sunshine on a cloudy day: citrus with a crisp, shimmering finish. Esterlina ('sterling' in Spanish) is named for its owners, the Sterling family of African-American vintners who struck gold with pomegranate-and-star-anise Anderson Valley Pinot ($45) at the 2008 SF Chronicle Wine Competition.

☕ CLAUDIA SPRINGS WINERY

☎ 707-895-3993; www.claudiasprings .com; 1810 Hwy 128, Navarro; ☺ 11am-5pm Fri-Mon summer, Fri-Sun winter

Step up to the old-time soda-fountain counter at this micro-winery, and let Claudia treat you to limited-release favorites. The Redwood Valley Viognier ($18) is spared malolactic fermentation to keep flavors as crisp and intense as biting into a chilled apricot, while Claudia's Mendo Zin blends ($22) bring Syrah and Petit Sirah along for a Hwy 128 joyride.

BOONVILLE

Locals made light of hard work in Boonville's hop fields with a lingo called Boontling, and developed a historic fondness for beer right in the heart of Mendo wine country.

◉ SEE

◉ ANDERSON VALLEY BREWING COMPANY

☎ 707-895-2337; www.avbc.com; 17700 Hwy 253; tasting $5, applicable to purchase; ☺ 11am-6pm Thu-Mon, tours 11:30am & 3pm Thu-Mon

Drink up at Mendocino's famous solar-powered regional brewery. Come to taste Brother David Belgian-style ales, and stay for twice-daily tours of their energy-conserving gravity-flow facility, featuring vintage German copper brew tanks. There's an 18-basket disc-golf course ($5) alongside their shire horse pasture, though you might want to limber up before, during and after with signature Boont Amber Ale.

◉ ANDERSON VALLEY MUSEUM

☎ 707-895-3207; www.anderson valleymuseum.org; 12340 Hwy 128; ☺ 1-4pm Fri-Sun

Get schooled in local lore at this 1891 one-room schoolhouse and

THE VALLEYS

ANDERSON VALLEY

learn how the native Pomo wove watertight baskets, how Philo farmers made fortunes during Prohibition from 'jackass brandy' and how dreamy-eyed hippies changed Mendocino horticulture. You can even pick up a few choice words in Boontling (boxed text, above).

SHOP

 FARMHOUSE MERCANTILE
Gifts & Crafts
☎ 707-895-3996; 14111 Hwy 128;
⏲ 11am-5pm Thu-Mon
Your best bet for rustic-chic souvenirs that are handmade, highly portable and under $35: x-shaped trivets made from fallen

Anderson Valley acacia trees, tiny diaries dangling from silver chains, lavender wands woven with ribbon and fetching framed cow silhouettes.

ROOKIE-TO GALLERY
Gifts & Crafts
☎ 707-895-2204; www.rookietogallery.com; 14300 Hwy 128; ⏲ 10am-5:30pm Mon-Sat, 11am-5pm Sun
Whether you're crafty or prefer to leave handiwork to the professionals, head here for DIY project ideas and original work at fair prices, from $9 for a wooden cheese knife carved like a Gothic cathedral window to $76 for silver earrings featuring cross-sections of Pacific manzanita twigs.

EAT & DRINK

BOONT BERRY FARM
Locavore Deli & Groceries $
☎ 707-895-3576; 13981 Hwy 128;
⏲ 9am-5:30pm
Hippies and yuppies chow down and make nice at this natural-foods shack. Longbeards load up on wild-crafted kelp and trail mix, urbanites stock up on Sonoma cheeses and Fair Trade chocolates for wine pairing, and everyone trades gossip and conspiracy theories over the best cappuccinos in the valley.

V

THE VALLEYS

ANDERSON VALLEY

TOP FIVE BAHL BEEMISHES (GOOD SHOWS)

> Alsace Festival (www.avwines.com; Feb) Aromatic whites (no, we don't mean hippies) make a comeback with winery open houses, creative food pairings and a Grand Tasting of Alsatian varietals in Boonville.
> Boonville Beer Festival (May) See p24.
> Boonville Farmers Market (www.mcfarm.org; May–Oct) Everyone swaps recipes while musicians freestyle and organic farmers proudly primp their produce like pageant contenders; from 10am to noon Saturdays in the Boonville Hotel parking lot (below).
> Wild Iris Folk Festival (www.humboldtfolklife.org; Jun) Get down and folksy in Boonville with bluegrass performers, singer-songwriters and acoustic rockers like Django Latino on his cigar-box guitar.
> Mendocino County Fair (Sep) See p25.

BOONVILLE GENERAL STORE
Sustainable Locavore Californian $

☎ 707-895-9477; 14077 A Hwy 128; 8:30am-3pm; V

'Hand pie' sounds like a scandalous Boontling euphemism, but it's pure breakfast goodness: fluffy eggs with potatoes and ham inside a crust that's flakier than a wine taster on a schedule. Thin-crust pizzas and poached-chicken salads get robust flavor from local, organic ingredients, and the staff dishes everything out with justifiable pride.

BOONVILLE HOTEL
Sustainable Farm-to-Table Californian $$

☎ 707-895-2210; www.boonvillehotel.com; Hwy 128 at Lambert Lane; 6-9pm Thu-Sat, noon-3pm Sun Mar-Nov, 6-9pm Fri & Sat Dec-Feb

As you'll guess from the garden out back, chef–owner Johnny Schmidtt keeps the daily menu brief, farm-fresh and succulently seasonal, stacking fresh berries atop shortcake in summer and slow-roasting suckling pig in winter. Come Thursday's $30 three-course prix-fixe dinner (no choices, but who's complaining?), linger over a drink at the bar and leave reluctantly after Sunday's farm-to-table lunch feast.

LAUREN'S
Sustainable Locavore Californian $$

☎ 707-895-3869; 14211 Hwy 128; 5-9pm Tue-Sat

'Country picnic gone Zen in a '50s diner' describes the decor, but dishes like braised-beef stew and pork tenderloin with organic applesauce are simple, generous

Discover your inner chef at the Apple Farm (p156)

and comforting to the core. Wine-makers you met over tastings greet you the next booth over, and everyone gets down and funky with weekend musical acts.

🍴 MOSSWOOD MARKET
Sustainable Locavore Californian $

☎ 707-895-3635; www.mosswood market.com; 14111 Hwy 128;
🕒 7am-3pm Mon-Fri, from 8am Sat
Good vibes, just-baked blueberry-corn scones, organic fennel salad and tasty hot-pressed salami

sandwiches are sure bets here. Take advantage of rare Anderson Valley wi-fi access ($1 for 15 minutes) and local Stella Cadente olive oil samples from bulk dispensers – you can fill your water bottle with fragrant Meyer lemon oil for $1.50 an ounce.

PHILO

Small farms, mighty redwoods and the last stop for picnic supplies on the wine-tasting route make Philo a must.

🎢 HENDY WOODS STATE PARK
☎ 707-937-5804; www.parks.ca.gov; 18599 Philo-Greenwood Rd;
🕒 9am-5pm
A lumber baron named Hendy couldn't bear to fell these towering redwoods carpeted with purple irises and red trillium, and instead donated 100 acres as state parkland. Big Hendy Grove is wheelchair-accessible via the All-Access Trail, and the 1.6-mile Loop Trail is level enough for hardy toddlers to handle. Hermit Hut Trail is named for a Russian recluse who lived inside two large redwood logs, but you can reserve Huckleberry Cabin instead, with room for four and a wood-burning stove.

PHILO APPLE FARM
☎ 707-895-2461; www.philoapple
farm.com; 18501 Philo-Greenwood Rd;
⏰ 9am-dusk

Local-food pioneer Sally Schmitt
sold French Laundry (p56) to
farm this 32-acre biodynamic
orchard. Today daughter Karen
Bates organizes culinary weekends
that include cooking classes,
farm-to-table feasts, orchard hikes
and accommodations in designer
sheds ($2000 per couple, all-
inclusive). Granddaughter Sophia
keeps an eye on the farm, horses
and a fearless bunny that chases
the farm scaredy-cat. You can visit
the orchard and buy organic cider,
apples and chutney from the farm
stand – just leave cash in the box.

LEMONS' PHILO MARKET
Locavore Deli & Groceries $
☎ 707-895-3552; 8651 Hwy 128;
⏰ 8am-6:30pm Mon-Fri, 10am-6pm Sat

Putting the 'super' back into
supermarket with local products
galore: sandwiches with artisanal
deli meat and cheeses, golden
jars of Sonoma honeycomb, fresh-
roasted Thanksgiving Fair Trade
coffee and the wild catch of the
day just in from the coast.

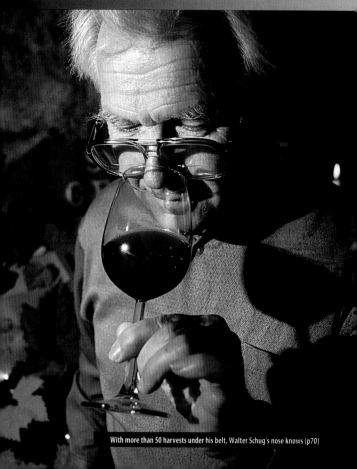

>WINE-TASTING BASICS

With more than 50 harvests under his belt, Walter Schug's nose knows (p70)

GETTING STARTED

Never mind if you don't recognize many NorCal wine labels yet: few people know many Napa and Sonoma brands besides the 25 mega-producers responsible for 90% of Californian wines on the world market (mostly industrially produced Chardonnays and Merlots). From some 750 wineries in the region, we've distilled a list of 100-plus vintners of distinctive artisan wines that are seldom seen outside California or swanky restaurants, yet generate a whole lot of buzz (in more ways than one). With strategic wine-club subscriptions and case shipments, your NorCal wine cellar may soon be the envy of master sommeliers.

But with over 100 wineries and 70 varietals to choose from, where do you begin? You could organize your drinking discoveries around a favorite wine – such as Syrah, Alsatian whites, Pinot Noir or bubbly – or you might check out new varietals at www.wine.appellationamerica .com/varietal-index.aspx and find a NorCal classic to suit your personality. Or go with the Californian flow and become an equal-opportunity drinker, taste-testing whites and reds, blends and single-varietals, much-hyped Cabs and cult-hit Meritages.

UNSPOKEN TASTING ROOM RULES

Have fun Some tough-guy tasters arrive prepared to criticize, but why waste good wine on a bad mood? Give yourself a chance to be delighted, and enjoy the company of your pourer and fellow drinkers. If you're not enjoying the wine or the scene, move on to another winery or activity – a redwood-forest stroll or grapeseed-oil massage perhaps.

If you're driving or cycling, don't swallow 'But it was juss my firsss tasting, ociffer...' Yeah, Wine Country cops have heard that one before. Sips are hard to keep track of at tastings, so perfect your graceful arc into the spit bucket.

You don't have to buy anything, unless you picnic You may get a bit of a sell on a wine club, but no one expects you to buy, especially if you're paying to taste or take a tour. That said, it's customary to buy a bottle before winery picnics, since they're paying to upkeep picnic grounds.

Take it easy Wine tasting is not an Olympic sport, so there's no need for speed. Plan to visit three or four wineries a day maximum, and if you don't make it to all the wineries on your agenda that just means you're having a great time.

WINERY CRITERIA

Savvy boozers will notice most wineries in this book are microproducers (under 2000 cases produced annually), small producers (under 5000 cases) and medium-sized producers (under 10,000 cases), plus a few larger producers with bold artisanal ventures. If future vintages don't exactly match review descriptions, that means artisan winemakers are doing their job adapting to the fertile but fickle NorCal *terroir* renowned for capricious coastal mists, sun-drenched valleys and rocky, volcanic hillsides. We've sought out wineries that consistently produce outstanding wines, but also think outside the bottle in some areas:

Great value Not necessarily the cheapest wines, but ones that represent the best ratio of price to quality.

Memorable tasting experiences Knowledgeable and friendly pourers, scenic locations, historic venues and inspired art help make a tasting worth toasting.

Sustainability Vintners who take pride in their product and responsibility for its impact, raising industry standards with sustainable growing practices, low-impact production methods, good labor practices, rigorous recycling efforts, and partnerships with local businesses and nonprofits to enrich local communities.

If you note efforts that deserve acclaim or seem to have gone awry, please email us at talk2us@lonelyplanet.com.

Practicing the three Ts – Taste the wine, Talk to the vintner and Take notes of your faves – at Amphora (p124)

NORCAL VARIETALS

Tastings (aka flights) are usually poured white to red, light to heavy. Look for cameo appearances by Rhône classics, Tuscan favorites and late-harvest dessert wines, plus star turns by these NorCal specialties.

Sparkling Call it ticklish, bubbly or Brut – just don't call it Champagne, or you'll be breaking the 1919 Treaty of Versailles, which confirmed that Champagne must come from the eponymous region of France.

Sauvignon Blanc Lemongrass, Italian parsley or caramel apple: you never know what you'll find in this mysterious white, also marketed as Fumé Blanc.

Chardonnay This blonde bombshell scandalized the planet when Chateau Montelena Chardonnay (p47) beat French Chardonnays in 1976 (see p189). Malolactic fermentation and new oak barrels gave Chardonnay buttered-popcorn flavors and blockbuster success – followed by a backlash against 'over-oaked butter bombs,' ushering in trendy 'steely' Chardonnays aged in steel tanks. The latest Chardonnay buzzword? Balance.

Dry Gewürztraminer Not your grandmother's favorite sweet white, but a dry, satiny palate-cleanser Californians call Gewürz, with hints of Sierra Beauty apples, lemon zest – even lavender.

Rosé Disco ruined Rosé's reputation with cloyingly sweet blends beloved by club kids, but modern Californian Rosés range from watermelon-ripe pinks to sultry, smoky Rosés of Pinot Noir.

Wine isn't just for the taste buds – educate your sense of smell at Mondavi (p42)

Pinot Noir A foodie favorite with meats, fatty fish and robust vegetables, Pinot is prized by oenophiles (wine geeks) for unusual hints of rose petals, redcurrant, and 'forest-floor' flavors like moss and black truffles.

Merlot Never mind the diatribe against this venerable French grape in the movie *Sideways:* laid-back Merlot offers full flavor without a fire-and-brimstone finish, and shows true charisma with meats, cheeses and vegetables.

Meritage A blend featuring Bordeaux reds (Cabernet Sauvignon, Cabernet Franc, Merlot, Petit Verdot and Malbec), this Napa invention rhymes with heritage and showcases winemakers' talents in tantalizingly limited productions.

Zinfandel A cousin of the Italian *primitivo* grape that flourishes in stubborn soil, Zin is a Gold Rush success story, dazzling New World drinkers with juicy blackberry and hints of dark chocolate, black pepper and pyrite (Fool's Gold).

Syrah The French grape known as Shiraz in Australia leads a life of international intrigue in California, with spice-route flavors such as star anise, ancho chili and wild blueberry.

Cabernet Sauvignon Napa's celebrated red makes imbibers wax weirdly poetic about humidors and dusty boots, with signature long finishes of cedar, tobacco, earth and leather.

WINE COMPLIMENTS THAT SOUND LIKE INSULTS

> 'Like licking a cigar box' – high praise for Napa Cabs renowned for the raspy mouthfeel of 'Rutherford dust' and a lingering aftertaste usually associated with late nights in a smoky gentleman's club – or in the company of certain racy Russian River Pinots.

> 'Furry mouthfeel' – the plush, mouth-coating sensation left behind by decadent unfiltered Alexander Valley Zinfandels and cashmere-blend swigs of Dry Creek Syrah.

> 'A barnyard finish' – also known as 'horse sweat,' technically this may be the result of *Brettanomyces* (*Brett* for short), a yeast that can occur during maturation in oak barrels; when too stinky it's considered a fault, but many connoisseurs seek it out as a subtle musky note in complex Napa Meritages and Sonoma Syrahs.

> 'Hints of freshly poured concrete' – bracing flavors of fossilized minerals and crushed seashells that distinguish certain Dry Creek Viogniers and Anderson Valley dry Gewürz-traminers from flowery or sweet versions; and not incidentally, helps market these whites to macho men.

> 'Cat urine on the nose and gunpowder on the palate' – describes sneaky Sonoma Sauvignon Blancs that smell astringent but deliver an unexpected flash of flinty flavor.

TASTING TIPS

1. Swirl Before tasting a vintage red, swirl your glass to oxygenate the wine and release the flavors. To avoid splashing, put your hand palm-down on the bar, grip the stem of your wineglass between your thumb and forefinger, and move the glass in circular motion without lifting it.

2. Sniff Dip your nose (without getting it wet) into the glass for a good whiff. Your nose signals your taste buds what's coming, but wine aromas can be deceptive: a Pinot with a bouquet of violets and wet redwood may taste like raspberries and porcini mushrooms – the olfactory mystery adds drama to tasting.

3. Swish Take a swig, and roll it over the front of your teeth and sides of your tongue to get the full effect of complex flavors and textures. After you swallow, try breathing out through your nose to appreciate the lingering aftertaste ('the finish'). You don't need to drink it all – pour leftovers into a spit bucket. Pourers are gratified when you enjoy wine thoroughly and responsibly, and might reward you with bonus tastes of reserves, food-pairing suggestions or free tasting passes for neighboring wineries.

Bonus round: Assess Aficionados taste twice to check first reactions, though some claim the third sip is the 'honest taste,' unclouded by eager anticipation or second thoughts. Make notes describing wines you liked by their aromas and flavors, and note what foods they make you crave – there's your next dinner-party pairing.

SUSTAINABLE WINEMAKING

Eco-cred is all the rage for NorCal wine, but the specifics of the various labels, such as the difference between 'organic' and 'organically grown,' can be confusing. Many vintners who don't use synthetic fertilizers and pesticides do not pursue official California organic certification, an intensive three-year process that can be tainted by a neighbor's pesticide use and leaves vineyards vulnerable to bunch rot. Other vintners who scrupulously observe certified organic growing practices choose not to make certified organic wine – this label limits the addition of naturally occurring sulfites that allow the wine to develop with age, meaning wines are subject to spoilage and best drunk within a year or two of release.

Biodynamic wines are made from grapes grown without synthetic fertilizers or pesticides according to principles outlined by philosopher-agronomist Rudolph Steiner. Biodynamic methods can sound esoteric (composting with herbal-tea mulches and manure fermented in cow horns during specific moon cycles), but the simple definition for biodynamic farms given by biodynamic-certifying agency **Demeter** (www.demeter-usa.org) is those farms that promote biodiversity and function as self-sufficient ecosystems while reducing their carbon footprint. Certification can prove prohibitive for smaller farms, but vintners of all sizes are adopting common-sense biodynamic practices such as planting cover crops to attract beneficial insects and to deter pests. Biodynamically produced wines may include minimal naturally occurring sulfites for aging, but happily, drinkers aren't required to wait for a full moon to enjoy them.

READ BETWEEN THE WINES

The best way to learn about wine is by drinking. But after you taste, compare your notes with the experts' to see whose opinions match yours: those recommendations could direct your taste buds toward worthy finds. Following are some of the most respected resources on California wines.

MAGAZINES & WEBSITES

Food & Wine (www.foodandwine.com) Wines that have instant romantic chemistry with modern menu favorites top F&W's hit lists.

Wine Advocate (www.erobertparker.com) *The Atlantic* described Robert M Parker Jr as the most influential critic in any field: a difference of five points on his scale can make or break wine sales. Many winemakers craft wines to please the Parker palate, but be warned: his preferences may not always match yours.

Wine Enthusiast (www.winemag.com) *WE* is refreshingly egalitarian – they don't play favorites, judging each wine on its own merits – but like a kindly professor, *WE* grades on a curve. We estimate their grade inflation at five points.

Wine News (www.thewinenews.com) When you're suffering from purple-prose overload, head here for pithy, insightful reviews. Their thorough California coverage and best-of lists feature lesser-known gems.

Wine Spectator (www.winespectator.com) Based in Napa, this mag gets the scoop on California winemaking, from new releases to collector favorites – and their value picks under $15 are reliable, too.

COMPETITIONS

San Francisco Chronicle Wine Competition (www.winejudging.com)
Sonoma County Harvest Fair (www.sonomacountyfair.com/hf_home.php)

WINE SEARCH ENGINES

Able Grape (www.ablegrape.com) The 'Google of grapes' lets users search wine-tasting notes and press, ranging from wine-geek blogs to scientific publications.

CellarTracker (www.cellartracker.com) Aficionados compare notes on more than 10 million bottles.

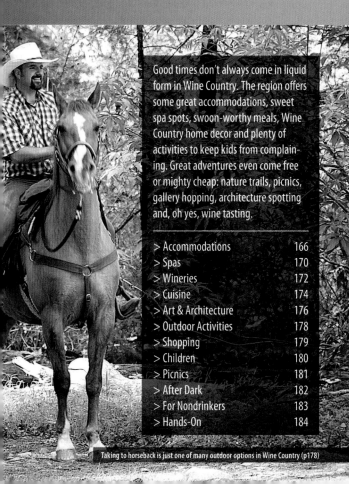

Good times don't always come in liquid form in Wine Country. The region offers some great accommodations, sweet spa spots, swoon-worthy meals, Wine Country home decor and plenty of activities to keep kids from complaining. Great adventures even come free or mighty cheap: nature trails, picnics, gallery hopping, architecture spotting and, oh yes, wine tasting.

> Accommodations	166
> Spas	170
> Wineries	172
> Cuisine	174
> Art & Architecture	176
> Outdoor Activities	178
> Shopping	179
> Children	180
> Picnics	181
> After Dark	182
> For Nondrinkers	183
> Hands-On	184

Taking to horseback is just one of many outdoor options in Wine Country (p178)

ACCOMMODATIONS

Indulgence is the whole point of Wine Country, so don't be shy. If you want to sleep naked, surrounded by giraffes or in a caboose like a high-class hobo, be Wine Country's guest at clothing-optional Harbin Hot Springs (p57), Calistoga's Safari West wildlife preserve (p57) or Yountville's **Railroad Inn** (www.napavalleyrailwayinn.com). Find your own Wine Country style at the following destinations:

Cottage charm Calistoga (Napa Valley) and Glen Ellen (Sonoma Valley).
Nature lovers Russian River and Anderson Valleys.
Organic chic Anderson Valley and Carneros (Sonoma Valley).
Spa spiffy See Spas, p170.
Va-va-voom Victorians Cloverdale (Alexander Valley), Healdsburg (Dry Creek Valley) and downtown Napa.

Rentals can be found via visitor information bureaus (p200), with additional listings at the following:
BeautifulPlaces (www.beautiful-places.com)
BirdSong Property Management (www.birdsongpropertyservices.com)
craigslist (http://sfbay.craigslist.org/nby/vac)
Healdsburg Vacation Homes (www.healdsburgvacationhomes.com)
NapaGetaway.com (www.napagetaway.com)
Russian River Getaways (www.rrgetaways.com)
Sonoma County Vacation Rental (www.sonomacountyvacations.com)
Wine Country Getaways (www.getaway2winecountry.com)

 Hotels & Hostels

Need a place to stay? Find and book it at lonelyplanet .com. More than 40 properties are featured for Napa and Sonoma Counties – each personally visited, thoroughly reviewed and happily recommended by a Lonely Planet author. From hostels to high-end hotels, we've hunted out the places that will bring you unique and special experiences. Read independent reviews by authors and other travelers, and get practical information including amenities, maps and photos. Then reserve your room simply and securely via Lonely Planet Hotels & Hostels – our online booking service. It's all at www.lonelyplanet.com/accommodation.

BEST NAPA STAYS

> Indian Springs (p62)
> Old World Inn (www.oldworld inn.com)
> Carneros Inn (p49)
> Lavender Inn (www.lavender inn.com)
> Safari West (p57)

BEST SONOMA STAYS

> Gaige House Inn (www.gaige.com)
> Beltane Ranch (www.beltaneranch .com)
> El Dorado Hotel (www.hoteleldorado .com)
> Thistle Dew Inn (www.thistledew.com)
> Glen Ellen Cottages (www.glenellen inn.com)

NAPA VALLEY

Victorian B&Bs, cottages amid vineyards and spa getaways: Napa isn't lacking for options, but for best choices and rates, go off-season or midweek. Summer rates increase by 50% or more and vacancies are scarce – see lonelyplanet.com and www.legendarynapavalley.com for backup options.

Calistoga's **Brannan Cottage** (www.brannancottageinn.com) and **Bear Flag Inn** (www .bearflaginn.com) offer country charm without floral overkill, and **Calistoga Inn** (www.calistogainn.com) has rooms over a lively brewery for $95. Carneros Inn (p62) offers luxury guest-sheds with private patios and outdoor showers.

Downtown Napa offers B&B stays in Victorian charmers like **Old World Inn** (www.oldworldinn.com) and **Beazley House** (www.beazleyhouse.com) and Arts and Crafts bungalow **Blackbird Inn** (www.blackbirdinnnapa.com).

Hotel St Helena (www.hotelsthelena.net) offers period-furnished rooms with shared bath for $95, and **Bothe-Napa Valley State Park campsites** (www.reserve america.com) provide bucolic splendor on a budget.

Try Yountville's **Lavender Inn** (www.lavenderinn.com) for deep tubs and last-minute deals, rest tired cabooses at the **Railway Inn** (www.napavalleyrailwayinn .com), or nod to Napa's ranching days at Rutherford's **Rancho Caymus** (www .ranchocaymus.com) with its adobe fireplaces and oak-beamed ceilings.

SONOMA VALLEY

Idyllic cottages in Sonoma's green hills seem worlds away from the traffic jams of Napa's Hwy 29. The plaza beckons from balconies of rustic-chic **El Dorado Hotel** (www.hoteleldorado.com), while B&Bs such as **Hidden Oak Inn** (www.hidden oakinn.com), **Victorian Garden Inn** (www.victoriangardeninn.com) and **Thistle Dew Inn** (www .thistledew.com) offer hideaways off the plaza. **Beltane Ranch** (www.beltaneranch.com) is a 100-acre, 1890s ranch where guests can watch the horses graze.

BEST RUSSIAN RIVER STAYS

> Dawn Ranch (www.dawnranch.com)
> Boon Hotel (www.boonhotels.com)
> Tea House Inn (www.teahouseinn .com)
> Green Apple Inn (☎ 707-874-2526)
> Vine Hill Inn (www.vine-hill-inn.com)

BEST DRY CREEK STAYS

> Inn on the Plaza (www.healdsburg inn.com)
> Hotel Healdsburg (www.hotel healdsburg.com)
> Piper Street Inn (www.piperstreet inn.com)
> Madrona Manor (www.madrona manor.com)
> Best Western Dry Creek Inn (www .drycreekinn.com)

BEST ALEXANDER VALLEY STAYS

> Vintage Towers (www.vintagetowers .com)
> Old Crocker Inn (www.oldcrockerinn .com)
> Geyserville Inn (www.geyservilleinn .com)
> English Tea Garden Inn (www.tea gardeninn.com)
> Cloverdale Wine Country KOA (www .winecountrykoa.com)

BEST ANDERSON VALLEY STAYS

> Philo Apple Farm (p156)
> Boonville Inn (www.boonvilleinn.com)
> Hendy Woods (p155)
> Long Valley Ranch (www.sheepdung .com)
> Anderson Valley Inn (www.avinn.com)

Glen Ellen is the same distance from Oakville and Rutherford as Napa downtown, via Oakville Grade – and you'll have better luck with high-season reservations. There's rural romance to cottages along the creek at **Gaige House** (www.gaige.com) and **Glen Ellen Cottages** (www.glenelleninn.com).

Kenwood stays range from high-end spa retreats (see p170) to camping at **Sugarloaf Ridge State Park** (www.reserveamerica.com).

RUSSIAN RIVER VALLEY

Sunny riverside resorts attract fogged-in San Franciscans, while redwood-shaded cabins draw burnt-out Napkins. For summer bargains, try motels along Santa Rosa's Cleveland Ave.

Bohemian Highway getaways come with homemade breakfasts at Free-stone's **Green Apple Inn** (☎ 707-874-2526), antiques at the **Inn at Occidental** (www .innatoccidental.com) or hot tubs at Monte Rio's **Tea House Inn** (www.teahouseinn.com).

Guerneville's eco-retreats include **Boon Hotel's** (www.boonhotels.com) solar-heated cabanas or **Dawn Ranch's** (www.dawnranch.com) vintage cabins with wood stoves and organic dining. Armstrong Woods (p114) has cold-water campsites with ridgeline views by Bullfrog Pond, while **Santa Nella House** (www.santanellahouse.com) overlooks redwood stands from canopy beds.

Sebastopol's **Vine Hill Inn** (www.vine-hill-inn.com) is a Victorian farmhouse with vineyard views and farm-fresh omelets, while **Sebastopol Inn** (www.sebastopolinn .com) features rustic pine furniture, outdoor hot tub and holistic spa access.

DRY CREEK VALLEY

Healdsburg is as fancy as California-casual Wine Country gets, with snazzy downtown hotels and mansion B&Bs on sprawling estates. Budget-friendly motels and B&Bs are west of the Plaza.

The central **Hotel Healdsburg** (www.hotelhealdsburg.com) goes for an industrial-sexy look with polished concrete and mood lighting, while the **Inn on the Plaza** (www.healdsburginn.com) has high ceilings, double-paned bay windows and gas fireplaces. **Madrona Manor** (www.madronamanor.com) offers suite stays on an 8-acre Victorian estate, but for value and eclectic flair, try **Piper Street Inn's** (www.piperstreetinn.com) botanically-themed garden cottage or reflective Mirror Suite. Motels that go the extra mile are **Best Western Dry Creek Inn** (www.drycreek inn.com), where some rooms feature whirlpool tubs, and **L & M Motel** (www.landm motel.com), with retro-Vegas looks and barbecue grills on the lawn.

ALEXANDER VALLEY

Relive the glory days of the Wild West at former stage-coach hubs of Cloverdale and Geyserville in sumptuous B&Bs – or if you're just passing through, stay at one of the area's value-priced motels. Cloverdale offers lavish breakfasts and gilded-age decor at **Vintage Towers** (www.vintagetowers .com) and the turreted **English Tea Garden Inn** (www.teagardeninn.com). Mosey off the tourist trail to **Old Crocker Inn** (www.oldcrockerinn.com), a historic ranch with Wild West–themed rooms, or to **Cloverdale Wine Country KOA** (www.winecountry koa.com), where sites and cabins come with a pool, hot tub, trails and bikes.

Geyserville Inn (www.geyservilleinn.com) is a motel with Wine Country twists: a vineyard setting, hot tub and surprisingly cushy remodeled rooms.

ANDERSON VALLEY

Wine Country's hidden valley offers hotels tucked in amid orchards and redwoods. Go for organic fare in downtown Boonville at places that simple-but-refined **Boonville Inn** (www.boonvilleinn.com), with a restaurant that grows its own ingredients. On the Ukiah road, **Long Valley Ranch's** (www.sheepdung.com) two-bedroom hillside cottages are dog-friendly and offer ranch views.

In Philo, Apple Farm (p156) offers eco-glamorous sheds in a biodynamic orchard. Neighboring Hendy Woods (p155) features camping or cabins, and well-kept rooms are under $100 at **Anderson Valley Inn** (www.avinn.com).

SPAS

A recent study from Cambridge University identified Californians as the 'least neurotic' people in the world, and Wine Country spas are surely responsible for skewing that curve. Where else can you get naked, muddy and slathered in Chardonnay shea butter?

For quintessential California spa experiences, head for the clothing-optional wilderness of Harbin Hot Springs (p57) or indoor–outdoor pools at Wilbur Hot Springs (p57), go organic at Sumbody & Sumtime Spa (p108), or immerse yourself in a cedar-flake bath at Osmosis (p111). Natural hot springs bubbling up among the vineyards in Sonoma and Napa Valleys will leave you glowing, and day spas in Russian River and Dry Creek Valleys offer specialty wraps involving a happy by-product of winemaking: ultraemollient grapeseed oil. Lavender is Sonoma's specialty, and its naturally soporific scent magnifies Wine Country's mellow mood.

BEST SPA HOTELS
> Indian Springs (p62)
> Spa at Carneros Inn (p49)
> Spa Solage (p62)
> Spa at Hotel Healdsburg (p129)
> Kenwood Inn & Spa (p94)

BEST LUXURY TREATMENTS UNDER $100
> Cedar Enzyme Bath – Osmosis (p111)
> Swedish massage with organic oils – Sumbody & Sumtime Spa (p108)
> Lavender-scented mud baths – Lavender Hill Spa (p62)
> Grapeseed, sea salt and cocoa butter polishing treatments – Akoia Day Spa (p128)
> 'The Works': mud bath, whirlpool, steam and blanket wrap – Dr Wilkinson's (p62)

BEST HOT SPRINGS
> Wilbur Hot Springs (p57)
> Harbin Hot Springs (p57)
> Calistoga Spa Hot Springs (p65)
> Fairmont Sonoma Mission Inn & Spa (p81)
> Morton's Warm Springs (p91)

BEST REHYDRATING WINE COUNTRY TREATMENTS
> Crushed Zinfandel Body Polish – Spa at Hotel Healdsburg (p129)
> Zen Harmony Facial – Osmosis (p111)
> Red Wine Grapeseed Massage – Garden Spa at MacArthur Place (p82)
> Organic facials – Sumbody & Sumtime Spa (p108)
> Riesling grapeseed sugar scrub – Kenwood Inn & Spa (p94)

Calistoga is the best spot in Wine Country to get plastered…in mud. Native Wappos took mud baths centuries before the first local spa-resort was built in 1861 by Gold Rush millionaire Sam Brannan, and today Indian Springs (p62) remains the best place in Napa to roll in volcanic mud and paddle in a mineral-spring pool. Calistoga's most appealing hotel-spas are Solage (p62), eco-deluxe **Mount View Hotel & Spa** (www.mountviewhotel.com) and retro-motel Dr Wilkinson's p62 and associated **Hideaway Cottages** (www .hideawaycottages.com). In most mud baths, mud is heated and reused; if that makes you squeamish, go for single-use mud applications instead.

Sonoma has its own ancient Wappo hot springs at historic adobe-style Fairmont Sonoma Mission Inn & Spa (p81), built in 1927 on the site where San Franciscans have taken the waters since the 1840s, and Morton's Warm Springs (p91), a draw for families since 1938 with geothermic pools. Sonoma accommodations with snazzy spas range from the cozy Cottage Inn & Spa (p81) and laid-back Garden Spa at MacArthur Place p82 to **Gaige House Inn's** (www.gaige.com) spa suites with hewn-granite tubs and chateau-chic Kenwood Inn & Spa's (p94) Romeo-worthy balconies and waterfall hot tub. Check websites for spa-accommodations packages, especially midweek and midwinter.

Indulge in splish, splash, and scenery at the Spa at Carneros Inn (p49)

SNAPSHOTS

WINERIES

A great bottle of wine calls for friends, tasty food and a proper toast – but a boring bottle is just filler, the liquid equivalent of talking about the weather. Since stores don't usually let you try before you buy and restaurants inflate bottle prices, wine purchases can seem like risky investments. But in Wine Country, you get to taste-test at wineries without having to commit to a bottle or dinner party: it's like gourmet speed-dating.

You can't always tell a top-notch winery on looks alone, though some are worth a peek for wow factor. Tasting rooms with the most intriguing architecture and impressive art collections are listed in Art & Architecture

Grapes are sorted by hand at Stag's Leap Wine Cellars (p41)

(p176), and wineries with prime picnic spots are in Picnics (p181). But some memorable tasting-room experiences are inside unassuming farm sheds serving specialty wines, such as Porter Creek (p101) and Vincent Arroyo (p47), or outside where you can see and taste the landscape, such as at Iron Horse (p99) and Lazy Creek (p150).

A well-versed tasting-room pourer will be delighted to suggest wine to match any recipe or occasion you have in mind. Mention your preferences – red, white, sparkling, dry, spicy – but don't be bound by them: you may never know a great Merlot until you try. To maximize your tasting experience, skip perfume, chewing gum and flavored lip gloss, and follow the basic procedure on p162. Prices are usually on the tasting menu, but don't forget to factor in shipping. Foodies will appreciate tasting rooms that offer tasty small bites to pair with wines and spark menu ideas. See p162 for the finer points of sustainably produced, organic and biodynamic wines.

When you find the right wine, your taste buds will rejoice, and you'll feel a sudden rush of gratitude toward your pourer, the winemaker, the vineyard workers and the land that produced those two perfect bunches of grapes that wound up singing your tune in the glass. The best wine makes people generous and garrulous, so you'll know you're onto something when you turn to complete strangers in the tasting room and gush, 'You've gotta try this!'

BEST FOR REDS
> Joseph Phelps (p45)
> Piña (p44)
> Stag's Leap Wine Cellars (p41)
> Unti (p123)
> Hartford Family Winery (p99)

BEST FOR WHITES
> Grgich Hills (p44)
> Navarro Vineyards (p150)
> Groth (p42)
> Breggo (p148)
> Schramsberg (p46)

BEST FOR WINES UNDER $25
> Wine Garage (p47)
> Amphora (p124)
> Claudia Springs Winery (p152)
> Wellington (p74)
> Sausal Winery (p138)

BEST FOOD PAIRINGS
> St Francis Winery (p76)
> Marimar (p99)
> J Vineyards & Winery (p102)
> Robert Sinskey (p41)
> Dutton Estate & Sebastopol Vineyards
  Tasting Room (p99)

CUISINE

Wine Country is actually a misnomer: this is Farm Country, with the produce to prove it. Roadside farm stands including the Patch (p88), Philo Apple Farm (p156) and Oak Hill Farm (p93) are bursting with local flavor May through October, with heirloom apples, flowering herbs and wildcrafted mushrooms. Farmers markets are raucous street celebrations of local food with live music and local crafts, and you can find Sonoma County farms that welcome visitors and harvest-time volunteers at www.farmtrails.org.

Farm-to-table dining (see p13) whisks ingredients from the field to your plate, sometimes within hours of being picked from the farmers market or kitchen garden. Supermarket produce that's been in transit for weeks and cold storage for months can't compete for flavor or nutritional value. Every chef dreams of working with heirloom ingredients like dry-farmed Burbank tomatoes, powerfully tangy and still the most nutritious American tomato a century after its development by pioneering Sonoma horticulturalist Luther Burbank (see p104). You can pick up farm-to-table prep skills at Relish (p128), perfect some new recipes at Ramekins (p82) or dive into a pre-professional program at the Culinary Institute of America (p63).

BEST MEALS UNDER $10
> Bovolo (p132)
> Boonville General Store (p154)
> Pica Pica Maize Kitchen at Oxbow Public Market (p52)
> Glen Ellen Village Market (p93)
> Taylor's Automatic Refresher (p63)

BEST FOR LOCAL FLAVOR
> Ubuntu (p52)
> Zazu (p105)
> Ad Hoc (p54)
> Jolé (p67)
> Vineyards Inn Bar & Grill (p95)

BEST FOR ROMANCE
> French Laundry (p56)
> Underwood Bar & Bistro (p119)
> Barndiva (p131)
> Bistro des Copains (p112)
> Café la Haye p86

BEST EDIBLE SOUVENIRS
> Woodhouse *ras el hanout* chocolates (p61)
> Dry Jack from Vella Cheese (p90)
> Beekind Sonoma lavender honey (p109)
> Philo Apple Farm chutney (p156)
> BR Cohn organic olive oil (p72)

On Wine Country menus, you'll notice the names of local farms on the menu alongside star chefs and famed wineries. Just as a top Rutherford Cab would never be shortchanged as 'red wine' on a menu, a Sebastopol-grown organic Gravenstein apple pie gets full billing. Local source name-dropping is proof that the meats, produce and cheese you're about to enjoy are fresh, seasonal and sustainably sourced, with your taste buds, the community and the planet in mind.

You don't need to spend a lot to go gourmet in Wine Country, whether you're craving sustainably farmed Hog Island oysters (Oxbow, p52), artisan salami sandwiches (Bovolo, p132), or that Gravenstein apple pie (Mom's Apple Pie, p110). While you're in the neighborhood, don't miss free tastings of local delicacies: artisan olive oil at Oxbow Public Market (p52), chocolate at Wine Country Chocolates (p91) and aged cheeses at historic Vella Cheese (p90).

Fresh herbs, marvelous mushrooms and vibrant vegetables yearn to grace the plates at Ubuntu (p52)

ART & ARCHITECTURE

If you picture Wine Country as rolling vineyards interrupted by the occasional castle winery or farmstead, you're not far wrong – but to make it NorCal, you'd have to throw in a Persian palace (Darioush, p39), a Mexican adobe mission (Adobe Barracks, p78), a giant Elvis made from junk (Florence Ave, p107) and dreamscape gardens behind a twisted white-picket fence (Cornerstone Sonoma, p76). Sonoma's adobe Mission of San Francisco Solano is one of the earliest surviving local landmarks, followed by gilded, gussied-up 'Painted Lady' Victorian mansions built in Napa and Cloverdale by prospectors who struck it rich in California's Gold Rush. Historic hop kilns can be glimpsed in Dry Creek and Russian River, with giant chimneys used to dry hops for beer. But from the 1980s onward, Wine Country has been subject to sudden outbursts of inspiration from Tuscany (p46) to Persepolis (p39), and protomodernist Frank Lloyd Wright (p139) to green postmodernist Friedensreich Hundertwasser (p41).

Some of Napa's splashiest architectural landmarks aren't open to the public, though when you're passing Yountville, you might catch a glimpse of the low-slung Dominus Winery, with walls constructed of stainless-steel cages (called gabions) filled with basalt rocks by Pritzker Prize–winning architects Herzog & de Meuron. Green building is the newest trend, with solar panels glinting from winery rooftops, and Frog's Leap Winery (p43) raising the bar with its LEED gold-certified tasting room built from reclaimed lumber.

But if Wine Country seems quirky and eclectic from the outside, wait until you see the inside. Local art collectors have been building important collections of contemporary art since the 1960s, and di Rosa Preserve (p47) overflows with key pieces of California art history, from early Beat collages to Tony Oursler's freaky video projections onto a Lenin statue. For 35 years, Hess (p40) has amassed works by the likes of Robert Motherwell and Anselm Kieffer. Sonoma County Museum (p104) features important works done by photographer Ansel Adams and *Running Fence* artist Christo, while the Sebastopol Center for the Arts (p108), Sonoma Valley Museum of Art (p80), and Nest (p50) showcase local talent with themed shows ranging from altars to art cars. Fine craft is a local specialty, from jewelry to funerary urns.

BEST LOCAL LANDMARKS
> Sonoma Adobe Barracks (p78)
> Darioush (p39)
> Hop Kiln (p102)
> Quixote (p41)
> Stryker Sonoma (p139)

BEST LOCAL ART
> di Rosa Preserve (p47)
> Hess Collection (p40)
> Sebastopol Center for the Arts (p108)
> Sonoma County Museum (p104)
> Nest (p50)

Top left Artwork of Andy Goldsworthy and Per Kirkeby at the Hess Collection Art Gallery (p40)

SNAPSHOTS

OUTDOOR ACTIVITIES

Not since your mom had to call you in for dinner has playing outside been so totally engrossing. With redwood groves to hike in Anderson Valley, a winding river to canoe in Russian River and sculpture to discover in Napa's di Rosa Preserve (p47), you may find it hard to tear yourself away from the wilds of Wine Country, even for wine tasting. Once you start cycling down idyllic West Dry Creek Rd, with dappled sunlight filtering through the trees, you might forget even the most serious Syrah intentions.

But you don't have to go inside if you don't want to: you can sip wine outdoors at Lazy Creek (p150) and Iron Horse (p99), shop at farmers markets for picnics (p181), sleep outside at prime camping spots (p166), and even bathe *au naturel* at several spas and hot springs (p170).

Wine Country's state parks offer attractions for all ages and ability levels, from watching fish hatch at Lake Sonoma (p133) to overnight trail rides and ridge hikes above the old-growth redwoods of Armstrong Woods (p114). After breathing in cool forest-floor air and mountain wildflowers, you'll have a whole new appreciation for Wine Country's distinctive *terroir* (territory).

BEST WINE COUNTRY WORKOUTS

> Armstrong Woods Trail Rides (p114)
> Cycling Westside Dr (p129)
> Tubing or canoeing Russian River (p115)
> Hiking Hendy Woods (p155)
> Skateboarding at Carson Warner Skate Park (p128)

BEST OUTDOOR ADVENTURES

> Touring the sculpture gardens at di Rosa Preserve (p47)
> Overnight safaris at Safari West (p57)
> Calistoga Lighted Tractor Parade (p26)
> Exploring the Pig Palace at Jack London State Park (p90)
> Santa Rosa Human Race (p26)

SHOPPING

Except for the vineyards, Wine Country style is surprisingly portable. Wine country has gotten over its fixation with wrought-iron, French-country furniture, maxed out on the Tuscan castle look with Castello di Amorosa (p46), and gone rustic modern with fluid lines and whimsically repurposed vintage items.

Birdcages are used to hold books, jewelry, chandeliers and pretty much everything else besides birds, as you'll notice at Ma(i)sonry (p54) and Chateau Sonoma (p83). Twine is a recurring theme, with artfully frayed lengths tying back curtains and tightly wound balls heaped in wooden bowls at Farmhouse Mercantile (p153) and Artists & Farmers (p130) Anything you might need around the house – forks, pencils, candelabras – is shaped like a twig at Zipper (p78) and the cave shop at Bella Vineyards (p126). Tastemakers seem to be taking their cues from the di Rosa Preserve (p47), with its outdoor sculpture blending into the valley and a stack of literature in the living-room corner painted half-scarlet and titled *Partially Red Books*.

Wine Country souvenirs are graduating from grape-cluster jewelry, wineglass tags and winery-logo fleeces to more practical, stylish finds. Look for straw fedoras at Coppola's Rubicon (p42), pleated wool evening wraps at Darioush (p39), and grapeseed sugar scrubs and tasty Merlot mustard at Napa General Store (p52). For more foodie finds, see p174. Wine labels aren't often decoupaged onto trays anymore – they're individually framed, whether they're new labels by local artists commissioned by Imagery (p73) or vintage lithographs from Sonoma Antique Society (p109).

BEST WINE COUNTRY HOME DECOR
> Farmhouse Mercantile (p153)
> Artists & Farmers (p130)
> Geyser Arts Gallery (p143)
> Chateau Sonoma (p83)
> Artefact Design & Salvage (p77)

BEST WINE COUNTRY SOUVENIRS
> Barrel-stave wine racks from Napa General Store (p52)
> Mudd Hens volcanic mud (p66)
> Reclaimed barrel cheeseboards from Kenwood Farmhouse (p95)
> Wine Country Chocolates (p91)
> Cabernet Soapignon from Napa Soap Company (p60)

CHILDREN

People over 21 don't get to have all the fun in Wine Country. For the younger set, there are cannibals to conquer at Pee Wee Golf (p116), cartoonists to meet (p104) and river otters to spot (p118). Hot spots for tots include Monte Rio for the beach (p113), family movie nights at the Rio cinema (p113) and kid-friendly Café des Jumelles (p113), but also downtown Sonoma, with Traintown (p83), the Plaza farmers market (p79), ice cream at El Dorado Kitchen (p86) and retro toys at Tiddle E Winks (p85) – not to mention day spas for tuckered parents. The teen scene is best in Russian River, with tubing at Johnson's Beach (p115) and vintage PacMan at Pee Wee Golf & Arcade (p116), plus parent–teen bonding on overnight trail rides in Armstrong Woods (p114) or lazy river kayaking trips.

Kids of every age and interest will find their niche in Wine Country. Calistoga keeps kids busy with bike rides to visit Old Faithful Geyser (p65), short hikes through the Petrified Forest (p65) and safaris in Calistoga's backwoods (p57). Young imaginations can run wild here, what with the outdoor art collection at di Rosa Preserve (p47), junk sculptures on Florence Ave (p107) and art workshops at Nest (p50), Sonoma County Museum (p104) or the Schulz Museum (p104). Budding foodies will appreciate St Helena, with sushi-rolling classes at Go Fish (p61), corn-grinding at Bale Grist Mill (p59), cooking classes at the farmers market (p59) and curry-coconut chocolate at Woodhouse Chocolates (p61).

As for wine tasting, many vintners (especially outside Napa) welcome well-behaved children. Look for the 👶 in this book, and for more family-friendly options check out www.napavintners.com.

BEST ACTIVITIES WITH KIDS

> Russian River Adventures with inflatable canoes (p129)
> Watching Venus flytraps in action at California Carnivores (p107)
> Pee Wee Golf & Arcade (p116)
> Mommy and Me Mondays at the Schulz Museum (p104)
> Riding boxcars through shrunken Western towns at Traintown (p83)

BEST RESTAURANTS FOR FAMILIES

> Taylor's Automatic Refresher (p63)
> Oxbow Public Market (p52)
> Café les Jumelles (p113)
> East-West Café (p110)
> Mom's Apple Pie (p110)

PICNICS

The great outdoors only get better when there's food involved. Napa has stringent regulations to control wine tasting and drinking outdoors – most Napa tasting rooms require appointments and enforce strict drinking regulations – but in Sonoma County, restrictions are more lax and many wineries have picnic tables strategically positioned outside tasting rooms or in scenic spots overlooking the vineyards. The accepted etiquette is to buy a bottle of your hosts' wine when using their picnic facilities, though you're not obliged to drink it on the spot unless you want a leisurely lunch. In Dry Creek and Anderson Valleys there aren't many restaurants or markets near vineyard tasting rooms, so plan ahead for picnics. Some wineries have outstanding picnic supplies: Preston (p126) has house-baked organic bread, estate olive oil, local cheeses and jugs of house red wine on Sundays, while Ledson (p76) and Korbel (p101) have gourmet delis on the premises.

State parks are another prime picnic option, though tables tend to be positioned near parking lots. Bale Grist Mill (p59) and Bothe-Napa Valley State Park have scenic picnic tables, but the most picturesque picnic areas are the Beauty Ranch overlook at Jack London State Park (p90) and the redwood ridgeline by Bullfrog Pond in Armstrong Woods (p114).

BEST PICNIC SUPPLIES
> Farmers markets and farm stands (p21)
> Wild Flour Bread (p111)
> Glen Ellen Village Market (p93)
> Paninoteca Ottimo (p56)
> Boont Berry Farm (p153)

BEST PICNIC SPOTS
> Jack London State Historic Park (Beauty Ranch overlook; p90)
> Bartholomew Park Winery (p71)
> Arista (p102)
> Preston (p126)
> Casa Nuestra (p45)

v

SNAPSHOTS

AFTER DARK

After drinking all day in Wine Country, panic starts to set in among wine-tasters as wineries close their gates: what is everyone supposed to do now? You could make like a local and switch to beer (see p128), or go for a spa treatment and early dinner before collapsing into bed. But then you'd be missing out on a movie night at one of Wine Country's vintage art-deco cinemas, live music at one of Wine Country's top performing-arts venues, and a late-night bar scene that proves the West still has its wild streak.

Music halls have been popular around here since the Gold Rush, and cinemas have attracted date-night crowds since the 1930s. Wine Country is close enough to San Francisco and Los Angeles to draw top-tier talent, and with support from wine moguls like Robert Mondavi and nearby Silicon Valley engineers, the theaters are thoroughly up to date.

Many breweries and bars in Wine Country close scandalously early at 9pm, but Napa Valley locations stay open later to accommodate the influx of staff after restaurants close, and Russian River places carouse into the wee hours with the regular GLBT crowd. Dive bars with pool tables are perennially popular across Wine Country, but night owls also splash out on upscale cocktails and bar bites at Bouchon (p55) and Cyrus (p133).

BEST AFTER 10PM
> Rainbow Cattle Co (p117)
> Cameo Cinema horror movie Saturdays (p64)
> Silverado Brewing Company (p63)
> Pancha's (p57)
> Bouchon (p55)
> Cyrus (p133)

BEST LIVE MUSIC
> Napa Valley Opera House (p54)
> Lincoln Theater (p57)
> Wells Fargo Center for the Arts (p106, pictured above)
> Hopmonk Tavern (p110)
> Ace-in-the-Hole Cider Pub (p109)

FOR NONDRINKERS

Three kinds of people offer to be designated drivers in an area as rife with drinking temptation as NorCal Wine Country: those who expect you to promptly return the favor, people who don't drink anyway, and altruists bucking for sainthood. Everyone else should be sweet-talked and lavishly rewarded for driving services rendered in Wine Country, because let's be honest: it can be tough work jockeying for parking in Napa, driving defensively around people pulling U-turns for Pinot, and looking for wineries in areas where GPS systems and cell phones still don't work all that well.

But with plenty of pit stops for scenery, nonalcoholic beverages and other treats, a Wine Country drive makes a terrific adventure – especially along tree-lined, sun-dappled West Dry Creek Rd, a truly stunning stretch of asphalt. To make the most of a wine-free trip to Wine Country, nondrinkers may prefer to veer off Napa's slow-moving Hwy 29 to Russian River, which has scenic Bohemian Hwy (p19) and the best roadside attractions. For travels with under-21s, check out p180.

BEST REWARDS FOR DESIGNATED DRIVERS

> Early-evening mud bath – Lavender Hill Spa (p62)
> Mom's Apple Pie à la mode (p110)
> Napa date night – Cameo Cinema (p64)
> De-stress stroll through lavender fields – Matanzas Creek (p75)
> A foodie field trip – Relish Culinary Adventures (p128)

BEST ROADSIDE ATTRACTIONS

> Monte Rio Community Beach (p113)
> Florence Ave (p107)
> Johnson's Beach (p115)
> Pee Wee Golf & Arcade (p116)
> California Carnivores (p107)

BEST TASTINGS FOR NONDRINKERS

> Farmers markets (p21)
> Vella Cheese Company (p90)
> Round Pond (p43)
> Oxbow Public Market (p52)
> Beekind (p109)

BEST NONALCOHOLIC BEVERAGES

> Pinot Noir grape juice – Navarro Vineyards (p150)
> Cappuccino – Flying Goat Coffee (p133)
> Mint-chip milkshake – Taylor's Automatic Refresher (p63)
> Calistoga bubbly water with fresh lemon – Oakville Grocery (p58)
> Kombucha – Bohemian Market (p112)

HANDS-ON

For an up-close experience of Wine Country, you should be prepared to get some wine-stains on your teeth and some under your fingernails. Dive right into the local winemaking and culinary action with cooking classes, wine-blending workshops and hands-on tasting tours. If you want to dig deeper, you might volunteer at harvests with **Sonoma Farm Trails** (www.farmtrails .org), enter the annual Wine Tasting Competition (p150), or jump in with both feet at the annual World Championship Grape Stomp competition.

You've come to the right place to make yourself handy, so don't worry if you don't have a lot of experience. You might discover a natural knack – that's how a lot of local winemakers, chefs, farmers, craftspeople and musicians got started. The best souvenirs you bring home from Wine Country are the ones you'll learn how to make yourself here, whether it's a California Meritage, beeswax candle, ukulele tune or a perfect peach pie.

BEST WINE IMMERSION
> Greenwood Ridge Wine Tasting Competition (p150)
> World Championship Grape Stomp Competition at Sonoma County Harvest Fair (p26)
> Frog's Leap Winery tour (p43)
> Benziger biodynamic farming tour (p73)
> St Francis Aroma Workshop (p76)

BEST FOODIE EDUCATION
> Chats with farmers about recipes at farmers markets (p21)
> Culinary immersion weekends at Philo Apple Farm (p156)
> Paula Wolfert workshops at Ramekins (p82)
> Dry Creek day trips with Relish Culinary Adventures (p128)
> 'Sophisticated Palate' classes at the Culinary Institute of America (p63)

BEST DIY SOUVENIRS
> Blend your own Meritage at St Francis Winery (p76)
> Handcraft your own beeswax candles with Beekind (p109)
> Grow your own bug zappers with California Carnivores (p107)
> Make your own art at Nest workshops (p50)
> Play your own ukulele theme song with lessons at People's Music (p109)

BEST EDUCATIONAL TOURS
> di Rosa Preserve (p47)
> Anderson Valley Brewing Company (p152)
> Round Pond olive mill (p43)
> Ranger-led Lake Sonoma Fish Hatchery Tours in February (p133)
> Luther Burbank Home audio tours (p104)

>BACKGROUND

Wine making is a hands-on affair in the Napa Valley

BACKGROUND
HISTORY
SONGS & GHOSTS

Between the rumbling of volcanoes eight million years ago and the clinking of wineglasses today, there was singing in Northern California. Native Californians sang of romance but also practical matters, including where to fish and hunt. Agreements among Native groups in the San Francisco Bay Area were passed along by song and story in 22 dialects, from redwood houses in the northwest to subterranean saunas further south.

Northern California's tune changed when Franciscan missionaries arrived in Sonoma in 1823, equipped with hymnals and Mexican military support to establish the Mission of San Francisco Solano (p79). Some 900 Native Californian workers were conscripted to construct adobe buildings and plant Northern California's first vineyard, and by 1832 Sonoma's mission covered 10,000 acres. The mission was meant to pass into Native receivership, but many Native Californians died from introduced diseases during the construction process, and cultivated mission lands were in demand by Mexican and American settlers. Mexico sold off mission lands to settlers, and by 1840 Mission Solano had become Northern California's first commercial vineyard.

MAKE WINE, NOT WAR

Mexico's General Mariano Guadalupe Vallejo was given a fancy title and a thankless task in 1840 as Comandante of Northern California: to maintain control over an unruly region with independent-minded American settlers, free-flowing local wine and a few poorly paid and frequently bored soldiers (p78). What started as a drunken prank on June 14, 1846 became an international incident when Sonoman settlers sneaked into the barracks, tied up Vallejo's soldiers and replaced the Mexican flag with a makeshift flag featuring a hastily drawn bear. They captured the General who, being an independent thinker and a hospitable fellow besides, signed a letter of surrender and invited the rebels to dinner. The next morning, Sonomans awoke to find they were living in a rogue nation apparently ruled by a pig, shrugged, and went about their business more or less unperturbed until the US intervened a month later.

In the ensuing Mexican–American war, Northern California mostly stayed out of the hostilities, and General Vallejo symbolically burned his uniform. Mexico finally ceded California to the US in 1848, just days before gold was discovered in California. The General stayed in Sonoma and was elected to California's first state senate, and after US forces abandoned Sonoma's adobe barracks, Vallejo reopened them as a winery.

GOLD! TIMBER! PARKS!

The Gold Rush fast-tracked California as the 31st state in 1850, but when gold was discovered in Australia in 1851, the market for gold plummeted, and prospectors turned to the next available resource: trees. According to 1860s accounts, shouts of 'Timber!' could be heard for miles around the logging camp of Guerneville, aka Stumptown. Situated on the stagecoach line from San Francisco to redwood logging camps in Anderson Valley, Cloverdale boomed with 100 saloons, 100 brothels and 20 churches. In Sonoma's countryside, the boom left hillsides bare, erosion wiped out vegetation, and silt and mercury from mining flowed into streams.

But in California's forests, lumberjacks were undergoing a change of heart. While sawmill worker John Muir began studying California's forests in the 1870s, lumber barons Colonel James B Armstrong and Joshua P Hendy decided they couldn't in good conscience cut down hundreds of acres of old-growth redwoods. Muir founded the Sierra Club in 1892, but it took Armstrong and his daughters almost 50 years of lobbying to preserve his 440-acre grove as a state park (p114). Hendy intended to preserve his Anderson Valley groves, but they were sold and logged after his death until 1958, when 100 acres were preserved as Hendy State Park (p155).

MUD-SLINGING & SOUR GRAPES

Meanwhile in northern Napa, Gold Rush speculator extraordinaire Sam Brannan glimpsed the next big thing: hot water and dirt. He transformed Native Wappo mud baths into a spa for San Francisco's nouveau riche in 1862, and local wine from neighboring Schramsberg (p46) helped make Calistoga the toast of society. By the mid-1880s, Napa surpassed Sonoma's 100 wineries, becoming the largest California wine region. But Napa didn't have long to gloat: phylloxera wiped out 105 of the valley's vineyards in 1889, and in 1919 the 18th Amendment to the US Constitution prohibited 'the manufacture, sale, and transportation of intoxicating liquors.'

Prohibition was enforced in the Napa and Sonoma Valleys, where most vines that had survived phylloxera were ripped out from the roots. But Italian communities in Alexander Valley, Dry Creek Valley, and Anderson Valley found a workaround: wine could be made for sacramental purposes for the Catholic Church, and grapes were shipped with wine-making instructions to 'parishes' run out of speakeasies. This explains why some

TOP FIVE WINE–VIDEO PAIRINGS

> *Bottle Shock* (2008) — Mostly shot in Sonoma and loosely based on the true story of the Napa Chardonnay that rocked the world (opposite). With bad blond wigs and a gratuitous love triangle, Alan Rickman's wry performance and the gorgeous countryside are saving graces. Pair with Chateau Montelena Chardonnay (p47).

> *Corked* (2009) — Sonoma wine mockumentary about four wine 'types' vying for the fictional Golden Cluster Award: the obsessive-compulsive solo winemaker, clueless Hollywood celebrity vintners, the spoiled heir to family vineyards, and wine geeks who don't want to share their wine with anyone. Pair with Kaz Hooligans Grenache (p75).

> *Falcon Crest* (1981-90) — Campy '80s soap set in Napa-esque 'Tuscany Valley' starring Ronald Reagan's ex-wife Jane Wyman as the winery matriarch, Lorenzo Lamas' waxed chest, and ozone-penetrating quantities of hairspray. Pair with Chateau St Jean Chardonnay (p75).

> *Mondovino* (2004) — Documentary about the globalized wine industry revealing how a handful of tastemakers influence what the world drinks. Despite queasy handheld camerawork and heavy-handedness overall, director and master sommelier Jonathan Nossiter presents a compelling case for artisan wines. Pair with Porter Creek biodynamic Fiona Hill Vineyard Pinot Noir (p101).

> *Sideways* (2004) — Snicker-worthy midlife-crisis rom-com set amid Santa Barbara vineyards. Paul Giamatti is so convincing as a cantankerous aficionado, he actually swayed public opinion with a one-liner: 'If anyone orders Merlot, I'm leaving!' The negative impact on Merlot sales still irks NorCal wineries – sniffs one pourer, 'Napa Merlot is better than Santa Barbara's.' Napa snags top billing and Merlot gets fairer treatment in the Japanese version, *Yoko-ni* (2009). Pair with Frog's Leap Merlot (p43).

old-growth Zinfandel vineyards are still alive and producing today – and why Catholic saints are revered by nonbelievers in Wine Country.

After Prohibition was repealed on December 5, 1933, NorCal vintners hoping for a comeback were soon disappointed. American tastes shifted to cocktails and European wines, especially during WWII. By 1960, just 35 wineries remained across Napa and Sonoma.

FLOWER POWER & FARM WORKERS

In the 1960s, civil rights and war in Vietnam brought protests to cities across America, and unexpected changes to California's countryside. Empowered by the example of Martin Luther King, César Chávez organized the United Farm Workers in 1965 to establish living wages for California grape-pickers. Meanwhile, California hippies looking for a peaceful way of life away from political clashes and police harassment began hitching rides to farms in the Sonoma and Anderson Valleys.

The two movements happened independently, but together they changed California's agricultural outlook. Fair pay helped professionalize farms and wineries, and attracted new talent to the fields. 'Back to the land' idealists began small-scale experiments in low-impact farming in the 1970s, while farm workers rallied to eliminate harmful chemical pesticides on large-scale operations. Traditional ideas about crop rotation, composting and biodiversity were revisited and revived, and organic farming took root in Northern California. When phylloxera struck Napa and Sonoma in the 1980s, some leading Wine Country vintners replanted vineyards with these principles in mind (p11).

JUDGMENT OF PARIS

As *Time* journalist George Taber observed, hippies not only looked different from their parents: they drank differently, too. Instead of swilling highballs to put world wars and office politics behind them, hippies preferred the shared pleasures and bonding rituals of wine. By 1972 groundbreaking winemakers from Mondavi (p42), Chateau St Jean (p75), St Francis (p76) and Joseph Phelps (p45) were cultivating America's new taste for fine wines. In 1979 Sally Schmitt jumpstarted a trend when she opened a restaurant in Yountville's old French laundry with an all-California wine list (p56).

California's upstart wines might have gone unnoticed beyond American shores if not for British wine merchant Stephen Spurrier's challenge to French critics to compare California and French wines in a 1976 blind tasting. While the results are still disputed, two of the surprise winners were 1973 Chateau Montelena Chardonnay (p47) and Stag's Leap Wine Cellars Cab Sav (p41). A 1978 blind tasting Spurrier conducted in San Francisco yielded similar wins, and in a 30th anniversary expert blind tasting in 2006, California Cab again prevailed – including 1973 Stag's Leap.

HIGH TECH MEETS SLOW FOOD

The Judgment of Paris helped innovative California wine and cuisine earn a global reputation. But in the contrarian spirit of the Bear Flag Republic, Wine Country is now attempting to return to its local roots, without losing its daring edge. Many Wine Country chefs were early adopters of slow-food ideals, focusing on organic kitchen gardens and partnerships with local farmers and vintners. While embracing technical innovations such as solar power and screw tops, some winemakers are taking a rather radical zero-manipulation approach to grapes, letting organic farming, wild yeasts and gravity assist in the winemaking process. Tradition and innovation seem at odds in theory, but they may be the ultimate Wine Country pairing.

LIFE AS A WINE COUNTRY RESIDENT

Top chefs, Silicon Valley millionaires and Hollywood movie moguls: yes, Wine Country has a few of those. But statistically speaking, if you lived here, you'd probably live in Sonoma, and get up early for your half-hour commute to work at a farm, winery or eatery. Your neighborhood is culturally diverse and, like most Californians, you probably speak a second language.

Though you may work making high-end wines or gourmet foods, according to a recent UC Berkeley study, many of those luxuries would be beyond your family budget. Sonoma County's working families are eight times more likely to be impoverished than families elsewhere in California. Despite César Chávez' success organizing farm workers, farm wages have fallen 20% in the past two decades.

But in Sonoma and Napa, fortunes can change within a generation. Most family incomes have grown over the past 20 years, and the founders of notable wineries including Ceja (p39) and Grgich Hills (p44) are immigrants who worked their way up. Local kids who dream of becoming top chefs and winemakers have a range of role models: Wine Country's stars reflect California's vibrant cultural diversity, and many groundbreaking chefs and winemakers over the past 30 years have been women.

FURTHER READING

The Art of Eating (2004) MFK Fischer, the legendary food writer from Sonoma gave America permission to enjoy eating with decades of classic essays and recipes covering the art of scrambled eggs, the ministry of minestrone, and the search for one perfect oyster.

The House of Mondavi (2008) This *New York Times* bestseller by Julia Flynn Siler chronicles the fortunes of Napa's famed winery from Cesare Mondavi's 1906 immigration through blights and breakthroughs, philanthropy and family feuds, and the shocking corporate takeover that left a billion-dollar fortune in dispute.

Judgment of Paris: California vs France and the Historic 1976 Paris Tasting that Revolutionized Wine (2005) A meticulous, fascinating account of how California farmers, a Croatian winemaker, British playboys and French critics started a liquid revolution that broadened minds and taste buds, by George Taber, the journalist who witnessed the historic events firsthand.

The Omnivore's Dilemma (2006) Michael Pollan's bestseller, which introduced America to locavore movements and farm-to-table dining, examines the US food system through four meals: a drive-thru burger, an organic meal sourced from Whole Foods, a Virginia family farm feast and dinner hunted and foraged by the author in Northern California.

The Way We Lived: California Indian Stories, Songs & Reminiscences (2001) Find out how California lived before ranches, gold and grapes, through Native Californian love songs, witty cautionary tales and revealing anecdotes; edited by Malcolm Margolin.

DIRECTORY
TRANSPORTATION
ARRIVAL & DEPARTURE
AIR
San Francisco International Airport

All flights from Asia, Europe and Latin America go through the International terminal; the North and South terminals handle domestic flights. The entire **airport** (SFO; ☎ 650-821-8211; www.flysfo.com) is nonsmoking.

SFO is 14 miles due south of downtown San Francisco (SF) on Hwy 101 at the San Francisco International Airport exit. The drive can take 20 minutes to an hour, depending on traffic. Taxis to downtown SF cost $35 to $45; taxi stands are on the lover level, outside baggage claim.

The most convenient, inexpensive way to travel between SFO and downtown SF or the East Bay is Bay Area Rapid Transit, or **BART** (☎ 415- 989-2278; www.bart.gov). The SFO BART stop is signed near the International terminal; tickets to downtown SF destinations cost $3.75.

To take in the sights en route to Napa, take BART to the downtown SF Embarcadero stop, and exit to the Ferry Building. Here you can catch the **Vallejo Ferry** (☎ 877-643-3779; www.baylinkferry.com; adult/senior & child $13/6.50), which departs about every hour from 6:30am to 7pm Monday to Friday and every two hours 11am to 7:30pm weekends and holidays; travel time is about an hour. From the Vallejo terminal, catch Napa Valley Vine buses (p197) to downtown Napa or Calistoga.

You can also reach Napa from SFO or the East Bay by taking BART to El Cerrito (30 minutes), transferring to **Vallejo Transit** (☎ 707-648-4666; www.vallejotransit .com) for the 30-minute ride to Vallejo, then hopping Napa Valley Vine buses (p197) to downtown Napa or Calistoga.

Other travel options from and to SFO:

CLIMATE CHANGE & TRAVEL

Travel – especially air travel – is a significant contributor to global climate change. At Lonely Planet, we believe that all travelers have a responsibility to limit their personal impact. As a result, we have teamed with Rough Guides and other concerned industry partners to support Climate Care, which allows travelers to offset the greenhouse gases they are responsible for with contributions to energy-saving projects and other climate-friendly initiatives in the developing world. Lonely Planet offsets all staff and author travel. For more information, turn to the responsible travel pages on www.lonelyplanet.com. For details on offsetting your carbon emissions and a carbon calculator, go to www.climatecare.org.

ALTERNATIVE TRANSPORT TO/FROM WINE COUNTRY

Amtrak (below) offers a few low emission, leisurely ways to travel to Wine Country. The Coast Starlight provides scenic overnight services from Seattle, Portland and LA to Oakland, and the California Zephyr takes its sweet time (51 hours) traveling from Chicago through the ruggedly handsome Rockies and Sierra Nevada en route to Emeryville (near Oakland). Both have sleeping and dining/lounge cars with panoramic windows, and you can stop along the route and resume your journey. These train journeys are lower in emissions than air travel, and Lonely Planet travelers have dubbed the Zephyr 'the trip of a lifetime.' Once you arrive in Oakland or Emeryville, connecting buses take you to Martinez and onward to Napa, Santa Rosa and Healdsburg.

Airport Express (☎ 707-837-8700; www .airportexpressinc.com) runs shuttle service from SFO to Santa Rosa (adult/senior & child 13-21yr/child under 12yr $32/30/free). **Sonoma Airporter** (☎ 707-938-4246, 800-611-4246; www.sonomaairporter.com) operates door-to-door shuttle service (adult /child $50/35) between SFO and Sonoma Valley; reservations required. Rides take about 90 minutes, and scheduled departures are listed online.

Sonoma County Charles M Schulz Airport

Daily nonstop services to **Sonoma Airport** (STS; ☎ 707-565-7243; www .sonomacountyairport.org; 2290 Airport Blvd, Santa Rosa) from Los Angeles, Las Vegas, Portland and Seattle on 76-seat commuter planes are provided by **Horizon Air** (☎ 800-547-9308; www.horizonair.com). And yes, that is Charlie Brown out front – the airport is named for the *Peanuts* cartoon creator.

STS is about 4 miles north of Santa Rosa and 65 miles north of San Francisco. To get to the air-port from Santa Rosa, drive north on Hwy 101 and take the Airport Blvd exit. Head west on Airport Blvd for about 1.5 miles until it dead-ends at the airport terminal. Taxis are available outside the terminal.

Sonoma County Transit (p197) bus 62 runs to/from STS to Healds-burg and Cloverdale Monday to Friday from 6:30am to 5pm, with departures about every 1½ hours; fares run $1.25 to $2.75. For Russian River and Sonoma Valley destinations, transfer in Santa Rosa at the Transit Mall stop.

TRAIN

Amtrak (☎ 800-872-7245; www.amtrak .com) trains travel to Martinez (south of Vallejo), with connecting buses to Napa (45 minutes), Santa Rosa (1¼ hours) and Healdsburg (1¾ hours).

GETTING AROUND

To cover your choice of wineries in a limited time, you'll need a car –

DRIVING DISTANCES BETWEEN KEY DESTINATIONS (IN MILES, APPROXIMATE)

	San Francisco	Napa (downtown)	St Helena	Calistoga	Sonoma (downtown)
San Francisco	–	46	65	74	44
Napa (downtown)	46	–	19	27	42
St Helena	65	19	–	9	31
Calistoga	74	27	9	–	30
Sonoma (downtown)	44	15	31	30	–
Glen Ellen	51	22	18	24	7
Guerneville	60	78	40	32	48
Healdsburg	65	57	35	26	38
Geyserville	74	64	42	35	52
Boonville	96	80	61	52	72

preferably with a designated driver. Public transportation gets you to major towns in Napa, Sonoma, Russian River, Dry Creek and Alexander Valleys, but most wineries are out of town and spaced miles apart. The most scenic winery bike routes are in Dry Creek, Russian River, Napa (around Calistoga) and Sonoma (around Kenwood). For the best selection of tasting rooms within easy walking distance, head to Healdsburg, downtown Napa or downtown Geyserville.

TRAVEL PASSES

Sonoma County Transit (p197) offers a 31-day pass (available at www.sctransit.com/purchase .htm; adult/student/seniors & disabled $57/42.50/28.50) for unlimited travel within Sonoma County.

CAR

The Napa, Sonoma and Russian River Valleys are approximately 90 minutes' drive from San Francisco. Dry Creek and Alexander Valleys are about 1¾ hours' drive, and Anderson Valley is about 2½ hours' drive. Time your trip to avoid midweek rush hours (from 6:30am to 9:30am and 3:30pm to 6:30pm) across the Golden Gate and Bay Bridges.

Glen Ellen	Guerneville	Healdsburg	Geyserville	Boonville
51	60	65	74	96
22	78	57	64	80
18	40	35	42	61
24	32	26	35	52
7	48	38	52	72
–	36	30	38	65
36	–	20	28	41
30	20	–	8	30
38	28	8	–	22
65	41	30	22	–

Driving Directions

From San Francisco, take Hwy 101 north then:

Napa and Sonoma Valleys Take Hwy 37 east to Hwy 121 north, and continue to the junction of Hwys 12 and 121. For Sonoma Valley, take Hwy 12 north; for Napa Valley, take Hwy 12/121 east. Hwys 29 and 12 back up weekdays 4pm to 7pm, slowing return trips to San Francisco.

Russian River Stay on Hwy 101 past Petaluma to Cotati and take Hwy 116 west to Sebastopol.

Dry Creek and Alexander Valleys Stay on Hwy 101 to Healdsburg and Geyserville exits (respectively).

Anderson Valley Stay on Hwy 101 past Cloverdale, and take Hwy 128 west toward Mendocino.

From the East Bay (or from downtown San Francisco), take I-80 east to Hwy 37 west (north of Vallejo). From Hwy 37 west, follow the signs:

Napa Valley Take northbound Hwy 29.

Sonoma Valley Hwy 121 north, then Hwy 12 north.

Russian River Hwy 121 west, then Hwy 116 west.

Dry Creek Hwy 121 west, then Hwy 116 west, then Hwy 101 north.

Alexander Valley Northbound Hwy 29 to Hwy 128 west of Calistoga.

Anderson Valley Northbound Hwy 29 to Hwy 128 west of Calistoga, then Hwy 101 north to Hwy 128 and west toward Mendocino.

A few key shortcuts will save you some time:

Between Napa and Sonoma Valleys From Oakville to Glen Ellen, take Oakville Grade to Trinity Rd.

Between Napa and Russian River From St Helena, take Spring Mountain Rd into Calistoga Rd, which takes you to Hwy 12 through Santa Rosa and west to Freestone.

Between Napa and Dry Creek, Alexander and Anderson Valleys Take Hwy 128 west of Calistoga, then Hwy 101 south to Healdsburg, north to Geyserville and Cloverdale, and further north onto Hwy 128 and west toward Mendocino to Anderson Valley.

Rental Cars

Most rental car agencies are represented at SFO. If you're arriving at STS, the following rental agencies are located at the terminal:

Avis (☎ 707-571-0465; www.avis.com; ☽ 8am-7pm Mon-Fri, 9:30am-5pm Sat & Sun)

Enterprise (☎ 707-570-3600; www .enterprise.com; ☽ 8am-5pm Mon-Fri, 9am-5pm Sat & Sun)

Hertz (☎ 707-528-0834; www.hertz.com; 780 McDonnell Rd; ☽ 8am-10pm Mon-Fri, 9am-10pm Sat, 10am-10pm Sun)

LIMOUSINE & CAR SERVICE

Hiring a limousine lets you wine taste without having to drive afterwards, but most wineries don't welcome limousines – they take up too much parking, and the people in them tend to get rather schnockered. Many limo drivers hit wineries where they have parking arrangements or earn commissions, and these options may not suit your tastes.

To visit boutique wineries that shower visitors with personal attention, and wineries off the usual Napa tourist trail – including many wineries recommended in this book – recruit a friend and take turns as designated drivers, or bike it (opposite). For tours where the itinerary is set for you, see p200.

Four of the more reliable and flexible Wine Country limo/car service operators:

Antique Tours Limousine (☎ 707-226-9227) Hit the highway in style in a vintage 1947 convertible limo ($130 per hour, minimum five hours).

Beau Wine Tours (☎ 707-938-8001, 800-387-2328; www.beauwinetours.com) Custom winery tours in sleek black town cars, stretch limos and 'executive coaches' ($50 to $100 per hour plus $30 fuel surcharge, minimum three/six hours on weekdays/weekends).

Magnum Tours (☎ 707-753-0088; www .magnumwinetours.com) Custom tours of restaurants, sights and wineries in Mercedes sedans, Lincoln town cars and SUV limos ($65 to $110 per hour plus $30 fuel surcharge, minimum four/five hours on weekdays/weekends).

Napa Valley Hoppers (☎ 707-224-4677; www.nvhoppers.com) Want to hit the Silverado Trail, shop Napa Outlets, or try dinner in Yountville? Your chariot awaits – only it's a motorized rickshaw for two. Rickshaw excursions with three to four winery stops depart daily from 10am to 2pm ($89 per person, five hours); downtown Napa excursions are $15 one-way; and Napa to Yountville dinner rickshaw shuttles are available on weekends ($40 round-trip); reservations required. Music, lap blanket and refreshments are included.

BUS

For public-transit information, dial ☎ 511 from Bay Area telephones or get information online at www .transit.511.org. Nighttime, weekend and holiday services are less frequent.

For travel from/to San Francisco:

Golden Gate Transit (☎ 415-923-2000; www.goldengate.org) Operates bus 70/80 from San Francisco to Petaluma ($8) and to Santa Rosa ($8.80); catch it at 1st and Mission Sts, across from the Transbay Terminal in San Francisco.

Greyhound (☎ 800-231-2222; www .greyhound.com) Operates from San Francisco to Santa Rosa ($21 to $26) and Vallejo ($16 to $20); transfer for local buses.

For travel within Wine Country:

Napa Valley Vine (☎ 800-696-6443, 707-251-2800; www.nctpa.net) Operates bus 10 from the Vallejo Ferry Terminal and Vallejo Transit bus station to Napa or Yountville ($3.50) and north to St Helena or Calistoga ($4.50). For stops within the Valley, rides cost $1.25 to $2; exact change is required. The Vine operates the free Yountville Shuttle, which runs the length of Yountville and over to the Lincoln Theater on show nights (p57); just hail it in the street when you see it. The Vine also runs the **Downtown Napa Trolley** (☎ 800-696-6443, 707-251-2800; www.nctpa.net; adult/child/senior $1.25/1/0.60), which is free when picked up at Oxbow Market or Napa Premium Outlets. The Trolley makes a downtown loop every

20 minutes, 11am to 6pm Monday through Wednesday, until 8pm Thursday and Sunday, and to 10pm Friday and Saturday.

Sonoma County Transit (☎ 707-576-7433, 800-345-7433; www.sctransit.com) Operates buses from Santa Rosa to Petaluma (70 minutes), Sonoma (1¼ hours) and western Sonoma County, including the Russian River Valley towns (30 minutes). Fares range from $1.25 to $3.25, depending on distance covered.

BICYCLE

Touring Wine Country by bicycle is unforgettable, especially on back roads. The most spectacular ride in Wine Country – and pretty much anywhere else we can think of – is sun-dappled, tree-lined West Dry Creek Rd. This country road meanders from golden hills and bio-dynamic Dry Creek vineyards with top-notch Syrahs to the Russian River Valley, with its elegant Pinots and stirring redwood groves.

Cycling between wineries isn't demanding – the valleys are mostly flat – but crossing between Napa and Sonoma Valleys is intense, particularly via steep Oakville Grade and Trinity Rd (between Oakville and Glen Ellen). Within Sonoma Valley, take Arnold Dr instead of busy Hwy 12. Through Napa Valley, take the Silverado Trail instead of Hwy 29 with its manic drivers U-turning into winery driveways.

For rentals and self-guided tours, check out Sonoma Valley Cyclery (p82), Calistoga Bike Shop

DIRECTORY

(p65) or Spoke Folk Cyclery (p129). Daily rentals cost $25 to $40; make reservations.

Guided bike tours start at around $135 per six-hour day tour, including bikes, tastings, lunch and occasionally a wine delivery service; gratuities are extra. Reputable guided tour outfits:

Backroads (☎ 800-462-2848; www.back roads.com) All-inclusive guided biking tours cover Alexander Valley, travel from Anderson Valley to the Russian River Valley, and do a Sonoma–Coast–Dry Creek–Napa loop.

Getaway Adventures (☎ 707-568-3040, 800-499-2453; www.getawayadventures.com) Single- and multi-day trips, including easy Sip-n-Cycle tours around Calistoga or Dry Creek ($149 for six hours, tastings not included) and a more ambitious Pedal and Paddle tour biking Alexander Valley and kayaking the Russian River ($175 for six hours, tastings not included).

Goodtime Touring (☎ 707-938-0453, 888-525-0453; www.goodtimetouring.com) Take a leisurely 12-mile ride to wineries clustered around downtown Sonoma and Kenwood, with a stop for cheese tasting at Vella Cheese (p90) and at California historical landmarks ($135 for six hours).

Napa Valley Adventure Tours (☎ 707-259-1833, 877-548-6877; www.napavalley adventuretours.com; Oxbow Public Market, 610 1st St, Napa) Bike along the Napa River and hit the Silverado trail to taste right out of the barrel, or add a twist to the usual Napa wine-tasting experience and meet local artisans and organic farmers ($139 for 6½ hours). Tours are led by your 'Experiential Architect,' and include organic lunch, wine tasting and wine-purchase drop-off services. Rentals, kayaking and hiking are also available.

Napa Valley Bike Tours (☎ 707-944-2953, 800-707-2453; www.napavalleybiketours .com; 6488 Washington St, Yountville) Mostly off-road bike tours provide a moderate challenge while hitting three to four Napa wineries; fee covers wine-purchase drop-off and one wine-tasting fee ($149 for 6½ hours).

You can also BYOB (bring your own bike) to Wine Country. Bicycles can be checked in boxes on Greyhound buses for $20 to $30; bike boxes cost $10. You can transport bicycles on Golden Gate Transit buses, which usually have free racks available (first come, first served).

TRAIN

See the Napa Valley roll by and toast the good life aboard the **Napa Valley Wine Train** (☎ 707-253-2111, 800-427-4124; www.winetrain.com; adult/child under 12yr $49.50/25, plus lunch $44.50/23, plus dinner $49.50/23, plus Vista Dome observation deck upgrade $30). Vintage 1915–17 Pullman dining cars chug from Napa to St Helena and back in three hours, with an optional stop at one of three wineries along the route ($25 extra): we recommend biodynamic champion Grgich Hills (p44). In case you get bored or thirsty watching all those vineyards go by, there's a bar on board ($10 for a tasting of four wines). Trains depart from McKinstry St near 1st St, Napa.

TAXI

Whether you've missed your Wine Train or lost count of your tastings, you'll need to call a taxi – in Wine Country they keep busy, so you won't have much luck flagging one down. Fares usually start at $2.50 at flag drop in town and cost $2.50 per mile, plus 10% to 15% tip; some offer out-of-town winery drop-off/pickup service at about double the usual fare. For nights on the town, taxis can usually be reserved for four hours starting at around $45:

Healdsburg Taxi Cab (☎ 707-433-7088)
Napa Valley Cab (☎ 707-257-6444)
Vern's Taxi Service (☎ 707-938-8885, Sonoma)

PRACTICALITIES

BUSINESS HOURS

Any exceptions to the following hours are noted in specific listings.
Banks 9am to 6pm Monday to Friday and 9am to 4pm Saturday.
Pubs and bars 11am to midnight.
Restaurants Lunch 11:30am to 3pm and dinner 6pm to 10pm.
Shops 10am to 6pm.
Tasting rooms 10am to 4pm.

EMERGENCIES

Alcoholics Anonymous Napa (☎ 707-255-4900)
Alcoholics Anonymous Sonoma (☎ 707-938-2027)
Police, fire & ambulance (☎ 911)

Queen of the Valley Medical Center (Map p37, C5; ☎ 707-257-4038; 1000 Trancas St, Napa)
Sonoma Valley Hospital (Map p80; ☎ 707-935-5000; 347 Andrieux St, Sonoma)

INTERNET

This close to Silicon Valley, there's wi-fi access at almost any café or hotel, and the entire town of Healdsburg offers free (if weak) wi-fi. For the latest word on Wine Country, surf these sites:

www.71miles.com Local-insider tips on spas, hikes, hotels, restaurants and adventure from SF to Anderson Valley, Napa to Sonoma.
www.alexandervalley.org Maps, events and wineries in Alexander Valley.
www.avwines.com Anderson Valley wines, festivals, history and lodging.
www.bohemian.com Events, festivals, food and wine reviews, green-living features, and irreverent commentary.
www.bohemianconnection.com Festivals, inns, spas, food, recreation and history along Russian River's Bohemian Highway.
www.napavalleyregister.com News, arts and entertainment listings, local profiles, foodie tips, and raging debates about wine.
www.napavintners.com Handy maps and winery-finder tool to locate wineries to suit every style including green, pet-friendly, arty, family-friendly or historic.
www.russianriver.com Latest events and happenings around the Russian River Valley.
www.sfbay.craigslist.org Find activities partners, short-term apartment rentals, freebies and more.
www.sfgate.com *San Francisco Chronicle*'s website covers Wine Country festivals and event listings, restaurant reviews, wines and news.

www.silveradotrail.com Wineries, lodging, dining and exploring along the Napa road less traveled, with customizable maps and video.
www.wdcv.com Maps, barrel tastings, festivals and background on the wine growers of Dry Creek Valley.
www.wineroad.com Lodging, wineries, events, arts and maps for the Russian River, Dry Creek and Alexander Valleys.

MONEY
For updated exchange rates see www.xe.com. Costs are cited throughout this guide, and current exchange rates are listed on the inside front cover.

TELEPHONE
The US country code is ☎ 1, and Napa and Sonoma's area code is ☎ 707. To make an international call from the Bay Area, call ☎ 011 + country code + area code + number. US cell phones operate on either CDMA or GSM, but on different frequency bands, so be sure to check compatibility with your phone manufacturer and/or service provider. For useful operator services, see the inside front cover.

TIPPING
Winery tasting-room staff don't expect tips.
Airport and hotel porters $2 per bag, $5 minimum per cart.
Bartenders 10% to 15% per round, $1 minimum per drink.
Restaurants 15% to 20%, unless a gratuity is already included in the bill.

Taxis 10% to 15%, rounded up to the next dollar.

TOURIST INFORMATION
Check out these sources of info, spa coupons and passes for free wine tasting:
Calistoga Visitors Center (Map p37, D1; ☎ 707-942-6333; www.calistogavisitors .com; 1506 Lincoln Ave)
Healdsburg Chamber of Commerce and Visitors Bureau (Map p80, B5; ☎ 707-433-6935; www.healdsburg.org; 217 Healdsburg Ave, Healdsburg)
Napa Valley Visitor Information Center (Map p50; ☎ 707-226-5813; www .legendarynapavalley.com; 1310 Napa Town Center, Napa)
Russian River Chamber of Commerce and Visitors Center (Map p97, A4; ☎ 707-869-9000; www.russianriver.com; 16209 1st St, Guerneville)
Sonoma Valley Visitors Bureau (Map p80; ☎ 707-996-1090; www.sonomavalley.com; Sonoma Plaza, 453 1st St E, Sonoma, also at Cornerstone Place, 23750 Arnold Dr, Carneros)

TOURS
See Wine Country as never before on these unusual tours:
Balloon Balloons above the Valley (p51).
Canoe or kayak Burke's Canoe Trips (p118), King's Sport & Tackle (p115) or Russian River Adventures (p129).
Horse Armstrong Woods Trail Rides and Pack Trips (p114) or Triple Creek Horse Outfit (p91).
Horse-drawn carriage (☎ 707-849-8989; www.flyinghorse.org) With the Flying Horse Carriage Company you can clippety-clop through Alexander Valley ($145, four hours).

Jeep (☎ 707-546-1822, 800-539-5337; www.jeeptours.com) Wine Country Jeep Tours cover Wine Country's back roads and your pick of 24 boutique wineries, year-round at 10am and 1pm ($75 for three hours). Alternatively, try Safari West (p57).

Segway (☎ 707-938-2080; www.sonoma segway.com) With Sonoma Segway you can cruise downtown Sonoma like Steve Wozniak on your high-tech, two-wheeled Human Transporter ($99 for 2½ hours), with stops at Vella Cheese (p90)and historic Gundlach Bundschu Winery (p71). Don't get too tipsy though: wherever you lean is where the Segway will go.

TRAVELERS WITH DISABILITIES

All the Bay Area transit companies offer travel discounts for disabled travelers, along with wheelchair-accessible services. For further information about wheelchair accessibility in the Bay Area, contact the **Independent Living Resource Center of San Francisco** (☎ 415-543-6222; www .ilrcsf.org; 🕑 9am-5pm Mon-Fri).

>INDEX

See also separate subindexes for Do (p204), Eat & Drink (p205), Play (p206), See (p206), Shop (p207) and Wineries (p207).

A

accommodations 166-9
activities 178, 184, *see also* Do *subindex*
Ad Hoc 53, 54
Adobe Barracks 78
air travel 192-3
Alexander Valley 136-45, **137**
 accommodations 168, 169
 festivals 24
 itinerary 140
 wineries 138-42
ambulance 199
Anderson Valley 146-56, **147**
 accommodations 168, 169
 festivals 24, 25, 154
 itinerary 31
 wineries 148-52
Anderson Valley Brewing Company 152
Annual Legendary Boonville Beer Festival 24
Apple Blossom Festival 24
architecture 20, 176-7
Armstrong Woods 114, 187
art 176-7, *see also* See, Shop *subindexes*

B

B&Bs 166-9
Bale Grist Mill Park 59
ballooning 51
bars 57, 88, 135

000 map pages

BART 192
beaches 113, 115
Bear Flag Republic 186-7
beauty treatments, *see* day spas, Do *subindex*
beer 24, 128, 152, *see also* Eat & Drink *subindex*
bicycle travel 197-8, *see also* Do *subindex*
biodynamic farming 10-11, 162, 189-90
Bohemian Hwy 19
 itinerary 30-1
books 83, 84, 190-1
Boontling 153
Boonville 152-5
bus travel 197
business hours 199, *see also* inside front cover

C

California Gold Rush 187
California Wine Tasting Championships 25
Calistoga 64-7
 mud baths 14-15, 170-1
Calistoga Lighted Tractor Parade 26
canoeing 115, 118, 129
car rental 196
car travel 194-6
cell phones 200
Chateau Montelena Winery 47
Chávez, César 188-9
cheese 87
children, travel with 180

chocolates 61, 85, 91
cinemas, *see* Play *subindex*
Cloverdale 143-5
Cloverdale Citrus Fair 24
cooking courses 82, 128, 156, 184
Cornerstone Sonoma 76
costs, *see* inside front cover
craft 26, *see also* Shop *subindex*
cycling 197-8, *see also* Do *subindex*

D

day spas 14-15, 62, 170-1, *see also* Do *subindex*
designated drivers 183
di Rosa Preserve 17, 47, 48
disabilities, travelers with 201
drinking 182, *see also* beer, wine, Eat & Drink, Wineries *subindexes*
driving 194-6
Dry Creek Road 135
Dry Creek Valley 120-35, **121**
 accommodations 168, 169
 festivals 24, 126
 itinerary 124
 wineries 122-7

E

economy 190
emergencies 199, *see also* inside front cover
events 23-6
exchange rates, *see* inside front cover

F
farm-to-table dining 12-13
farmers markets 21, 107,
    see also See *subindex*
festivals 23-6
film 188
fire services 199
fishing 115
Florence Ave 107
food 12-13, 21, 174-5, *see also*
    Eat & Drink *subindex*
    Alexander Valley 143,
        144-5
    Anderson Valley 153-5, 156
    Dry Creek Valley 131-5
    festivals 24, 25, 26
    Napa Valley 49, 52, 54-7,
        58, 59, 61-4, 67
    Russian River Valley 104-6,
        109-10, 111, 112-13,
        116, 118, 119
    Sonoma Valley 78, 85-90,
        92-3, 95
Forestville 117-18
Freestone Vineyards 98, 111
French Laundry 56

G
galleries, *see* See *subindex*
gardens 89, *see also*
    Do, See *subindexes*
gay travelers 114, 117
Geyserville 142-3
Glen Ellen 90-3
Graton 119
Gravenstein Apple Fair 25
Grgich Hills 44
Guerneville 113-17

H
Harmony Fest 25
Healdsburg 127-35

Hendy Woods State Park
    155, 187
history 186-90
Holiday Open House 26
horseback riding 91, 114
hospitals 199
hot springs 57, *see also*
    day spas, Do *subindex*
hotels 166-9

I
internet access 199
internet resources 163, 199-200
itineraries 27-31

J
Jack London State
    Historic Park 18, 90
Jimtown Store 142
Joseph Phelps 45
Judgment of Paris 189

K
kayaking 115, 118, 129
Kenwood 93-5

L
LaHaye Art Center 79
Lake Sonoma Fish Hatchery 133
lavender 75
lesbian travelers 114, 117
limousine services 196-7
live music 182, *see also*
    Play *subindex*
    festivals 24, 25
Luther Burbank Home &
    Gardens 104

M
Ma(i)sonry 54
markets 21, 107, *see also*
    See *subindex*
massage, *see* day spas,
    Do *subindex*

Mendocino County Fair 25
Mission San Francisco
    Solano 79
mobile phones 200
Mondavi 42
money 200
Monte Rio 113
movies 188
mud baths 14-15, 62, 170-1,
    see also Do *subindex*
museums, *see* See *subindex*
music 182, *see also*
    Play *subindex*
    festivals 24, 25
Mustard, Mud & Music 24

N
Napa 49-54, **50**
Napa Carneros 47-9
Napa Valley 36-67, **37**
    accommodations 167
    Calistoga mud baths
        14-15, 171
    festivals 24, 26
    itineraries 29
    wineries 38-47
Napa Valley Cinco
    di Mayo 24
Napa Valley Museum 54
Napa Wine and
    Crafts Faire 26
national parks, *see* parks,
    gardens & reserves
Native Californians 186
Nest 50
nightlife, *see* Play *subindex*
nondrinkers 31, 183

O
Oakville 58
Occidental 111-13
Old Faithful Geyser 65

opening hours 199, *see also inside front cover*
organic farming 10-11, 162, 189-90
outdoor activities 178, 181, *see also Do subindex*

P
parks, gardens & reserves 57, 89, 187, *see also Do, See subindexes*
Petrified Forest 65
Philo 155-6
picnicking 181
planning 30, 158
police 199
population 190
Prohibition 187-8

Q
Quicksilver Mine Co 117

R
redwood forests 16, 114, 155, 187
restaurants 174-5, *see also food, Eat & Drink subindex*
Robert Louis Stevenson State Park 65
Russian River, the 22
Russian River Blues Festival 25
Russian River Valley 96-119, **97**
accommodations 168-9
Bohemian Hwy 19
festivals 24, 25
markets 107
wineries 98-102
Rutherford 58-9

000 map pages

S
Safari West 57
Santa Rosa 104-6
Schulz Museum 104
Sebastopol 107-10
Sebastopol Center for the Arts 108
shopping 142, 179, *see also Shop subindex*
Sonoma 78-90, **80**
Sonoma Carneros 76-8
Sonoma County Harvest Fair 26
Sonoma County Museum 104
Sonoma International Film Festival 24
Sonoma Valley 68-95, **69**
accommodations 167-8
festivals 24, 25, 26
itinerary 29
wineries 70-6
Sonoma Valley Museum of Art 80
spa retreats, *see day spas, Do subindex*
sporting activities 26, *see also Do subindex*
Stag's Leap Wine Cellars 41
St Helena 59-64
Sugarloaf Ridge State Park 94
sustainable winemaking 10-11, 162, 189-90

T
Taste of Yountville 24
taxis 199, *see also limousine services*
telephone services 200, *see also inside front cover*
theater, *see Play subindex*
tipping 200
tourist information 200

tours 196-7, 200-1
train travel 193, 198
travel passes 194

V
Vallejo, Mariano 186-7
visual arts, *see See subindex*

W
websites 163, 199-200
Wildwood Farm Nursery & Sculpture Garden 93
wine 10-11, 157-63, 172-3, *see also Wineries subindex*
descriptive terms 161
festivals 24, 25, 26
tours 196-7, 200-1
Wine Country 7, 34, **35**, 73
winemaking 10-11, 162, 189-90
Winter Wineland 24

Y
Yountville 54-8

🏃 **DO**

Ballooning
Balloons Above the Valley 51

Beaches
Johnson's Beach 115
Monte Rio Community Beach 113

Bike Riding
Calistoga Bikeshop 65
Sonoma Valley Cyclery 82
Spoke Folk Cyclery 129

Canoeing & Kayaking
Burke's Canoe Trips 118
King's Sport & Tackle 115
Russian River Adventures 129

Cooking Courses
Philo Apple Farm 156
Ramekins Sonoma Valley
   Culinary School 82
Relish Culinary Adventures
   128

Day Spas
Akoia Day Spa 128
Calistoga Spa Hot Springs 65
Cottage Inn & Spa 81
Fairmont Sonoma
   Mission Inn & Spa 81
Garden Spa at
   MacArthur Place 82
Kenwood Inn & Spa 94
Morton's Warm Springs 91
Napa Massage & Bodycare 51
Osmosis 111
Spa at Carneros Inn 49
Spa at Hotel Healdsburg 129
Sumbody & Sumtime Spa 108

**Family-Friendly
Attractions**
Bale Grist Mill Park 59
Morton's Warm Springs 91
Pee Wee Golf & Arcade 116
Traintown 83

Fishing
King's Sport & Tackle 115

Horseback Riding
Armstrong Woods Trail Rides
   & Pack Trips 114
Triple Creek Horse Outfit 91

Mini Golf
Pee Wee Golf & Arcade 116

Orchards
Philo Apple Farm 156

Parks & Gardens
Bale Grist Mill Park 59
Robert Louis Stevenson
   State Park 65

Sporting Activities
Carson Warner Skate Park 128
Infineon Raceway 77

🍴 EAT & DRINK

Bakeries
Artisan Bakers 85
Model Bakery 62
Mom's Apple Pie 110
Sweetie Pies 52
Wild Flour Bread 111

Barbecues
Ace-in-the-Hole Cider Pub 109
Buster's 67

Bars
Dry Creek General Store &
   Bar 135
Mondo 88

Cafés
Barking Dog Coffee 85
Dry Creek General Store &
   Bar 135
English Garden Tea Rooms 67
Flying Goat Coffee 133
Napa Valley Coffee Roasting
   Company 63
Oakville Grocery 58
Paninoteca Ottimo 56
Roasters Espresso 118
Yo El Rey 67

Cal-European
Bistro des Copains 112
Bouchon 55
Bovolo 132

Cook 61
East-West Café 110
Estate 87
Olive & Vine 93
Vineyards Inn Bar & Grill 95
Zazu 105

Californian
Ad Hoc 53, 54
Barley & Hops Tavern 112
Barndiva 131
Boonville General Store 154
Boonville Hotel 154
Cyrus 133
El Dorado Kitchen 86
Farmhouse Inn &
   Restaurant 118
Fig Café 92
French Laundry 56
Harvest Moon Café 87
Jolé 67
Lauren's 154
Mosaic 118
Mosswood Market 155
Redd 56
Sage Fine Food &
   Provisions 78
Saint Rose 110
Underwood Bar & Bistro 119
Wine Spectator Greystone
   Restaurant at the Culinary
   Institute of America 63

Diners
Garden Court Café 92
Pat's Diner 116
Pick's Drive-In 145
Taylor's Automatic Refresher 63

Gourmet Foods
Bohemian Market 112
Boont Berry Farm 153
Food for Humans 116

Glen Ellen Village Market 93
Lemons' Philo Market 156
Long Meadow Ranch 59
Oak Hill Farm 93
Oakville Grocery 134
Oxbow Public Market 52
Patch 88
Sonoma Market 89
Vella Cheese Company 90

Italian
Diavola 143
Red Grape 89
Santi 143
Scopa 134

Locavore
Ad Hoc 54
Barndiva 131
Boont Berry Farm 153
Boonville General Store 154
Bovolo 132
Café La Haye 86
Estate 87
Fig Café 92
Harvest Moon Café 87
Lauren's 154
Lemons' Philo Market 156
Mosaic 118
Mosswood Market 155

Mexican
La Hacienda 144
La Luna Taqueria 59
Taqueria El Sombrero 135

New American
Boon Fly Café 49
Café La Haye 86
Café les Jumelles 113

Dawn Ranch Roadhouse 116
Market 62
Moore's Landing 49
Ravenous Restaurant 134

Pubs
Ace-in-the-Hole Cider Pub 109
Barley & Hops Tavern 112
Bear Republic Brewing Co 132
Murphy's Irish Pub 88
Russian River Brewing Co 105
Silverado Brewing
   Company 63

Seafood
Glen Ellen Inn Oyster Grill and
   Martini Bar 92
Go Fish 61

Sushi
Shiso 89

Thai
Jhanthong Banbua 104

Vegetarian
Ubuntu 52

PLAY

Cinemas
Cameo Cinema 64
Clover 145
Raven Film Center 135
Rio Theater 113
Sebastiani Theatre 90

Dive Bars
Pancha's 57

GLBT Entertainment
Rainbow Cattle Co 117

Live Music
Hopmonk Tavern 110

Performances
Lincoln Theater 57
Napa Valley Opera House 54
Wells Fargo Center
   for the Arts 106

SEE

Brewhouses
Anderson Valley
   Brewing Company 152

Farmers Markets
Cloverdale Farmers Market &
   Art Fair 144
Farmers Market at
   Sonoma Plaza 79
Healdsburg
   Farmers Market 128
St Helena
   Farmers Market 59

Galleries
di Rosa Preserve 47
Florence Ave 107
Funeria 119
Geyser Arts Gallery 143
Graton Gallery 119
LaHaye Art Center 79
Ma(i)sonry 54
Nest 50
Quicksilver Mine Co 117
Sebastopol Center
   for the Arts 108
Sonoma Valley
   Museum of Art 80

Museums
Anderson Valley Museum
   152
Cloverdale Museum 144
Hand Fan Museum 127
Napa Valley Museum 54

Schulz Museum 104
Sonoma County Museum 104
Sonoma Valley
  Museum of Art 80

Natural Phenomena
Old Faithful Geyser 65
Petrified Forest 65

Notable Buildings
Adobe Barracks 78
Mission San Francisco
  Solano 79

Parks & Gardens
Armstrong Woods 114
California Carnivores 107
Cornerstone Sonoma 76
Hendy Woods State Park 155
Jack London State
  Historic Park 90
Luther Burbank
  Home & Gardens 104
Sugarloaf Ridge State Park 94
Wildwood Farm Nursery &
  Sculpture Garden 93

SHOP

Antiques
Mr Ryder and Co 119
Sonoma Antique Society 109

Arts & Crafts
Farmhouse Mercantile 153
Hand Goods 111
Renga Arts 111
Rookie-To Gallery 153

Body & Bath Products
All Things Lavender 83
Beekind 109
Mudd Hens 66
Napa Soap Company 60

Books
Chanticleer Books 83
Readers Books 84

Candy & Chocolates
Tiddle E Winks 85
Wine Country Chocolates 91
Woodhouse Chocolate 61

Clothing
Arboretum 130
Betty's Girl 51
Haus 84
Lolo's 60
Napa Premium Outlets 52

Gifts
Artists & Farmers 130
Baksheesh 131
Chateau Sonoma 83
Cheese Shop 131
Farmhouse Mercantile 153
Guerneville 5 & 10 116
Kenwood Farmhouse 95
Napa General Store 52
Rookie-To Gallery 153
Tiddle E Winks 85
Zipper 78

Gourmet Foods
Beekind 109
Cheese Shop 131
Napa Valley Olive Oil 61

Home Decor
Artefact Design &
  Salvage 77
Artists & Farmers 130
Calistoga Pottery 66
Chateau Sonoma 83
Sign of the Bear
  Kitchenware 85
Zipper 78

Jewelry
Studio Collections Jewelry 85

Musical Instruments
People's Music 109

WINERIES

Alexander Valley
Alexander Valley Vineyards 138
Fritz Underground Winery 142
Hawkes 138
Locals Tasting Room 140
Meeker Vineyards 141
Robert Young 138
Rosso & Bianco 139
Sausal Winery 138
Silver Oak 142
Stryker Sonoma 139
Terroirs Artisan Wines 140
Trentadue 139

Anderson Valley
Breggo 148
Brutocao 149
Claudia Springs Winery 152
Esterlina 152
Greenwood Ridge
  Vineyards 150
Handley Cellars 151
Husch Vineyards 151
Lazy Creek Winery 150
Meyer Family Cellars 148
Navarro Vineyards 150
Roederer Estate 150
Scharffenberger Cellars 148
Toulouse Vineyards 149
Zina Hyde Cunningham 148

Dry Creek Valley
Amphora 124
Bella Vineyards 126
Kokomo Winery 125

La Crema 122
Longboard Vineyards 122
Peterson Winery 124
Preston of Dry Creek 126
Quivira 123
Seghesio Family Winery 122
Topel Winery 122
Truett-Hurst 125
Unti 123

Napa Valley
Artesa 38
Casa Nuestra 45
Castello di Amorosa 46
Ceja 39
Chateau Montelena
  Winery 47
Darioush 39
Domaine Carneros 38
Etude 38
Frog's Leap 43
Girard Winery 40
Goosecross Cellars 41
Grgich Hills 44
Groth 42
Hall 45
Hess Collection 40
Honig 42
Joseph Phelps 45

Mondavi 42
Mumm Napa 44
Piña 44
Quixote 41
Robert Sinskey 41
Round Pond 43
Rubicon Estate 42
Schramsberg 46
Stag's Leap Wine Cellars 41
Vincent Arroyo 47
Vintner's Collective 39
Wine Garage 47

Russian River Valley
Arista 102
Bottle Barn 98
Dutton Estate & Sebastopol
  Vineyards Tasting Room 99
Dutton-Goldfield &
  Balletto Tasting Room 98
Freestone Vineyards 98, 103
Gary Farrell 101
Hartford Family Winery 99
Hop Kiln Vineyards 102
Iron Horse 99
J Vineyards & Winery 102
Korbel Champagne
  Cellars 101
Marimar 99

Martinelli 100
Moshin 101
Porter Creek Vineyards 101
Rochiol 102
Sophie's Cellars 100

Sonoma Valley
Bartholomew Park Winery 71
Benziger 73
BR Cohn Winery 72
Chateau St Jean 75
Cline Cellars & California
  Missions Museum 70
Eric Ross Winery 73
Gloria Ferrer 70
Gundlach Bundschu 71
Imagery Estate Winery 73
Kaz Winery 75
Ledson Winery 76
Muscardini Cellars &
  Ty Caton 75
Roshambo 70
Schug Carneros Estate 70
St Francis Winery 76
Valley of the Moon Winery 72
VJB Cellars 74
Wellington 74
Wine Exchange of Sonoma 71
Wine Room 74

000 map pages